THE RED BLACKBOARD

The Red Blackboard

An American Teacher in China

by
RUTH KOENIG

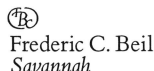
Frederic C. Beil
Savannah

FIRST EDITION

Library of Congress Cataloging-in-Publication Data
The red blackboard: an American teacher in China/
by Ruth Koenig
p. cm.
ISBN 0-913720-88-7 (acid-free)
1. China—Description and travel. 2. Koenig, Ruth,
1927–   —Journeys—China. I. Title.
DS712.K628   1994
951.05'9—dc20   93-37123
                  CIP

951.59   10/10/96
Koe

For Don, who made it all possible

Acknowledgments

I am grateful to my two sons: to John for his encouragement to write the book in the first place and for his invaluable editing; to Doug for his computer expertise and his patient attempts to help me become computer literate.

I am especially grateful to our Chinese students, friends, and colleagues who welcomed us and shared their lives and experience. They have given me a new understanding of courage and appreciation for the endurance of the human spirit.

I

We had taken off from Chicago at mid-morning on this August day of 1990. Now we were high over the Pacific, halfway to Hawaii. We'd already been amply fed a couple of times by dutiful flight attendants, and I was several chapters into the latest Tom Clancy novel. Nothing, however, could completely submerge my excitement. After nearly two years of planning, we were actually on our way to China.

I looked over at Don, asleep, seemingly relaxed and unconcerned about this momentous undertaking in our lives. How could he sleep at a time like this? All of our married years I'd vacillated between resentment and envy at his ability to drop off within minutes and wake refreshed a short time later. He was as excited as I about our adventure and perhaps as apprehensive, but most of the time he didn't let on—about the apprehension, that is. For the past year he'd made everyone within earshot aware we were going to China, to the point people were probably glad we had finally gone.

Whether or not he was apprehensive, I certainly was. That's not to say I wasn't eager, just realistic.

We were going to Chengdu, a city of two million people in Southwest China, to teach conversational English at the Chengdu College of Geology (now called the Chengdu Institute of Technology). That we were going at all came about through a serendipitous occurrence. For a number of years we had participated in a program that brought international students from Chicago-area colleges and universities to outlying areas over the Thanksgiving holiday. The intent was to give them a taste of American life outside of a metropolitan area. For the past couple of years Don and I had even chaired the program in Danville, the small downstate Illinois city where we live. About twenty students, sometimes with their families, would be bused in on Wednesday evening to stay with Danville families until the following Sunday.

In 1988 we hosted three Chinese people. One of the Chinese women learned that I was soon to retire from Danville Area Community College, where I'd taught composition and speech for nearly two decades.

"Why don't you come to China and teach conversational English?" she asked.

"I'd love to," I replied without hesitation.

I said that, of course, thinking the possibility was quite remote. I didn't reckon on the drive and tenacity of this woman, Jiang Zhirong. A gynecologist, Dr. Jiang (the family name is listed first in China) was married to an English teacher at the Chengdu college. At the time, she was visiting her son, a graduate student at Northwestern University in Chicago, and he had signed her up for the weekend program. Zhirong, as we came to know her, spoke little English but had ambitions to become fluent and return to the United States as a visiting scholar herself. As I later realized, she saw me as a potential tutor.

Zhirong collected my vita and Don's and sent them to her husband. She explained that the college might put to good use Don's skills as a retired industrial maintenance manager. Two months later, when Zhirong was back in China, we began receiving letters from Hu Jilin, her husband, and shortly after that we got an invitation from the head of the Foreign Language Department to teach the following academic year, 1989–1990.

We were delighted, but I hadn't planned to retire for another year. Dare we risk turning down the offer? No problem, was the response from Chengdu. We would be just as welcome a year later.

Even then, I couldn't help but be apprehensive. Although I'd taught composition and speech, I knew teaching English in a foreign country would be a far different matter. I confessed my reservations in a letter to the head of the Foreign Language Department at Chengdu. Again, I was told, in effect, not to worry.

Then, to our surprise, we discovered that the college also wanted Don to teach conversational English. A more unlikely English teacher would be hard to find. His education beyond high school consisted solely of trade school and a multitude of short courses, all in the area of electronics, engineering, and refrigeration; and his teaching experience consisted only of instructing first-aid and CPR courses and one semester in a vocational high school in between jobs.

Don does have vast experience and competence in construction and industrial maintenance. He is, in fact, something of a wizard in that field. But when it comes to language, he has two left tongues. He is cavalier about the fine points of grammar. And once he has incorrectly pronounced a word, he seemingly is incapable of ever fixing the error.

It's as if his mind is a write-protected computer disk. He has numerous language idiosyncrasies. For example, people play "chest" and "SEE-attle" is a city on the West Coast. To this day, he mispronounces my maiden name, Fissel.

Once again, however, the Chinese would not be dissuaded. And if the college was so determined to have us, we were not about to turn down the offer.

We felt truly lucky for the opportunity, although I suspect you could have found dozens among our friends and relatives who considered us out of our minds and even irresponsible to be undertaking such a venture. Count among this group the oldest of our two sons, Doug, and Don's mother, who was in her mid-eighties and living in a nursing home. Initially Doug avoided even mentioning the subject. It was as if he thought if he didn't talk about it, maybe Mom and Dad would get over this crazy idea.

It *was* a bit crazy. Don was sixty-five years of age, I was sixty-three, and neither of us was in great health. During the past six years, Don had had knee replacement surgery, angioplasty three times to clear blocked arteries, and had been put on medication for heart disease. Meanwhile, five months before I was to retire and seven months before we were scheduled to leave for China, I began having difficulty walking and discovered my left hip joint was degenerating rather quickly from arthritis. Rejecting immediate surgery to replace the hip out of fear that it would jeopardize our plans, I opted for medication and a cane instead. My hip joint hurt, but not badly enough to keep me at home.

Normally I like to think we are sensible people, and I suppose if we'd heard about someone else with the kind of medical histories we have, we too would have raised our eyebrows. But somehow we were undeterred. It was as if we thought we had amnesty where ill health was concerned.

As if concerns for our health were not enough to make our family and friends doubtful of our sanity, a year before we were to go, the Chinese government launched its brutal crackdown in response to the student demonstrations in Tiananmen Square.

"Surely, you're not going to go now?" friends queried. Admittedly, we read and watched for news of China carefully those next few months and sent for information about the Peace Corps program in Hungary, just in case. But we were never seriously deterred.

Why was going to China so important? Chinese scholars have long noted Americans' naïveté and sentimentality concerning China. I couldn't speak for Don, but I seemed to fit into that category. I've always had a soft spot for China. Although my mother died when I was five, she was president of her church missionary society, which supported missions in China. I had read novels and essays by Pearl Buck, and when I grew older I met Helen Huntington Smith, a missionary who was born in China and remained there until she was forced to leave in 1950. Everyone I had ever read or talked with had spoken with great affection for China and its people. Somehow that, to use a Chinese expression I would see and hear many times from my students, "gave me a very deep impression."

Although it seems pompous to say so and I didn't even admit it to Don at first, I felt as if we were destined to go to China. Even though we had idly discussed the prospect of some kind of overseas service project for years, the opportunity to go was nothing we sought; it just fell upon us. Countless things, seen first as possible obstacles, resolved themselves. For example, we had thought we might have to leave our home in Danville empty while we were gone, since it was difficult to find suitable renters in a small, economically depressed community. Yet, unsolicited, we were approached by a young optometrist who was moving to town to begin practice and was seeking temporary quarters. He asked to be our live-in caretaker-groundskeeper. Likewise, we sold our car on the first day it was advertised. Finally, the opportunity just seemed to offer too many rewards to be rejected.

Even though I was retiring willingly, I enjoyed teaching and hated to give it up entirely. I had gone back to school as an older student and felt I still had a contribution to make. After twenty years of teaching, I felt I was finally getting the hang of it. Certainly there were important volunteer opportunities awaiting me in Danville, but I didn't see any lifestyle among my retired friends that I wanted to emulate. I admit that I probably feared the loss of a meaningful identity along with the loss of a career. I wasn't ready to put my briefcase in mothballs and let my hair go gray. Going to China seemed to be a way of avoiding that fate.

I also envisioned another benefit. A friend had shown me an article written by a woman who, with her husband, had gone to China to teach. Although they stayed for only one semester, both lost weight. I thought of Don. For years his doctors and I had been urging him to lose twenty-five pounds or so. Our badgering was for naught. To make matters worse, he had picked up another ten pounds at all the farewell dinners we were given. He reasoned that since he was going to be living on rice for the next year, he had to eat in advance, like a bear going into hibernation. I couldn't imagine how the Chinese, who all appeared to be pencil slim, were going to react to this large, economy-size husband of mine. But I was counting on a rice diet to accomplish what Don's nagging doctors and I could not.

So here we were, winging our way across the Pacific. Don stirred to life and I reached over and squeezed his hand and said in a sentimental rush, "Aren't we lucky to have the opportunity to do this? A whole year to live in a country, to get to know the people, to travel all around, and to get paid for it besides!" (Well, admittedly the pay would be minimal, but it was something nonetheless.) We smiled at each other and he squeezed my hand in agreement. We would have been embarrassed had anyone heard my outburst.

2

Although there were hundreds of Americans teaching in China, most of them were affiliated with American educational institutions or organizations. We were coming as independents, receiving our invitation directly from the college in Chengdu. We didn't have the safety net of an American organization. Nevertheless, we weren't worried. We had a great deal of advance information about the college, and we knew we were going where we would be welcome.

The latter was confirmed for us when we landed in Beijing. Mr. He, a member of the college Foreign Affairs Department, had come from Chengdu to meet us and act as our tour guide for a few days. He took us to all the major attractions—the Great Wall, the Palace Museum, and so forth—giving us a nice introduction to China. One evening, he escorted us to a banquet for new teachers, hosted by the Ministry of Geology. We learned that Chinese banquets do indeed consist of endless courses and innumerable toasts. Fortunately the wine was good and the glasses small. Don had momentary doubts about continuing the venture, however, when we were served scorpion. I liked it, he didn't.

Three days later, Mr. He took us to the airport for our flight to Chengdu. He remained behind to meet two Canadian teachers who were scheduled to arrive in a couple of days.

While we waited for our flight, our first on China Air, we got an inkling that this might be a little different from what we were accustomed to. As departure time approached, people lined up early, then stampeded aboard when the gate was opened, as if they were worried that all the seats might be taken.

Although a jet, the plane was a cramped old Russian model, with three seats on a side. From the front entrance it seemed to take forever to reach Row 26, past all the curious onlookers who were stuffing bags overhead, while we dragged our own considerable hand luggage with us. The air-conditioning wasn't operating and since the outside temperature was about ninety degrees, the interior of the plane was stifling and occasionally smelly. We were given cold wash cloths as soon as we settled, which was momentarily refreshing. But when takeoff was delayed and we still felt no air-conditioning, Don observed that the cloths probably were for wiping off perspiration. Fortunately the air-conditioning came on soon after we were aloft.

When we approached our destination after two hours in the air, the flight attendant made the usual announcements and cautioned passengers to stay seated until the plane had come to a complete stop. Although she spoke in Chinese and then in English for our benefit, she might as well have addressed the passengers in Arabic. As soon as the plane touched down, people bounded out of their seats to retrieve their baggage and crowded into the aisle. The air-conditioning again was shut off, and since it was several minutes before the door was opened, the interior of the plane once more became very warm. I reminded myself of how glad I was that the college had promised us air-conditioned quarters.

It was a little after eight o'clock when we landed in Chengdu, but the sun had not yet set. Since the whole country is on Beijing time, and Chengdu is in southwestern China, day breaks and night falls late by the clock. As we left the plane we noticed that the weather was gloomy and the air heavy, what we'd heard was typical for Chengdu.

The plane had parked about fifty yards from the terminal, and since we were the last passengers to get off, we were slow in reaching the gate. Our welcome could not have been warmer, the temperature notwithstanding. Not only were Zhirong and Hu Jilin, her husband, there to meet us, but also the dean of the College Foreign Language Department, Mr. Zhou, and the head of the Foreign Affairs Department, Mrs. Yang, whom we would later come to know as "Emily." They practically fought over our luggage, wresting our cases out of our hands. I was sorry for every article of clothing I'd left behind because Don had told me we couldn't carry it all.

The tussle over our luggage was particularly ironic because Zhirong and Jilin were both shorter than either of us. Zhirong, a youthful and energetic fifty-year-old, with a disarming smile, probably weighed no more than a hundred pounds and may have reached five feet. Add two years, three inches, and thirty pounds and you have Jilin. They were both so excited at our arrival they could hardly contain themselves. They talked excitedly and could not stand still as they stowed our gear in the college van.

The ride to campus, about fifteen miles to the opposite side of the city, was harrowing. It was growing dark now and there were no street lights anywhere, not along the tree-lined airport road leading into the city, not even in downtown Chengdu. In spite of this, all of the motor vehicles, including our own, drove without headlights, so as not to blind bicyclers. The lack of lights did not slow anyone down until we got into the center city. Since it was a warm Saturday night, bicycles and pedestrians blocked the downtown streets, and the cars were forced to inch along, their horns blaring.

As we approached the college, Zhirong mentioned that the new Foreign Guest House, where we had been told we would be living, was not done. The significance of this announcement didn't immediately register.

The van parked outside of the old Foreign Guest House, a modern-looking building with a two-story glass exterior lobby. Once again, our Chinese friends snatched up the luggage and led us through the open doors of the lobby and up the stairs to our apartment on the third floor. Only as we entered our quarters did we realize this building was not air-conditioned.

Since the apartment was hot enough to bake bread in, our hosts set about hooking up two fans with which the quarters were furnished. The small fan in the living room plugged in with no problem, but the one in the bedroom, a floor model and a real Cadillac of fans, could not be used because the plug was incompatible with the socket. Our four companions fussed and discussed the problem in rapid-fire Chinese, but none knew what to do. In the meantime, we were growing hotter.

Finally they summoned a young woman, Chen Chen, from the Guest House staff, but she didn't seem to know what to do either. Don kept muttering under his breath that if they'd all just leave, he could have it going in five minutes. He's a veteran handyman, and there are few things around the house that he can't fix. After several more minutes of fussing, Chen Chen finally brought in an extension cord and, to Don's chagrin, strung it across the carpet. He views such makeshift arrangements as a disaster waiting to happen. But, at least, they got the fan going. Don could take care of the offending cord later.

Our hosts departed and, at last, we were alone to survey our dwelling place. The apartment consisted of an entryway, living room, bedroom, kitchen, and bathroom. The living room and bedroom were spacious, although the light from the overhead fixtures was so harsh we felt like we were in an operating room. We noted French doors in both the living room and bedroom, each leading onto a balcony, decidedly a nice feature. But then we saw that the screen doors didn't fit tightly, and we feared hordes of mosquitos, especially after we noticed the frilly blue mosquito nets suspended above each of the twin beds. We guessed they were not there for decoration. On the whole, though, we found the living room and bedroom satisfactory.

The rest of the apartment left another impression. In the small entryway, for instance, a small refrigerator, as well as a wall-mounted gas meter and water heater, created a boiler room ambience. The entryway, however, set the proper mood for viewing the kitchen and bathroom. The walls of both were covered with white ceramic tile to about four feet off the floor, with the rest being gray-white plaster. It would have looked rather sterile, except for the fact that none of the pipes were built into the walls; they were fully exposed.

The kitchen was equipped with a two-burner gas stove and a small sink, over which hung a single cold water faucet. The only food preparation space was a small tile ledge, running along two walls, and a long narrow student desk that served as a table.

The bathroom contained a small lavatory with a small mirror above, but no medicine cabinet. Between the mirror and lavatory was an inset, just big enough to hold some toilet articles. The bathtub was a footed model, huge and luxurious, and it came equipped with a shower, constructed of a galvanized pipe with a small portable plastic hose and nozzle. We weren't expecting something out of *House Beautiful*, and it appeared adequate.

That was all we cared to see at this point. We unpacked the few odds and ends we would need for the night, leaving the rest of the unpacking until morning, and settled in as best we could. The fans provided some relief from the heat and humidity, and we blocked the screen doors with our luggage to keep them as secure as possible against mosquitos. Exhausted from the travel and excitement, we climbed into bed and let down the mosquito nets. Looking across at me through the filmy blue haze, Don joked that he felt like he was going to bed with the queen of Sheba.

At that point we decided we were glad our sons and Don's mother couldn't see us. When our kids were growing up, we knew they didn't tell us everything they did, fearing we couldn't handle the truth. As we drifted off to sleep that first night in Chengdu, we surmised that we too would probably withhold a lot of information in the coming year, because we feared they couldn't handle the truth about our life in China.

3

I was awake at 4:30 A.M. A good night's sleep restored my spirits a little and, surveying our situation as day broke, I decided if we could just stay well, keep cool when it was hot, warm when it was cold, and maintain my hair color, we'd have it made.

By the time we had arrived in Chengdu, we had already sampled ethnic foods during our stopovers in Chicago, Hawaii, and Beijing, and we were ready to get back to familiar fare. We had made clear before coming to China that we wanted to have facilities in which to do our own cooking. But that was going to have to wait for the moment. We were to have breakfast in the guest house dining room that first morning.

Since it was Sunday and there weren't any conferences in progress, we were the only patrons for breakfast. We were ushered into the foreigner's small dining room, with the inevitable round table and lazy Susan, seemingly a fixture in China.

We waited while the cook-waiter brought out one dish at a time. First there was a large bowl of hot milk. (Don's only concession to milk is the least amount possible to get dry cereal to pass down his throat— and never hot milk.) Next came a succession of tough, deep-fried pastry, dried beef, boiled peanuts (I kid you not), and something Oscar Meyer wouldn't recognize, but which remotely resembled bacon. The last course, or at least the last one we stuck around for, was a small dish of green beans cooked in oil. There was probably more, but we decided we'd had enough and went back up to our apartment.

We were to be guests of Zhirong and Jilin for the other two meals that day, which meant more Chinese cuisine. But I vowed that first thing Monday I would go shopping so I could begin cooking American style.

Now that it was fully light, we had our first opportunity to view our surroundings. The window walls in both living room and bedroom, with French doors opening onto a balcony, provided us with a fascinating vista. Below us was a canal, part of a two-thousand-year-old irrigation system which ran through the campus, dividing it in half. On the opposite bank we could see an open-air market set up along a tree-lined street paralleling the canal. Long before daylight we had heard the chatter of farmers bringing in their produce on noisy carts, bicycles, or shoulder poles. Now we could see them hanging up their goods or spreading them out for display. In the sunny patches, vendors were putting up large, colorful umbrellas over their perishable stock. Other vendors were setting out their goods on concrete tables along the canal; still others were using their carts as display stands or spreading their wares on the ground.

From the balcony we could see a wide variety of produce, plus dressed chickens and sides of pork being hung up on lines. As I watched, one vendor carried a side of pork down the concrete steps to the canal and washed it in the dirty water before hanging it up. Right then I decided I'd postpone cooking any pork dishes for a while.

We were eager to explore the campus. After some initial unpacking, we went back down to the lobby with Zhirong and Jilin, who had arrived to be our guides.

The Foreign Guest House itself was a five-story building with a pale yellow glazed-tile facade. From the outside it appeared to be an imposing, quite modern building, with many reflective windows a dominant feature. Something had gone awry inside, however. I had the feeling an architect had been asked to design a luxurious high style building, but that halfway through, funding had been slashed.

Stepping into the two-story high lobby, with floor to ceiling windows on three sides, I was struck by the two large crystal chandeliers and a sweeping open staircase. But contrasted to that were the sparse furnishings: a dozen rather old-fashioned armchairs set around the periphery, covered with faded gray slipcovers. Two enameled spittoons on a tile floor reminded me of the chipped enameled wash-pans of my childhood. Both spittoons obviously were in frequent use— audibly so, I might add.

On the upper floors the white plastered walls in the hallways had never been painted nor had the terrazzo floors ever been polished or waxed. Maintenance apparently was minimal. The overall effect of the building's interior, then, with the juxtaposition of sparkling chandeliers and enameled spittoons was curiously contradictory—like someone wearing a chiffon scarf, rhinestone earrings, and factory coveralls.

With Zhirong and Jilin leading the way, we set out to tour the campus. We headed for the front gate. The campus was laid out roughly in the shape of a tree, although one with more rectangular dimensions. Starting at the front gate and working our way back along the main street—the trunk of this tree—we saw dormitories on the left. A few students played Ping-Pong in front on makeshift tables. Remembering that there were supposedly about five thousand students enrolled, I wondered if there was enough housing. I was impressed when they told us the sport area on the right included an Olympic-size swimming pool as well as an athletic field. A little farther on, the street forked where it met a handsome complex of three buildings. The center building was a new library, still under construction. Flanking it like forward leaning wings set at forty-five degree angles were two teaching buildings. Fronted by a broad expanse of lawn and some strategically placed palm trees, the three buildings provided an impressive entrance to the college.

Still other tree-lined streets fanned out on either side. We wandered past the college theater, the dining hall, the college museum, more dormitories and teaching buildings, as well as administrative support buildings. Not unlike large American universities, the college also has its own hospital and post office.

What is different, however, is that colleges and universities in China, as well as most other employer units, are complete communities. Anyone who has anything to do with the college lives on campus, from the college president to the gardeners. Housing there, as everywhere in China, is in short supply, and most of what is available is, by Western standards, abominable. Very quickly we found that everyone on campus constantly complained about housing. Their complaints usually concerned the size of their apartments. They probably could not have imagined how inadequate their dwellings appeared to our Western eyes.

Housing is assigned by seniority, education, position, and family status, although not necessarily in that order. Because Jilin was an associate professor, he rated a four-room apartment with a balcony in a building less than a year old. The old-timers among the staff are those who get to move into the new buildings. When a new building is completed, a game of musical chairs ensues, with many more moves taking place than the number of new apartments. Sometimes it isn't even a matter of an additional room, but a *bigger* room that impels a family to move.

The older staff housing on campus was made of red brick. But cement is the substance of choice for more recent Chinese construction, and it's mostly gray, in Chengdu as well as the rest of China. The buildings were uniformly five stories high. Newer housing was located at the outer edges of the campus. Since the professors who occupied them were older and had higher salaries and more leisure time, the small amount of land in front of those buildings was often filled with flowers, displaying colorful evidence of the tenants' gardening talents.

Since vegetables were quite cheap in the market, few bothered to plant them, but we did notice around some of the older housing, occupied by younger, less-prosperous residents, a few chickens confined in small pens. Although it supposedly was against regulations to keep chickens on campus, the crow of the cock was to become a familiar morning sound to us.

There were some attractive elements to the campus. Gardens and pools were integrated throughout, creating some restful and secluded areas for study or conversation. Small pavilions located here and there also appeared inviting.

The overall appearance of the college, however, was shabby and unkempt. We were astounded when we learned that the college was established in the 1950's, built from scratch, and that the Foreign Guest House was only three years old.

Many of the concrete buildings appeared grimy and could have used a fresh coat of paint. On the orange brick walls that surrounded the campus not nearly enough mortar was used, giving them a temporary, unsubstantial appearance. Broken window panes also punctuated many buildings, even those newly built.

Although the plantings were lush and flowers colorful, the blossoms and foliage were dusty or straggly and untamed. Grass, where grass existed, went unmowed, and bushes untrimmed. Pools, though sporting lily pads, were filled with mostly stagnant water.

My fastidious husband shook his head and said, "What I couldn't do around here with a crew, a few lawn mowers, clippers, rakes, and edgers."

The next few days we began the serious business of settling into the place we were going to call home for the next year. Although we'd sent two boxes of household goods from Illinois, they hadn't arrived yet. From a former teacher, we had inherited a wok, a tea kettle, assorted pots and pans, some enamel rice bowls, a few odd utensils, and about a dozen pairs of chopsticks, the use of which we'd not yet mastered. When we had supplemented this equipment with a luncheon set for six, a gift of the Hu's, some drinking glasses, a small oven, and a few knives, forks, and spoons, I felt we could put a meal together.

On Monday, Jilin volunteered to introduce us to the intricacies of shopping in a Chinese free market. We gathered up a couple of bamboo baskets—for the most part, you furnish your own containers—and set out.

Once we'd crossed the bridge, we turned right, along the canal, and plunged down a narrow street, crowded with vendors, shoppers, bicycles, and even an occasional car or truck, which proceeded slowly through the market, its horn beeping all the way. The three of us wound our way along, Don and I attracting attention from farmers and the other shoppers and creating our own little traffic jam. When we stopped to examine merchandise or make a purchase, curiosity seekers gathered round to listen to our conversation with Jilin, or to look at our clothes.

Consulting my list, Jilin kept an eye out for the freshest-looking produce. No prices were marked. If I saw something I liked, Jilin asked the price. If he thought it too much, he walked on. If he were interested, he started bargaining, sparring goodnaturedly with the vendors.

I asked Jilin how much something cost and quickly translated it into cents. It was so cheap I was prepared simply to pick out the best quality goods in the market and pay whatever price was asked. An American dime would buy enough of most kinds of vegetables for a meal. But Jilin insisted on haggling before every purchase.

Lots of produce I didn't recognize, but there was still much that was familiar to choose from. Peaches, apples, and watermelon were abundant that first morning; and I bought tomatoes, potatoes, onions, cabbage, bell peppers, and green beans. Not only were there chickens and sides of pork hung up for sale, but live chickens and fish were available, too; so was roast smoked duck, displayed in glass cases. Goods like sugar, coffee, detergent, clothespins, toothpaste, and notebooks could be bought at permanent, state-run shops along the street. In these, we learned, prices are fixed.

That first night I served a dinner of cabbage, potatoes, and onions, augmented with some mediocre canned ham, garnished with fresh tomatoes. From Don's reaction, you'd have thought I had served the finest French cuisine. It paid to have peasant appetites.

Back at the apartment, we had a visit from Emily, from the Waiban, pronounced Wy-bahn. That's the Chinese word for "foreign affairs." (We were learning the lingo.) Although her Chinese name was Yang Huidong, Emily had been named after poet Emily Dickinson by a previous American English teacher. She had spent a year at Berkeley studying English, and her experience in the States helped her to understand some of our requests and concerns. A stocky woman in her forties, Emily was blessed with an irrepressible laugh and an unfailing sense of humor. She found in Don's penchant for teasing a kindred soul.

We told her we wanted some things for the apartment. Most important on our list were three shelves that could be attached above the tile on the walls in the kitchen. That would free up the one table and the tile ledge for workspace.

Emily said she would tell the pertinent department. But she warned, "In China it takes time to get things done, so you must be patient. It's not so easy as in your country."

Given what she'd said, we were amazed when the very next day two young women from the housekeeping staff showed up with a solution to our problem. Instead of three separate shelves, however, they brought a three-shelf bookcase to replace the table. (We had, after all, requested three shelves.) As tactfully as possible, we tried to refuse the bookcase and make them understand that we needed the table *and* wall shelves.

In the end, we compromised on one long shelf in the kitchen, which at least was an improvement.

Next on my list of chores was attacking the grimy floor in the kitchen. I was determined to get the apartment in order before classes started, because I knew there would be little time thereafter. Using laundry detergent and the thin surgical gloves my hairdresser had given me to apply hair color, I set about scrubbing the tile on hands and knees. An hour and much perspiration later, the gloves were in shreds, and I could see only scant improvement. I longed for Spic and Span or a can of Comet and some steel wool. What I wouldn't have given, too, for a stiff scrub brush and a squeegie mop. The brush that Housekeeping gave me had less resistance than my toothbrush. The mop wasn't much better; it was a dirty rag type, and I didn't have a wringer. I could slop on lots of water, though, because there were floor drains in both kitchen and bathroom and I found that when I let water sit on the tiles for a while they did get a little cleaner. At least it showed there were possibilities.

I couldn't really consider myself settled in until the computer was up and going. But that required a stepdown electrical transformer, because Chinese voltage is higher than that of the United States. Getting a transformer necessitated a shopping trip downtown one steamy afternoon, accompanied by Emily. Even with Don's diagrams and Emily's translations, that quest was the biggest shopping challenge we had faced so far. After three hours and chasing all over town, we finally found one.

Now, to get it hooked up. Before Don could even think about how he was going to manage that, Jilin brought a friend to the rescue. Zhang Zhenggang, chairman of the Physics Department, studied our plight and within two days was back with a mounting board with outlets and a volt meter. We were in business . . . well, almost.

We suddenly remembered we would have no computer printer paper until our boxes of books and other supplies arrived. It seemed like that would be no problem, since China does have computers and where there are computers, there surely must be computer paper. That seemed a logical assumption, anyway.

On our next shopping trip downtown, we searched in vain. All we could locate was lined paper (of the type used in accounting) without side perforations. We mentioned our plight to a Chinese clerk in the American consulate, where we had gone to register our presence in the country. No problem, the clerk said, and he reached down beneath his own computer desk, and presented us with a short stack of paper from Uncle Sam's own store.

Ordinarily, the ethical transgression would have given me pause. But we feared that refusing the paper might cause embarrassment and more problems. Besides we *were* Americans, right? So now, with the computer up and running, we were ready to begin preparing for our classes.

4

Although we didn't plan it that way, we were introduced to China's health care system during that first week in Chengdu. One morning Don awoke with what he thought were mosquito bites all over his body. We were dismayed because we had used the mosquito nets above our beds consistently and thought we were safe. When the "bites" disappeared during the day, we realized they were hives.

The weather was extremely humid, aggravating the problem and making Don itch like crazy. He sat in front of the fan much of the time trying to get relief. As evening came on the hives got worse, so he tried bathing in cool water.

While he soaked, I went looking for Zhirong. Granted, she was a gynecologist, but it was no time to quibble.

Zhirong came later with a doctor from the campus hospital, a very attractive young woman with long black hair. Emily and another member of the Waiban staff also came along to act as interpreter for the doctor.

The doctor decided that Don should go to the campus hospital, so our whole entourage set off into the steamy night, cicadas humming incessantly on either side of us. Seeing the hospital was a memorable experience, one that would strike terror even in the heart of a well person. The two-story brick building was dimly lit, with only a single light bulb suspended from the ceiling in most examining rooms off the central hall. All of the entrances were unscreened and the doors stood wide open, admitting any kind of life that cared to wander or fly in. The woodwork, walls, and floors were dingy and dirty and the paint was peeling. The floors were cement, and if they had been mopped in recent weeks it wasn't readily apparent.

Don and I sat on a wooden bench in the hall, while the others animatedly discussed what to do with him. We avoided looking at each other, neither of us wanting to acknowledge to the other how horrible we found these conditions. A little girl, daughter of one of the doctors, was running around the examining room, hanging on to her mother's skirt or rummaging through a drawer of the one table. In an unlit examining room across the hall, several people were watching a TV played at peak volume. People walked bicycles past me in the hall.

I walked down the long dimly-lighted hall to the other end. The building was bleak and seemingly uninhabited, although Zhirong said there were in-patient rooms on the second floor. Jilin, who'd joined us, pointed out the dentist's office. Seeing it provided a big incentive to brush and floss every day.

From what we could see of the examining room, the equipment inside was minimal and what there was appeared antiquated, even dilapidated. On the floor, among other things, was the ubiquitous grimy teakettle—generic in China, it seemed—and an electric fan that was unplugged, despite the heat. An old wooden chair was provided for patients to sit on.

Of the three doctors on duty (there were no nurses), all were women. Only one was dressed in a white lab coat, and it was none too clean. The other two, including the one who had come to our apartment, wore pretty silk print dresses and high-heeled shoes. They looked as if they were ready to duck out to a party.

The first doctor readied a syringe, a big one, which she unwrapped from an unimpressive dingy looking cloth. (I remembered having to wrap such bundles for the autoclave when I worked in a hospital emergency room forty-five years ago.) Don said he hadn't seen a syringe that big since the local veterinarian used to come to inject his dad's dairy herd. The doctor got out several vials of the medication she intended to inject and came to the hall door. She knocked off the glass tip of one vial with a bandage scissors, aiming toward a wastebasket in the corner. She missed. All around the basket on the floor were other glass tips and discarded swab sticks that had missed their mark.

The doctor called Don into the examining room and searched futilely for a vein in his arm. She probed and poked. For the next forty-five minutes, all four doctors, including Zhirong, took turns searching and poking. None was successful. (To be fair, American doctors and nurses have had similar problems with my husband.)

I could see that Don was suffering from the stifling heat in the examining room. His face was pale and he kept cupping his forehead in his hand. The doctors were concentrating so hard on finding a vein in his arm, they didn't even notice the rest of him. Only when he confessed to being a little dizzy, did one of the doctors plug in the floor fan.

Finally, the doctors sent for a nurse, who came within minutes. The nurse succeeded on the first try.

When Don's injection began to take effect and ease his itching, the doctors gave him some additional medication and we went home, hoping it was a magic cure and that we'd seen the last of the hospital.

But the rash persisted. After a particularly bad night, Emily took us back to the hospital. The campus hospital looked even more appalling in daylight. When the nurse swabbed Don's arm with iodine before giving him a shot, she pitched the used swabs out the open window.

When Don continued to have the same symptoms for several days, we finally were referred to a downtown hospital. There he was examined by a dermatologist, the first and only male doctor we saw. After many questions, asked in a friendly and quietly capable manner, the doctor examined Don behind a screen. When he asked Don to drop his pants, all the white-coated personnel within ten yards scrambled to have a look—all in the interest of furthering medical education, I'm sure.

Eventually the dermatologist's prescription cured Don's rash. Although we suspected both heat and food allergies, we never really knew the cause.

5

We had arrived in Chengdu two weeks before the start of classes, on September 9, so we'd have plenty of time to settle in and make plans for teaching.

Those first few days while we furnished our nest, we also began meeting with the dean of the Foreign Language Department and with others who would be working with us. Since teachers do not have separate offices or telephones in their homes, most of these meetings occurred in our apartment. The phrase "my door is always open" took on new meaning for us in China. Every day a steady stream of people came calling.

Our first meeting with the dean and two vice-deans concerned textbooks. Between Don and me, we would be teaching three different courses. Yet they offered us the same text for all three.

The deans asked if the text was acceptable. Since there didn't seem to be any alternatives, what could we say? Besides, we had other supplemental materials coming.

Knowing that teaching materials were at a premium in China, I had taken advantage of offers of surplus written and audio-visual materials from my college in Illinois. My colleagues in various departments were generous in allowing me to choose unused texts from many disciplines, so I was able to pick a nice sampling of resources. I also included a number of English handbooks and dictionaries and a desk encyclopedia. These we had packed up and shipped off to China in July.

When we met with the deans our boxes had not yet arrived. But since we still had several days before classes were to start, we didn't panic.

In the meantime I could only shake my head over the lack of organization at the college in Chengdu. We received no handouts or printed instructions of any kind for classes—no course descriptions, no guidelines for grading, not even an exam schedule. Even our class rosters were handwritten on air-mail-thin white paper and the names weren't alphabetized. Obviously we weren't in a paper culture. It probably is the lack of equipment (typewriters, copying machines, computers) that has kept the Chinese from getting caught up in a paper chase. But while we Americans tend to overdo it, the Chinese definitely could benefit from a little more systematic approach to things.

As was my practice, I composed a course syllabus to be passed out to students, describing the nature and objectives of the course and my "rules of the road." I submitted it for approval to Mr. Kong, our liaison with the Foreign Language Department. He seemed a little surprised, but said nothing. I asked if it was acceptable. He studied the document a moment longer, then blurted our, "Well . . . I think it just makes you a professional."

I took that as approval. Evidently a course syllabus was unique. This particular syllabus was unique for me, too, because it was the first one on which I'd ever included the following declaration: "Spitting in the classroom will not be tolerated."

We did not actually see our classrooms until the day classes began. At our request and by prearrangement, we had walked down to Teaching Building One with Mr. Kong a few days beforehand. But when we arrived, although the building itself was open, we found all the rooms were locked. I learned later that rooms were always locked, so Mr. Kong had obviously made no attempt to have them opened. What I did see was dismaying, however. The walls were scuffed and dirty, with not so much as a picture or a poster or a calendar to relieve the visual monotony.

We were given lists of student names days before classes began, so we had time to study them. The lists were daunting, but not because of the number of students. In fact, my former colleagues would have been envious of the student-teacher ratio, which averaged sixteen to one. What was daunting to Western eyes were all those undecipherable, unpronounceable Chinese names. I like to go into class on the first day and call the roll and begin to learn students' names. Accomplishing that feat in China even in a semester seemed formidable.

Since it was a college of geology, every student enrolled was majoring in some aspect of geology. The college offered more majors than I even knew existed. Students in three of my classes were in the first year of a three-year program leading to a master's degree. My fourth class was composed of doctoral students who also were in the first year of a three-year program. Weren't they going to be impressed when they learned that my one and only course in geology came at Ohio State University years before most of them were born?

All of Don's students also had at least bachelor's degrees and were working geologists, returning to the college solely to study English. Many of his students were in their late twenties or early thirties. A few were even older.

Ever since China had embarked in 1978 on her program of opening to the outside world, the country had stressed the importance of learning English. Realizing how much they lagged behind developed countries in science and technology, China's leaders recognized that English was an essential tool for tapping into the global pool of technical knowledge. A massive campaign was begun to initiate or expand English instruction at many different levels. Students were introduced to English in middle school (comparable to high school in the United States), and college and university students were required to study English for two years.

Our students, then, were coming to us with anywhere from four to eight years of study already under their belts. They would be deficient, however, in speaking and in listening comprehension. Our main task, a charge given to us by the president of the college at a welcoming banquet, would be to get them to open their mouths and ears.

The first day of classes, a Monday, Don was free until the second period, so he came with me to my first class of master's degree students. I suspect he wanted to see how things went so he could decide whether he really wanted to stick around for the whole semester.

When we walked in, most of the students were already seated, reading aloud from the textbook that had been assigned. Customarily these minutes prior to the start of class, after the warning bell, were to be devoted to practice recitation of the day's lesson. The students were noisy, but orderly. A few looked up when we walked in and smiled shyly, but most went on with their recitation.

Mr. Kong had asked if I wanted him to be present to introduce me. I'd said yes. I looked around. He was nowhere in sight. So when the bell rang, I plunged into introductions. I pointed to my printed name and address on the board, and tried to remember to speak slowly.

I had made tent name tags out of note paper for my students to place in front of them on their desks. As I called the roll, I passed them out. I told the students we would use the name tags each week to help me to learn their names. We spent an inordinate amount of time on roll call, what with my fumbling attempts to pronounce their names, and their subsequent good-natured attempts to correct my pronunciation. I hoped it would make them feel better about their own inadequacy in speaking English to see how much trouble I had just pronouncing their names.

Although entire names are used in China in addressing someone, except among intimates, I decided to be easy on myself and compromised: I used only the surname with Mr. or Miss. That simplified one problem, but it didn't solve another. The family name is first in Chinese, but I couldn't tell from the list whether I should be saying Mr. or Miss. Was Chen RonGui a man or woman?

The students laughed good-naturedly at my goofs in that regard. (Later on, I would turn the tables on them. I wrote on the board a list of English first names and asked the students to tell me whether they were men's or women's names. They knew historical names like George and Abraham and currently popular names like Madonna or Michael, as in Jackson. But, overall, they scored no better than fifty percent. We all had a good laugh, and afterward they were a little more sympathetic to my blundering.)

After roll call I began with an informal autobiography. I told the students I would ask questions when I was finished in order to check their listening comprehension. I told them about my childhood, my education, my career, and my family. I referred to the map of the United States I had filched from the airline magazine to show them where we lived, giving them a minigeography lesson in the process.

The students looked interested, intent, and smiled throughout my presentation. I was encouraged and grew more confident. Then I began asking for information that I had covered.

"How many children do I have?"

Silence.

"Where do I live in the United States?"

Still no response. Blank expressions.

"What are my hobbies?"

They looked to each other for interpretation. Right then I realized I would have my work cut out for me with this class.

Having observed my students' less than stellar performance, Don left for his own class with dampened enthusiasm, even dread.

My class of eight doctoral students, plus a few auditors, which met the following two hours, was a welcome change. The students were more mature, far more comprehending and less shy. I followed somewhat the same lesson plan and found them much more responsive. Then I asked them to introduce themselves. Although their pronunciation sometimes made it necessary for me to ask them to spell a questionable word or write it on the board, we did actually communicate.

One student said, "I've been studying English for eight years and I still can't speak or understand."

They all acknowledged, however, that they had really had little chance to practice. Since we were going to be meeting at least eight hours a week in class, as well as sometimes outside of class, I assured them that this semester was going to make a difference. They clearly were pleased at the prospect.

Don too had a surprising and exhilarating second half of the morning. His first training class, dubbed Class A, consisted of eighteen students.

They had spent the previous semester studying English, but their teacher had been a French woman and the students were disappointed at the results. I guess they didn't like learning English with a French accent.

Many of the students had asked their respective work units to allow them to study a semester longer. Those who elected to come back were highly motivated and also had above-average language aptitude. Therefore, their skills were better and they were eager to get on with the opportunity to study with an American. After initial introductions, Don invited them to ask questions and they amazed him with their knowledge and interests.

"What do you think of the situation in the Gulf?" one student asked, referring to Iraq's invasion of Kuwait weeks before and the subsequent build-up of American forces in Saudi Arabia.

"Who do you think has been the best American president?" another asked.

The students told him they had already been through the book the college used for the course and they would like another. Don came home for lunch that day, worrying not about being able to communicate with them, but whether he would be able to keep up with them.

Needless to say, our mood at lunchtime was more optimistic than it had been two hours earlier.

We met the rest of our classes that week. I learned that my other two postgrad sections were superior in skills to the first one, but Don's were just the opposite. His other two classes, with widely varying skills among them, were just beginning their year of intensive English study, and it was going to be an uphill battle to help them achieve much progress. Nonetheless, his students were eager and appreciative of their opportunity to study. Because they had difficulty understanding Don's questions, their responses were often minimal and, therefore, frustrating to him. Don had two different, even contradictory responses. On the one hand, he became impatient and didn't always appreciate how difficult it was for the students; he suspected when they could not or would not respond in class that they hadn't done their homework and really weren't working very hard. On the other, when he thought about trying to learn their language, he was overwhelmed and hoped his students wouldn't discover his own weakness with language.

When we started collecting written assignments from all our classes, we found that almost without question the students' written work was far superior to their speech. We had assigned them to write on the topic, "One of My Proudest Moments," and Don was surprised and a little chagrined when he read in the conclusion of one student's paper that one of his proudest moments was when he was chosen to study under the tutelage of a real American professor, Don Koenig. As Lincoln said, you *can* fool some of the people all of the time.

The next few weeks were a time of discovery. I had never had a more satisfying teaching experience. For one thing, our students were bright—only the best and brightest, after all, are chosen for limited places at colleges and universities. They all had a good reading knowledge of English, with vocabularies that sometimes astounded me. Occasionally when a polysyllabic word came up in the reading, I'd write it on the board and ask if they understood. They often gave an equally obscure, but equally correct synonym as a definition.

All of our students had, at least, bachelors' degrees, and some were pursuing doctorates. Don's students who had been working for a while brought additional experience, maturity, and a different perspective. They added the enriching ingredient that my returning students at the community college level had brought to the classroom.

Furthermore, indoctrinated as they were with the propaganda emanating from the government for the last ten years or more, they were convinced that it was important and necessary to learn English. We did not have to spend time on motivation. Some students were doing it for patriotic reasons—they wanted to help the Party, or more likely, the Motherland—but others were interested in helping themselves by becoming fluent in English. All wanted desperately to go abroad to study, most frequently to the United States, so English was the sine qua non.

I had only half as many students as I had normally had in the United States, I made up the curriculum as I went along, I had considerable freedom to do what I liked in the classroom, and my students did their assignments almost without fail, to the degree that they understood the assignment. What more could a teacher want?

Like American teachers, a few Chinese teachers complained that students didn't respect teachers like they used to and didn't work as hard, but from my perspective, it was still a far different world than I was accustomed to in the United States.

If the blackboard wasn't clean when I walked into a classroom, before I could scarcely lift an eraser, a student would bound forward, take it from my hand, and finish the job. As the weather turned cooler and I, like everyone else, brought a tea jar to class, someone would take my jar during break periods and refill it with hot water. Seldom did students leave the classroom without a comment, or at least a smile. If I had many things to carry back to the apartment, a couple of volunteers sprang forward to be bearers.

Physically the buildings and classrooms were dismal, dreary places, not conducive to lofty thoughts—to my eyes, anyway. The classrooms were spartan, the only extra object in mine being a wooden map stand. The odor from the open doors of the toilets assailed the nostrils as I walked down the halls. There was spittle here and there on the floors and steps, both inside and outside the building. (You couldn't be outside long without hearing someone hawking and spitting.)

Yet, with all of that, the classroom was a magical place. When I got inside the classroom and faced the students, I forgot all my complaints. A smile was always met with a smile. The students were there to learn; they were polite, cheerful, and attentive, and I had a good time each and every day. As I said, what more could a teacher want?

6

A few weeks after we came to China, Peter Vaganov, a professor from the University of Leningrad, arrived at the college for a three-month stay. I asked if he were taking his meals in the dining room. He said he was cooking for himself most of the time, adding, "Chinese food isn't for every day."

My sentiments exactly.

For the American living in China who does not like to eat Chinese food as a steady diet, it's desirable not only to know how to cook, but to like to cook. Thank goodness I like to cook—there is something therapeutic about it for me, in the way that other people find relaxation in painting or knitting—because cooking in China represented a real challenge.

There are advantages in having learned to cook before the development of modern appliances and packaged food. I grew up on a farm in northwestern Ohio where we didn't have electricity until the New Deal made it possible through the Rural Electrification Act. Our vegetables came from the garden, fruit from the orchard, milk and butter from our own cows, and canned goods from the cellar.

In winter we cooked on a coal stove, equipped with a small tank on the end to provide warm water. In the summer, we enjoyed the luxury of cooking on a three-burner kerosene stove on the screened porch. Even after 1946, when Don and I were first married, we lived on a small farm where we too had a garden and I froze surplus fruits and vegetables for winter meals. In my spartan Chinese kitchen, I sometimes felt like I had returned to those days.

Now granted, by the time we went to China I was long removed from that rather primitive life-style. Even so, I had not realized how much I had come to depend on convenience foods. Maybe not entirely, but even in most modern-day recipes there are all kinds of shortcuts.

One of the first difficulties I ran into was the scarcity of familiar spices. While there was a wealth of spices and seasonings available in China, often I didn't know what they were. Even when I found out, they were still unfamiliar to the palate, particularly for rather unadventurous gastronomic spirits, born and bred in the Midwest.

I was indebted to Rich Marvin, the previous occupant of our apartment, for leaving behind a couple of seasonings, cinnamon and oregano. There were several little film canisters full of leafy spices and I eagerly opened each one and sniffed. It turned out they were all filled with oregano, probably having been salvaged when the original container self-destructed. Disappointed, I momentarily conjured up an ad: "Creative homemaker with oversupply of oregano would like to meet interested party in possession of dill weed, rosemary, thyme, or lemon pepper."

Knowing no place I could post such an ad, and still waiting for my own supplies to arrive from home, I set about seeing what I could do with what was available: salt, a strange variety of pepper, onion, chives, garlic, green and red peppers, soy sauce, and, of course, cinnamon and oregano. Not a whole lot.

Sometimes, as I chopped and stir fried and experimented with new combinations I felt like Julia Childs or the Frugal Gourmet. I never came up with anything worthy of a new cookbook, though.

When the box we had mailed from home arrived in September, the possibilities were enhanced, but I had misjudged what was available. For example, I had included a variety pack of salad dressing mixes. But only after several weeks did I manage to find white vinegar and cooking oil that didn't look and taste like it had been salvaged from a Beijing Jeep crankcase.

I also had not anticipated the problem with salad greens. We were warned not to use any raw vegetables. So I had to blanch everything, including cabbage, peppers and onion for cole slaw, and what sold there for lettuce and celery, when it was in season. The result was not that nice crisp salad we yearned for.

By this time we were eating pork; but my offerings, mostly in stir fry dishes, were pretty monotonous. I wanted some different cuts, but didn't know how to get them. Approaching a farmer in front of half a hog, with knife poised, was a lot different than buying prepackaged cuts at home. I had to tell the man where I wanted him to wield his knife. Unfortunately I didn't know much about a pig's anatomy. As a child, I hadn't been interested enough when the semiannual butchering was going on on the farm. I wasn't sure how tender the meat was, anyway, and I knew my Chinese oven was too small and too hot to do a pork roast.

Zhang Zhenggang, the physics professor who had become a regular at our house, came to our rescue once again. During one of his visits, he mentioned he had a food grinder and was ready to provide ground pork on order if I was interested. I was.

Not only did he provide ground pork, but when beef was occasionally available, he brought me hamburger as well. That opened up numerous possibilities: hamburger patties, cabbage rolls, spaghetti, chili, Spanish rice—all Chinese adaptations, of course. Nevertheless, things were looking up.

Whenever I needed guinea pigs to try a new dish, I knew I could count on Monique and Melinda, our Canadian neighbors, who lived in the apartment immediately below us. In their mid-twenties, they had come to China with the organization Educational Service Exchange with China and were assigned by the college to teach English to non-English teachers.

M & M, as we came to call them, were full of life and laughter, making us envious of their youth and, at the same time, grateful we were no longer young. They made fast friends with their students, and we teased them about their frequent wild parties. Every minute they weren't teaching they were off on their bicycles or playing badminton. When we visited them, stepping carefully over clothes strewn on the floor or brushing things from a chair in order to sit down, we stifled those not so dormant parental impulses that were yelling inside, "Why don't you clean up this mess?" Instead, we just relaxed and enjoyed their company.

Don's favorite card game is euchre, and to his delight we learned M & M were avid players. When we were in the mood for company or a Friday night card game, we had only to issue an invitation to dinner. I prepared a lot of food, hoping to have enough for the entire weekend. But like young people everywhere, they had ravenous appetites. They not only ate seconds, they ate thirds. So much for leftovers.

Little by little, we were developing a social life. We were beginning to enjoy Chinese home cooking as served in the homes of our friends. We had a standing weekly invitation from Chef Jilin, who, when we praised his cooking, offered to come back to the States with us and be our personal chef.

Since we had no telephone, people just dropped in unannounced. Sometimes it was convenient, sometimes it wasn't.

Professor Zhang was always a welcome visitor. We enjoyed his company, whether at our house or his. He and his wife, HuiXin, introduced us to some delectable dishes from their kitchen. She knew only about as much English as we knew Chinese, but one evening they showed up, bringing all the ingredients, and showed me how to make a sweet potato dish that we had relished at their house.

Professor Zhang's interests were many and his curiosity insatiable. He had been raised in Shanghai and like many others from the coast seemed more open and sophisticated than other Chinese. He liked most foods, and his interest in Western music was intense. It was music that brought us together as much as anything. Don's main hobby for years has been his premier stereo system and we have an extensive collection of jazz, big band, and classical recordings. He immediately warms to someone who has similar interests. Professor Zhang, too, was passionate in his liking for certain composers and singers. He had a phonograph and tape player and a sizeable collection of major works. He sang along with Pavarotti and conducted with Karajan. If a piece of music was playing when he came in, or began during a conversation, he would interrupt himself and identify it or sing along for a few bars.

Although music was a common bond, Professor Zhang's fluency in English helped a lot, too. He had studied English in middle school and then, as a young college student, he had studied Russian in preparation for going to Russia to study physics. He'd spent three years at the University of Leningrad in the late 1950's. Because he began speaking his mind too freely abroad, he was recalled in 1959. But his stay in Leningrad stimulated his appreciation of art and music. He visited museums and attended concerts at every opportunity.

Although like many others who had gone abroad, he was politically suspect for a while, he had been allowed to go to the States as a visiting scholar from 1983 to 1985 at Virginia Polytechnical Institute. He had traveled at every opportunity and he never ceased to surprise us by his observations and experiences.

Although we never asked him, we guessed that it must have been hard to adjust to the restrictions of life in China after living abroad. Like many others, he and a Chinese grad student had shared an apartment and a car in Virginia. He vacationed in the South, visiting Disney World and other attractions.

After he returned to Chengdu, he bought a small Honda motorcycle and later a new piano, both of which are prohibitively expensive for most people in China. Although his daughter was ready for college when he bought the piano, both she and he have learned to play, after a fashion.

Our informal conversations with him, which ranged from politics to philosophy to computers to karaoke, helped us to feel we were beginning to know China. Although we were temperamentally compatible, anyway, there is no denying the part that language facility plays in helping people communicate in a meaningful sense. Many of our relationships with other folks in China were sincere but superficial because of their limitations in our language and our ignorance of theirs.

7

Teaching was off to a good start. Although it was intriguing and satisfying, even fun at times, it also was a lot of work. Our students were motivated and tried hard, but teaching them still required patience and persistence.

Because they didn't always understand us the first time—or second or even the third—we found ourselves constantly repeating things. They read English well, but still had difficulty with the spoken language. Sometimes they would misunderstand a question and give an inappropriate response, forcing me to repeat or rephrase the question. Sometimes, even when they understood a question, they would misstate or mispronounce their answer, and I would have to help them again. Suffice it to say I used my voice a lot.

I found too that the students were reluctant to ask me to repeat things. Instead, they would ask each other. Sometimes a student who did understand would volunteer an interpretation for his or her classmates. All of this occurred in Chinese, of course, multiplied by however many people were in the room. The result was pandemonium, or to use one of my favorite words, cacophony. While we were in China, it occurred to me that "cacophony" describes perfectly the sound of five or more Chinese people speaking at once—a common occurrence.

I found that I could be in perfect control of the classroom one minute, then, a moment later, feel like a helpless bystander. I could clap my hands, ask the students to be quiet and listen for me to repeat what a student had asked, and ten seconds later have the classroom erupt in cacophony once again. There were days I just dissolved in laughter and told my students they were as noisy and uncontrollable as a flock of geese. I said I didn't know how Mao could possibly have gained enough control of the country to have mounted a revolution; I didn't think Chinese people could be still and listen to anyone that long. The students just laughed.

The upshot of all this voice-straining repetition and volume was that I would come home after a morning in class with my chest hurting and barely enough breath to make it up to our third floor apartment. On days when Don had a similar schedule, he had the same symptoms. We both suffered frequently from sore throats and hoarseness—mostly hoarseness. It seemed to go with the job. Emily and Zhirong gave us traditional Chinese medicine, proclaimed by all and sundry to guarantee a cure. We never knew what was in the stuff until one time when Emily got some laryngitis pills for us which had come from the Chengdu Traditional Chinese Pharmaceutical Factory. The ingredients and directions were written in both Chinese and English and provided enlightening reading: borax, toad cake, rhinoceros horn, cow bezoar, pearl, bear gall. We thought about all the TV nature programs we'd seen about rhinos, for example, being killed only for their horns and about the attempts to stop such poaching. We hated to think that we were contributing to that in any way, however small. But the medicine did, at least, seem to work.

We couldn't believe the complete fatigue we were experiencing. Although I have never been a person to take afternoon naps, I found myself hardly able to get through lunch before plopping on my bed for a luxurious snooze. Sushi (having a rest) is an institution in China. Between noon and two P.M. you need never worry about being disturbed.

Having just complained about how much my students talked, I must say too that sometimes it was extremely difficult to get them to speak. I might ask a simple question—for example, "Can you all come to the apartment on Thursday afternoon for conversation this week instead of Tuesday?"—and be met by silence, which I could only interpret as an affirmative answer. Only later might I learn that several students had another class or some other schedule conflict at that time. It was hard to get students to nod their heads yes or no or to raise their hands. I learned that my students would rather remain silent than tell a teacher "no" or disagree in any way.

I hate to perpetuate stereotypes, but I found there is a certain validity to the expression "inscrutable orientals."

When I was teaching in Illinois, I often cited a common communication breakdown that occurs between Eastern and Western people. It was that Asians, if asked, "You don't want to go?" will say "Yes," even though they do not want to go.

Their response is correct, grammatically. What they mean is "Yes, you're right, I don't want to go." But, of course, that's not how a Westerner would respond.

Sure enough, in China, I witnessed my example many times. To be certain I understood the intent of an answer, then, I would have to paraphrase the response, saying, for instance, "Yes, you don't want to go." *Urally*, it worked!

Urally?

That's the Chinese version of "usually." The "su" sound is one that Chinese find difficult to pronounce. Even now, Don and I find ourselves affectionately muttering "urally" whenever we feel nostalgic about China.

In the first few class periods teaching materials were no problem. Getting acquainted in all its aspects took time. But with the more accelerated groups, particularly my doctoral class which I was meeting eight hours a week, I quickly found myself scavenging for subject matter. Those boxes containing supplementary materials that we had mailed in July still hadn't arrived as of late September. We muttered darkly about slow boats to China.

In the meantime each day we faced bright and eager students whose minds we wanted to turn on. But what resources could we use?

First, I learned that many students, and especially the doctoral students, had shortwave radios. So one day a week we talked about current events—what they'd heard on VOA, BBC, or Radio Moscow. They listened to these radio services to improve their English, but in the process they also learned what was happening in the outside world. They learned from VOA, for example, days before there was anything in the Chinese newspapers, that some of the leaders of the Tiananmen Square demonstration were being tried. They also learned that the Chinese government had asked the American Academy Awards organization to withdraw nomination of *Ju Dou* as one of the best foreign films for 1989. They didn't even know there was such a film, let alone that it had been nominated for an award. It had not been shown publicly in China—and still has not, to my knowledge.

In late September and early October China hosted the Asian Games, a regional version of the Olympics. The event dominated TV for weeks, and all of China was preoccupied with the spectacle. China walked off with most of the prizes, and that set off a surge of patriotism, pride, and euphoria. Some students knew that China had been referred to as "the sick man" of Asia in the past and felt that the victories in the games showed that China was no longer sick.

In my search for supplementary materials I found an essay on sportsmanship by George Orwell. In his ironic style he wrote that while sportsmanship is supposed to promote brotherhood and goodwill, it usually has the opposite effect. The essay seemed appropriate and relevant, considering the games then going on in China, so I made copies and assigned it for discussion.

All of my students seemed to be regularly involved in some physical activity. There were several basketball and volleyball courts throughout campus, not to mention makeshift Ping-Pong tables, which were occupied daily when classes were not in session. I recognized many of my students among the players on our walks around campus.

Knowing this, I said, "Why do you play sports?"

"For exercise," they chorused. "To be strong," added others.

"Because it's fun," chimed still others.

"What if you don't win?" I asked. "Do you care if you don't win?"

They chorused, "Of course."

"Of course, we like to win," one fellow said, "but we just say we'll win tomorrow."

"Do you feel ashamed or disgraced if you lose?" I asked.

They looked at me, shaking their heads and laughing, as if I had said something foolish.

I asked what they thought of Orwell's claim that there is a dangerous linkage between sports and prestige, that the prospect of defeat, whether it be personal loss or one by a larger unit, such as a school or nation, of which a person is a member, arouses the most savage combative instincts.

I said, "Orwell says that nations seriously believe—for short periods, anyway—that running, jumping, and kicking a ball are tests of national virtue. Do you think he's exaggerating?"

When no one answered, I pressed further, "Do you think that if a nation is good at those things, that means it is a virtuous, a good nation?"

They remained quiet, some half shaking their heads.

When I asked if they knew what Orwell meant by his reference to the 1936 Olympic games as an example of how international sporting contests lead to orgies of hatred, I was surprised to learn they did. I hated to dampen their enthusiasm about China's triumphs in the Asian Games, but I thought Orwell's essay could be a thoughtful antidote to their euphoria.

China publishes one English language newspaper, the *China Daily*, which circulates worldwide. The Foreign Affairs Department provided us with a copy each day, and occasional articles there were a source of discussion. When I found something relevant or interesting, I typed it out, using my trusty little computer, and attached discussion questions.

Some topics, like the hazards of smoking, were quite prosaic. China is a nation of smokers. Many of my students were smokers; and while some wished they could quit, there was little awareness or concern about the health hazards of smoking. The cigarette vendors are everywhere along the streets. Even in the poorest of areas and in the countryside, a wide selection of cigarette brands is available, with American brands prominent among them.

While the Ministry of Health attempts an education program, students said, with some amusement, that the ministry probably will not be able to mount an all-out campaign until all the heavy-smoking octogenarians in the government are gone. One hardly ever saw a picture of Deng Xiao Ping on film without a cigarette in his hand.

Offering cigarettes is imbedded in the culture in various ways. At weddings the bride and groom offer cigarettes and candy to their guests. In trying to ease tension in either a business or social situation, cigarettes are passed around, preferably imported brands. When someone is attempting to persuade someone to do them a favor, a cigarette may be offered as an inducement. For example, during a road trip we kept having to stop because of landslides or equipment blocking the road. One time a tractor and trailer sat in the middle of the road beside a pile of rock. The crew was eating lunch. Mr. He got out of the van and sought out the foreman to persuade him to get his crew to interrupt their lunch to remove the obstacles posthaste. All the time he talked with the foreman, he was offering him a cigarette. The man at first kept waving it away, but in the end Mr. He distributed cigarettes to all members of the crew. The equipment was moved and we drove on.

In class, we discussed an article that detailed what Western countries have done to curtail smoking. I described the change that had occurred in the United States in the last twenty-five years—the legislation, the changing social attitudes, the public awareness of health hazards—and how surprised I was. I would never have thought such a change possible. However, they listened and reacted somewhat as if I were discussing unusual social customs of another nature. They were more amused or astonished than impressed.

When I talked about the danger to health, most students defended smoking as a means of revenue for the government and as a crop for farmers. When I acknowledged I had read that ten percent of China's budget comes from cigarette taxes (a figure I had gotten from a Hong Kong newspaper), they told me the figure was actually much too low. When I pointed out that smoking may cost society more in the way of medical and other social services for those smokers, I am not sure the possibility really registered. It was clearly a new thought.

Although in the United States it would no longer be considered in good taste to urge cigarettes on a nonsmoking colleague or even a subordinate, in China it is seen as a hospitable gesture—unless the person is female, that is. Reacting to an article in the *China Daily* reporting the increase in women smoking, a new phenomenon, students overwhelmingly opposed women smoking, including women themselves. There definitely is a double standard. Most oppose it on the basis that women bear children. Even though they were aware of the effects of passive smoking, they still let fathers off the hook.

Only a few students said, "If it's stupid and unhealthy for women to smoke, it's also stupid and unhealthy for men."

One prospective father had had part of a lung removed the previous year, but had begun to smoke again. He even admitted that smoking costs him one-third of his pitifully small teacher's salary. But still he continued buying cigarettes. I told him that he must have a very tolerant wife.

I was embarrassed by the abundant supply of American cigarettes available everywhere we went in China, even in remote rural areas. I was quick to confess to students that I think it highly immoral for our government to allow and even encourage American tobacco companies to freely advertise and market abroad a product that we acknowledge causes health problems and death.

Since there were several smokers in each class, we had lively, sometimes humorous discussions on the topic. Even though they know the hazards, some students still envy smokers and said that they would smoke if they could afford it. I referred to a previous class discussion of a Bertrand Russell essay entitled, "How To Avoid Foolish Opinions." I said whatever their views, I hoped they recognized that some of their justifications might be false, even "foolish." I must confess, though, that I made little headway in changing their attitudes. Such discussions helped students practice their English and gave us insight into their opinions about social issues.

Some newspaper articles even gave us an opportunity to indirectly discuss the Chinese political system—something we would never have been able to do directly. For example, one article described the experience of a Chinese-Japanese joint venture, which had had problems on both sides. While the two peoples share many cultural values and heritage, their national experience has been different in the past century and so there were conflicts and different perspectives that caused problems in the workplace. The Japanese owner complained about tardiness, apathetic work habits, and resistance to orders. The Chinese complained about being arbitrarily fired the first time they erred. The conclusion was that more than forty years of Chinese socialism, with its guaranteed jobs, had left people unprepared for the performance expectations of capitalist entrepreneurs.

A set of articles, from the *Columbus Dispatch* in Ohio, sent by a nephew, portrayed similar problems among East German workers who had flocked to West Germany after reunification. The scenario had a similar sound: absence of the work ethic; East Germans not used to paying taxes, feeling at sea without a paternal government to look out for them.

I used both the articles about the Japanese-Chinese venture and those about the German experience in class. While we confined our discussion to the East German situation, students could not help but make a connection between that situation and theirs.

In the college library, I also found a *Reader's Digest* article, written after the fall of the East German government, about the opulent lives of East German Communist officials. It described their luxurious homes, staffs of servants, Olympic-size swimming pools, and collections of antique automobiles. Again I brought the article to class for discussion. We stuck to the facts and not a word did we say about the Chinese government. We didn't have to. The inferences were clear.

My little laptop computer, which my sons had talked me into buying instead of a typewriter, turned out to be a marvelous tool, particularly when I considered the alternative. When we first started teaching, we took articles and quizzes to the Foreign Language Department to be typed and then sent to the campus print shop. Not only was turnaround time a whole week, but the quality of work was abominable. There could be a dozen misspellings in one item, including an error in the title itself. That was an unnecessary obstacle in the path of students struggling to learn a language correctly. At times, we bit our lip, not knowing whether to get angry or laugh.

Once, I made up a quiz that consisted of one short paragraph with blanks for some missing words that students were to fill in. When Don went to pick up the finished copies, he saw it had been typed, double-spaced, in the middle of oversized paper, with three-inch margins on both sides. In her halting English the secretary complained about the amount of paper it took, and she reminded Don that paper was expensive.

Of course the way she typed it *was* a waste of paper. She could have used smaller margins and changed the line space and easily have gotten two paragraphs to a page. Perhaps she didn't know how to adjust her old manual typewriter. Whatever, it struck me that the secretary should be grateful for her guaranteed job.

8

Before we went to China, when I thought about Don and me spending a whole year in a three-room apartment, after having lived in no less than seven rooms for the past forty years, I was understandably apprehensive. We have given each other lots of space in recent years, particularly the past twenty since our last child went off to college and our nest has been empty.

In addition to a sound system in the main part of the house, Don has a bedroom full of stereo and amateur radio equipment plus a TV, and a garage with a well-equipped, heated workshop. I have a study for school work, organizational activities, and my computer. We could enjoy togetherness or give each other a wide berth when the mood dictated. Although Don had been retired for three years already, I had continued to work, so we had not really tested what it was like to live together in retirement. In China, we would really be together.

Once there, however, we got along surprisingly well. We resolved at the outset that it would be pretty important to run a tight ship and keep things tidy. Both of us tend to get irritable in the midst of clutter. We also realized that we needed to stay out of each other's way. That is not easy to do in three rooms, particularly when the kitchen is no more than eight feet square. Although not intentionally, we tended to choreograph our movements.

When Don's internal alarm went off each day, he got up first and began his morning ritual in the bathroom. When I gained consciousness, I got up, moved into the kitchen to begin breakfast, and set the table. When he finished in the bathroom, he moved into the bedroom, dressed, and made the beds. I took my turn in the bathroom, and when he went to the kitchen to put the finishing touches on breakfast, I dressed in the bedroom. It was smooth, even without music. Other chores took on a similar routine.

Living in China, where there was so much talk of socialism, even though it isn't really socialism in the classic sense, and where the way of life reflects the social system to a great extent, I found myself looking at things in economic terms more than I might otherwise. We developed a real division of labor, none of which was ever spelled out in any discussion.

For instance, I cooked, Don did dishes. I cleared the breakfast table, and Don filled the bathroom water bottle with cold boiled water for teeth brushing. He gathered up wastebaskets and thermos bottles and set them outside the door each morning. When we came back from classes each morning, our ration of two thermoses of hot boiled water awaited us.

We took the same approach to washing our clothes. We did our laundry in the small portable washing machine provided. Don usually started the laundry process—and it was a process. First, he lit the water heater and then filled three buckets of very hot water from the bathtub spigot, which was the only outlet for hot water in the flat. While the first bucket was filling, he rolled the washer next to the sink, a few feet from its corner in the kitchen, and plugged it in. The machine was rectangular in shape, with the washer on one side and a small spin drier on the other. As soon as I heard the agitator in motion, I sorted the laundry in the bedroom and put in the first load of white clothes. By that time Don had moved into the living room, his task finished.

I decided early on, living in China, that there were some advantages to being older. I had gone to housekeeping in the late 1940's with an Easy Spindrier. One part was a conventional washer and the other was a spindrier, a kind of forerunner of automatic washers. I had used such a machine again in the mid-1960's, when we had lived in England for a year, and even then I felt I had stepped back in time. Now, here was the same machine in China twenty-five years later. Washing with this machine called for some ingenuity in order to achieve the most efficiency: from the soap, the hot water, the time and energy expended. But, at least, I had experience.

When one load of clothes was done, instead of draining the hot soapy water and rinsing the clothes immediately, I fished them out into a plastic bucket. Then I put another load of clothes into the hot water, and if the laundry pile that week was a big one (keep in mind that it was a very small washer), maybe even a third. Once I had finished washing, I put each batch of clothes back into the washer for a rinse, having to fill and drain the water off several times. Once the clothes were rinsed, I put them over into the spindrier. And the clothes did come out remarkably dry. It meant handling the clothes a lot, but it did save hot water.

Then it was drying time. Electric or gas driers? Forget it. Drying meant hanging up. When the weather was nice, we hung the clothes on a line strung across both balconies. Although I tried to hang more personal items on the bedroom balcony, I sometimes ran out of space and had to hang them on the more public living room one. I soon got over being embarrassed when callers and I had conversation in full view of Don's boxer shorts or my bras. People seemed oblivious to such things, perhaps because that's just the way it is in China.

You can't be in China very long and not be aware of the shortages and the tremendous efforts to economize on energy of all kinds. Although Chengdu fared better than some other communities, water sometimes was available only during certain hours of the day and always was off from midnight to 6:00 A.M. Occasionally electricity would be off for certain periods, and at times gas pressure was too low to cook effectively.

Back to my original comments about looking at things in economic terms. I don't know whether our division of labor was "socialist equality" or just making the most efficient use of resources to achieve maximum benefits. Whatever it was, it worked.

One deficiency in our apartment was the lack of storage space. There were no closets, although there was a row of hooks by the front door. There was only one medium-sized wardrobe and only a few drawers in nightstands and the footboards of the beds. It was not easy to keep our clothes separate, and our unisex underwear especially caused problems.

As the weather got colder, we started layering our clothes, beginning with long underwear. We brought four sets with us that we had bought from a surplus store, identical except that two were large, and two were medium size. Don was so used to thinking of long underwear as "his" that on two occasions he put on the medium pants and realized only afterward that they were "hers." Too late. The damage was done. His ample girth had stretched them irretrievably. So all winter I wore underwear that fit like a flour sack. All those layers under normal-fitting pants were bulky enough already, but tucking in those extra folds called for extra dexterity every time I visited the bathroom. We both had a rather lumpy appearance from November until March.

Wearing long underwear and trying to tuck the bottoms smoothly into my calf-length socks so there wasn't a bulky ridge reminded me of when I was a little girl. We had no central heating in our farmhouse in northwestern Ohio and I hated having to wear long underwear in winter. How I despised that telltale ridge around my ankles that showed the whole world that I was wearing those hated long johns. I envied the girls who had snow pants that matched their coats and that they could take off when they got to school. I was so ashamed and was glad when spring came.

I mentioned earlier that we both needed to maintain a certain sense of order in such close quarters. Whenever I've seen movies depicting colonial life in Africa or India, it always seemed ludicrous to see those regimented British serving tea from a silver service or having a house-boy serve from a chafing dish out in the bush. Now, however, I better understand the need of the colonials, who may have been away from home for years, to maintain some semblance of their accustomed life-style. It helps achieve a certain stability or normalcy in life when you can follow some of the same routines and habits you did at home concerning food, table settings, and the like.

After a few weeks' experience, we had not only developed our own routine, but also some rather mundane rules to stay happy, healthy, and reasonably comfortable in China: (1) never drink water that hasn't been boiled, (2) seldom eat anything that hasn't been cooked, (3) never go out of the house without toilet paper and a handkerchief or facial tissues, and (4) never leave the house in the morning until you have deposited at least part of your morning coffee in the bathroom.

9

Before we came to China I had read that there was both a Protestant and Catholic church in Chengdu, so we intended to attend the Protestant church at some time. We wanted to experience worship, but we were also interested and curious about the nature of the church in China where religion had been banned for so long. We did not anticipate, however, how much difficulty we would have getting there.

We were very busy for the first few weeks, but I did tell our Waiban (Foreign Affairs Department) that we were interested in going and asked them to check the location for us. Another American told us the church was near the Mao statue in downtown, but that it did not resemble a church building and was hard to find. She promised to meet us at the statue at 9:15 the following Sunday morning and lead us there. We asked Emily to arrange for a car. She reported that the non-English speaking driver knew where the church was and had taken many people there, so we didn't bother to discuss it any further.

On Sunday the driver picked us up at nine o'clock and made his way into town. Since most people work six days a week, they do much of their shopping on Sundays. The streets then were very crowded that morning.

We found ourselves winding around some narrow back streets. In a little while the driver stopped in front of a building, which looked like a kind of arcade. He got out of the car and asked something of a woman in front who was sweeping the street. She nodded, and he opened the car door, pointed toward the building, and gestured for us to get out of the car. In English he mentioned the Jinjiang Hotel, where we were to meet, pointed to three o'clock on his watch, and drove off.

We walked a little way inside the big archway, but saw no sign of any building or any activity that in any way resembled a church. That didn't put us off particularly because we had been told that the church was hard to find and didn't look like a conventional church building.

We decided we'd be better off to go out to the street to wait for several of the people we knew would be coming or, better still, to walk back to the Mao statue where the Americans had told us to meet them. We were sorry we hadn't followed their advice. Many times previously we had driven by the statue because it is on one of the main streets; and even though we had not seen it this morning, we assumed the driver had taken a short cut and that the statue must be up the street further. We started walking, but nothing looked familiar. After a while we walked back and waited in front of the building, wondering why we didn't see other Westerners coming along. A little later a Chinese woman approached, placed her hands together in a prayer position, and gestured inside. I nodded and smiled but stayed put.

We'd been told that the congregation practiced hymns beginning at 9:30 in preparation for the service at ten. When 9:30 came and went and we heard no singing and recognized no familiar faces, we realized we must be at the wrong place.

I went back through the arch into a big courtyard and walked toward the rear. I must have looked a little uncertain because a young woman approached me, said, "Good Morning," and asked if she could help. I said that we were looking for a church. She looked a little bewildered, turned to find someone to help, then led me to the back and side of the courtyard, turned a corner, and went through the open door of a small office. I saw a religious picture on the wall and decided we might be getting close.

The young woman said something to the handful of people inside. When I asked if this was a church, a small man, perhaps in his late sixties, and wearing a Mao cap and blue suit that always seems to complete that ensemble, came forward and assured me in halting English that it was. Since nothing there looked very ecclesiastical, I asked him where the service was and what time it would begin. He answered by leading me back to the courtyard in the direction we had come from.

I trailed along. I suspected that we might be at the Catholic church, but I found that, in itself, hard to believe. After all, we Protestants sometimes worship in the humblest of storefront churches, but never the Catholics. Somehow I thought that even Chinese Catholics would have a little more substantial accommodations.

"Is this a Catholic Church?" I asked, hurrying to keep up.

He said, "Yes, I'm a Catholic bishop."

I groaned inwardly and explained that we were Protestant and were looking for the church near the Mao statue. Immediately he looked a little stricken. But he indicated that he knew the church I meant. When I told him we were walking, he looked dismayed.

"The church is a long way," he said, "about five miles."

He led me out to the street where Don was waiting and pointed back down the street in the direction from which our car had come.

"When you reach the main thoroughfare, you can get a number 5 bus, which will take you toward the church," he told us.

We thanked him and left. I couldn't fault the driver. He had taken us to a church, and a church is a church, right?

It was a long way back to the main street. As we walked, our situation became clearer and more bleak. We had forgotten our city map. We didn't know the name of any of the streets. And though Don usually has an unerring sense of direction, Chengdu was having another of its cloudy days, so we had a hard time telling east from west. We realized too that once we got to the main thoroughfare we wouldn't know which direction to go on the bus. The narrow little street we were walking along was strictly residential and the people we passed did not appear likely to speak English. Furthermore, I had not thought to bring along my *Chinese for Travelers*.

We had no idea where we were, but we knew we were a long way from the church. Since it was almost time for the service to start, we realized we wouldn't make it. Now, we found ourselves wondering what we would do until three o'clock, when the driver was to pick us up—assuming we could find the hotel by three.

We continued walking and finally reached the main thoroughfare. Now, which way to start walking? On a whim we turned left, eventually reached a main shopping area, and continued. Don happened to see, in a shop window, a lighter he'd been looking for in order to light our small gas stove. As he paid for our purchase, he asked the young clerk where the Jinjiang Hotel was. That was a recognizable name. The young man pointed and we discovered with relief that we were going in the right direction.

We continued walking, asked directions to the hotel of a couple of soldiers, and were reassured again when they pointed in the same general direction.

Surprisingly we ended up near the Mao statue. From there we headed toward the hotel. We could at least look forward to a good lunch, the first Western meal since we had arrived in China.

Although the menu at the hotel's rooftop restaurant at the Jinjiang would not be mistaken for an honest-to-goodness Western restaurant menu, there were enough familiar items to give encouragement to food-starved American psyches, if not food for the soul that Sunday morning. It took no time at all for Don to decide on corn chowder and hamburger steak. I settled for tomato soup and a veal cutlet. The soup wasn't too bad, but my rather gristly veal made me resolve to stick to hamburger the next time. What made our eyes widen were the big puffy rolls and pats of *butter* that came with them. We asked for seconds on the rolls and butter, and lingered over the meal.

Since we were rather early for lunch, there were few other diners. Four Westerners who were having a late breakfast filed past our table as they left the restaurant. The last man paused to greet us, asking if we were there for the celebration. That was the beginning of a very informative afternoon with Dr. Howard Liljestrand, a retired surgeon living in Hawaii.

Slender and surprisingly energetic for his more than eighty years, he had grown up in Chengdu. Howard's father had been dean of the medical school at West China Medical and Science University, known as Huaxie, just down the street. The university, still one of the top institutions in the country, was started by several Christian denominations. Howard's father and mother had come to China in 1912 as medical missionaries. Howard was four at the time, his brother, two. Now, Howard and his brother, along with Howard's two sons, were back at Huaxie for the university's eightieth anniversary, the celebration he had referred to.

Our momentary encounter grew into a long conversation, and the other three men—Howard's sons and his brother—drifted back and gathered around our table. In a remarkable coincidence Dr. Liljestrand and his wife were good friends of a Danville physician and his wife, and had visited in Danville several times.

Before they left us to finish our lunch, Dr. Liljestrand invited us to accompany them that afternoon on a tour of the university grounds and to see the special exhibits.

In our personally guided tour, duly recorded by his two sons on video cameras, Dr. Liljestrand pointed out the original buildings, all magnificent and well maintained. The architecture was traditional Chinese; yet, ironically, the buildings were designed in London. Supposedly there had been no one in China at that time with the requisite design skills.

He also pointed out that the original cornerstones of the buildings, which had proclaimed them as missionary enterprises, had been removed to eliminate that association for the present-day population.

As we strolled around the campus, pausing now and then, Dr. Liljestrand told us more about growing up in China in the early 1920's.

Occasionally he and his brother reminisced about a particular happening. They had attended a boarding school on campus, which the university ran and where many children from various parts of China studied. Dr. Liljestrand spoke of the warlords who attacked each other endlessly until the outbreak of World War II and whose battles they could hear and see in the distance. He confessed that he had no sense of danger at that time. If his parents were worried, they gave no indication of it.

Dr. Liljestrand left in 1927 to study at Harvard. His parents remained in China until 1949, when they were forced to flee because of the Revolution. The opportunity to leave came suddenly, and they left on a plane that flew south into Burma. Even though it was a night flight, they couldn't fly over the mountains because the plane wasn't pressurized. The trip, through mountain passes, took hours. It was, Dr. Liljestrand said, his mother's first and last plane ride.

A few days later, we asked Monique and Melinda where the Protestant church was, since they had attended there the Sunday before, riding into town on their bicycles. They marked our Chinese map, and said we couldn't miss it. We planned to try again, sure that we now knew where it was.

This time we asked to be let out near the statue on the corner of the street where we were sure, from the map, that the church was located. Then we waited on the street corner down from the church where we thought M & M would be coming on their bikes.

No one came. So I went down the street to see if I could find the church, while Don remained behind acting as lookout in case someone did come along. Again, although there was a gateway down the block a short way and a building off to the left inside, similar to one described to us, there was no sign of a church. We mentally kicked ourselves for not being more thorough.

For a while we walked all around the area, convinced that we were in the right neighborhood. But, at last, we gave up and headed once more for the Jinjiang Hotel.

As we sat down to another relaxing lunch on the sunny roof terrace, we realized some people might have doubts about the sincerity of our attempts to worship on the Lord's day.

Another week went by. Emily resolved to see that we made it to church and decided to ride along with us. We also had the same driver, and even he was beginning to feel responsible for getting these dumb Americans to their destination. This time they delivered us to the right building, which indeed looked like it had been described and was near where we had been the previous week. Emily talked to the women at the gate who were there to greet people, to make sure we were in the right place. Then she and our chauffeur drove off, probably with a sigh of relief.

Although we were early, there were already a few people sitting on chairs in the courtyard, where a loudspeaker system was set up. We saw that there still were empty seats inside, however, so we made our way to the door.

The sanctuary was a long rectangle, seating about six hundred people. We were ushered to two almost vacant pews about ten rows from the front. That made us uncomfortable as we were uncertain why we were getting such preferential treatment. Later we learned that these pews routinely are reserved for foreigners. But on this Sunday an older Chinese man, who spoke a little English, was seated at the end.

The congregation was diverse, split between old and young. There were few middle-aged people. Those who sat in the rows in front of us were almost all older people. Most were women. By their dress and demeanor, it was clear that they possessed little of this world's goods. They sat reading their Bibles or visiting quietly amongst themselves. Other people wandered around the sanctuary at will. Younger people tended to sit in the back half of the church, either out of preference or because by the time they got there all the seats were taken, or perhaps to distance themselves from all those little old people in front. Those in the courtyard tended to be a mixed group.

The church inside looked not unlike the Ohio church I grew up in and many other churches in the Midwest that I remembered from my childhood in the pre–World War II era. The chancel had a communion or altar table against the back wall below a brass cross. A row of small vases of chrysanthemums lined the front of the table. A board attached to a post, off to the right and in full view of the congregation, held the page numbers of the three hymns that were to be sung that morning. The choir loft was off to the right, with chairs facing the pulpit, situated on the left. An upright piano stood on the platform to the extreme left.

Although the worship service did not begin till 10:00, we had intentionally gone early to be there for the congregational hymn practice at 9:30. At the appointed time a tall spare man, perhaps in his sixties, announced the first hymn from the pulpit, read the words, then went to the piano and proceeded to play the notes, half of them correctly, while the congregation sang. While he was introducing the second hymn, back at the pulpit, a young woman appeared at the piano, got out a hymn book, and took over the accompaniment, freeing him to lead the singing. She was only slightly better. I began to think that perhaps I should do a little practicing on Professor Zhang's piano and offer my services for the next Sunday. That thought was thankfully short-lived, saving both me and Chinese worshipers untold embarrassment, because another pianist, a middle-aged man, appeared and replaced the second. What he lacked in proficiency, this fellow made up for by his display of energy. Having practiced all three hymns, the song leader closed his hymnal promptly at 10:00, removed his glasses, picked up his papers, and, with some parting words to the congregation, left the chancel.

Almost immediately the pianist began a prelude, the choir filed in from the rear, and two members of the clergy followed, taking their places in the high-backed chairs behind the pulpit. The choir and ministers all wore robes.

Although the entire service was in Chinese, there was no problem in following what was happening. First there was an invocation, then a prayer, then an opening hymn. We were in luck. The first hymn was "Holy, Holy, Holy." We managed to sing the first verse from memory and sang the same words again through the second, third, and fourth verses. I'm sure the Chinese sitting around us didn't know the difference.

The first hymn was followed by scripture, then another hymn, the sermon, prayer, a closing hymn, and benediction. We could have been in a church in Ohio or Illinois, where presumably people were praying to the same God.

The Chinese man sitting beside us wrote the sermon text in English in his little book and showed it to me. From time to time in the future, when someone who spoke English, or a Westerner who knew some Chinese sat beside us, the person usually would fill us in on the main points of the sermon as we went along.

As soon as the service was over, people surged toward the doors, and we learned to hold back rather than risk getting trampled. We figured the congregation must have needed to get home quickly before the rice cooked dry.

Once outside in the courtyard, many people lingered, however, and engaged in leisurely conversation. Some English-speaking people approached us rather hesitantly and began conversations. Others just smiled and responded to our *Ni hao* (hello). We also met some Westerners who also were teaching at colleges and universities in the city.

Eventually some of these folks formed an informal fellowship, which we joined occasionally. They met a couple of Sundays a month for Bible study and conversation. Although we liked our situation at the College of Geology, we were located in the boondocks, as it were, and so we weren't able to socialize with other Westerners as much as we would have liked. Getting downtown was not easy.

As the autumn wore on, the weather got colder and we put on more clothes to attend church. We struggled to turn pages with our gloves on and saw our breath when we sang the hymns. We not only wore extra socks, we took something warm to sit on. We were having to sit longer because we continued to arrive at least half an hour early to ensure getting a seat inside. We marveled that people sat outside in such temperatures and wondered what church attendance would be like in the United States, if worshipers had to sit in unheated buildings or worse yet, outside.

10

In China you could hear firecrackers any hour of the day, almost any day of the week. At times I feared that another revolution had broken out and no one had told me. Firecrackers were used to celebrate weddings, new business ventures, and other special occasions. The intent was to scare off evil spirits.

Ironically, or so it seemed to us, given the American way of celebrating Independence Day, the one time we heard no firecrackers was October 1, China's National Day. The Chinese do make a big deal of their National Day. It's one of the few times people have a day free from work. Because of that, it's a popular day for weddings.

One of the first public events we went to after beginning our teaching duties was on the eve of National Day. We "Foreign Experts" were invited to a banquet sponsored by the Foreign Affairs Department of Sichuan province.

The banquet was held at the Jinjiang Hotel. About 250 people, both Chinese and Westerners, attended. When we entered the room, we saw that three rows of chairs were set up around the periphery. Since the number of people still outnumbered the seats, many people circulated, congregating between round tables heaped with food of all kinds.

After the guests had a short time to mingle and chat and sip drinks, provincial officials made welcoming speeches, with accompanying English translations.

It had not been made clear to us just what this event was about, so I stepped forward, hoping to find out. Good intention! Even though I pushed as close to the front as I could and all the speakers were using microphones, I still couldn't hear above the chatter created not by the Western guests but by the Chinese themselves. Even the Chinese officials who spoke rarely bothered to listen to the other speakers.

After the welcoming speeches were over and we had decimated the buffet, a program of Chinese entertainment followed: singers, dancers, and instrumentalists. Once again I wound my way to the front to try to enjoy the performances. But again the effort was futile. The roar of conversation among the Chinese in the audience was deafening.

Later I told Jilin we were amazed by the audience's behavior, particularly during the political speeches. "Oh, we've heard it all before," he replied.

The lack of consideration, the sheer rudeness, by audiences at public events was something I was to witness time and again in the coming months.

The holiday weekend was to get better. The next morning, accompanied by Melinda and Monique, we were to venture outside Chengdu for the first time, heading to Mount Emei, 125 miles to the southwest. We would not return until late Monday, the college being closed that day in celebration of National Day. The trip was planned by the Foreign Affairs Department.

Before we went to China, we had corresponded with people in the Foreign Affairs Department. I had been curious about what they did. Once in China, we learned that all colleges and universities have such departments and that their staffs are responsible for the welfare of visiting foreigners.

After arriving at the college, we learned our mail should be sent to Foreign Affairs, instead of the Foreign Language Department. When one of my friends noticed the change in the return address, she asked if there were any significance to our now being in Foreign Affairs. She thought it sounded titillating. I wrote back that I'd always had enough trouble managing my domestic affairs, so I wasn't about to take on any foreign ones. I couldn't speak for Don, however.

One of the main responsibilities of the Waiban was to plan and provide a number of diversions for us *waiguoren*—foreigners, that is. Travel opportunities, such as this trip to Mount Emei, were among the perks.

We set out Saturday morning with Mr. He, who had met us in Beijing, and Mr. Chen, the driver, in the college's blue Toyota van for the three-day trip to the mountain. Because this was our first trip outside the city, we were particularly eager to see the countryside, and how the peasants worked and lived.

Sichuan province, known as China's breadbasket, is a veritable plain ringed by mountains. When we got to open country, we found the land was a giant grid divided into small plots, bordered by low dikes. We had heard that Chinese farmers were enjoying greater prosperity under Deng Xiao Ping's policies. Some of the farmhouses we saw suggested this was true. They were relatively large, some being two stories tall. But we also saw dramatic examples of the extent of human toil that is expended to feed China's population. Occasionally we saw what we in the States call a garden tractor, and we saw many water buffalo pulling wooden plows, but most of what we witnessed was stoop labor. In some cases, men themselves pulled plows. We saw both men and women bent almost double, weeding or harvesting their plots, or dipping "night soil" (human excrement) to fertilize their crops. Men bearing shoulder poles, vegetable-laden baskets suspended from either end, trudged along the road. Other men bore baskets, almost as big as they were, or pulled carts, loaded with sand or bricks, their bodies taut from the strain. We saw humans doing tasks that would be performed by animals or machines in more developed parts of the world. Looking at the situation practically, China's farm plots are too small to lend themselves to mechanization. The word "field" is an inappropriate description. Still, the sight of so much hard physical labor was disquieting.

We arrived at the foot of Mount Emei about noon. Before leaving on this trip, we learned that most of our students had been to the mountain because the college maintains a field station nearby for geological research. Most had climbed to the top, a journey that can take several days on foot. They warned us of food-stealing monkeys dwelling on the mountainside. But the monkeys were not a problem for us. We climbed most of the mountain the easy way, in the Toyota van.

Still, the trip was not entirely comfortable. The mountain road was like a washboard, an expression from my childhood in rural Ohio, but which was a vast understatement applied here. It was good our breakfast had settled well before we started up. We went as far as we could by van, about one-third of the way to the summit, and then pulled into a parking area not nearly large enough to accommodate all the buses, trucks, and other vehicles attempting to squeeze in. We left our driver to sort it out.

From there, we climbed a steep, quarter-mile path that American park rangers would probably have marked "of medium difficulty." The path led to a lift station, built a year or two before. There, we boarded a gondola, big enough to hold about twenty people, and took a five-minute ride to the top.

Mount Emei is the highest of four sacred Buddhist mountains in the region, and the summit offered us a breathtaking vista. One vegetation-covered mountain range after another rolled on in all directions as far as the eye could see. Although the day was sunny, a blue-green haze filtered our view, creating a mystical panorama like those so often depicted in Chinese paintings.

As we drove down the mountain, thinking about the magnificent scenery, I asked Mr. He if there were plans to improve the roads and hotels and to develop the area so it would be more accessible to foreign tourists. (According to the *China Daily*, in 1991 there were less than four hundred miles of super highway in all of China.) Mr. He answered that there was no money.

It amounts to a Catch-22. China seeks and could realize a bonanza from tourism. But the nation can't develop tourism to its full potential without first investing capital.

Not that money is the only obstacle. The Chinese must also learn to meet Western standards for service and cleanliness. Our hotel in Emei was an example of China's shortcomings in these categories. It consisted of several rather widely separated buildings in a lovely setting, with hilly terrain, lush vegetation, and a rushing stream crossing the grounds. The hotel buildings themselves were spacious with wide porches and inner courtyards. From the outside the accommodations seemed quite nice. The interior spoiled it all, however. The walls were marked, fixtures were obviously long broken, and the rooms were filthy. A quarter inch of water covered the tile bathroom floor and the water in the toilet ran continuously. Thus, for want of a little maintenance, the appearance of a potentially beautiful place was, for us, sullied.

The next day we visited Leshan to see the Great Buddha, a colossal statue, 234 feet high, cut into the face of a sandstone cliff overlooking a wide river. Carved in the eighth century, the Great Buddha was intended to protect boatmen from drowning in the swift currents of the river below.

While our hotel in Leshan was newer and nicer, there was another problem with the commode. The flush lever kept coming loose. Out of three hotels we'd stayed in so far (including the one in Beijing), none was clean or in good repair. We could only conclude that this was typical.

In spite of these minor complaints, the weekend was enjoyable. My only real regret was that I had left behind at the Emei hotel a white turtleneck. The loss of one shirt may not seem like a big deal, but my wardrobe was pretty limited and, besides, the turtleneck was one of my favorites. I thought about all of those stories I'd read about honest Chinese who, after the Revolution, went to great lengths to return lost or forgotten items to foreigners. Supposedly, they did this to demonstrate their commitment to socialist principles. I found myself wishing that were still the case and that some diligent, honest Chinese would track me down, shirt in hand.

I I

I was intrigued by Don's teaching performance so far. While he wasn't exactly relishing his task, he seemed to be getting a positive response. I felt obliged about that time to reassure friends at home who may have worried about his inexperience in teaching English (he who couldn't recognize a split infinitive or a gerund if his life depended on it). Although he had not been enthusiastic about the prospect of teaching, he had tackled it like he tackles everything else—if a thing is worth doing, it's worth doing well, right? So this was no unprepared teacher who walked into the classroom.

He said some of his students complained that he was assigning too much homework—did he think his was the only course they took? In fact, I was ready to complain, too. I read and marked all his compositions.

We weren't expected to do much with composition the first semester, but we found those exercises particularly enlightening. Through their writing we learned a great deal about students' attitudes and experiences.

Don had an advantage over me in that all his students already had taken or been given English names by previous teachers, so whereas I was struggling with names like Tuo Fuzhi, he could call his students David and Mark. He even had a Napoleon and a John Smith. Frankly, though, I liked knowing my students' real names and thought it important to their sense of identity.

Class A, the class that had had the French teacher and was back for a second semester, turned out to be Don's favorite. His students warmed to him and he to them. Their relationship was such that they threw a party for us the day after Mid-Autumn Festival. Mid-Autumn Festival, whose date is determined by the phases of the moon, is a traditional rather than an official holiday. Everyone has to work, but anyone who can goes home for a family dinner.

The party was held in their regular classroom on the second floor of the museum. About seven, we made our way to the unlighted side entrance of the building and groped our way up the stairs to the second floor. We had not yet learned to carry a flashlight with us when we went out at night. We rounded a corner and headed toward a room at the end of the hall from which a light shown.

When we walked in, the students applauded, rather an unsettling experience for teachers. They had arranged the desks into a big U, with us at the "head table."

On each desk they had piled apples, mandarin oranges, sunflower seeds, and peanuts in the shell. They also had for each of us a "moon cake," a hard, flavored biscuit-like pastry, traditional for that holiday. And, of course, a jar of tea. (Traditionally, after dinner you are to sit under the moon with your loved one and eat a moon cake—if the moon appears, that is.)

Most of the students were far away from their families, and they thought it sad that we were away from our family on this holiday. The party was their way of making it up to us. Each student made a little speech of welcome and expressed gratitude that we had come to China to teach them. Then they played some music and each told a story, or recited a poem, or sang a song, or just generally joked around. Taking our turn, we harmonized on "Down in the Valley." It was do-it-yourself entertainment.

One could say it was all rather hokey, but their obvious enjoyment and their expressions of good will were so sincere it was disarming. The Chinese seem innocent and unsophisticated, but very real, as children are real. That they could have such a good time with so little was appealing.

Escorted by a student with a flashlight, we went home that evening, warmed, in spite of the chill October night air.

A few weeks after classes started, we met Ruth and Paul Benedict of Bellingham, Washington, who were also teaching oral English. Ruth taught classes similar to mine at Hua Xie (West China Medical Science University), and Paul taught at #7 Middle School, supposedly one of the best middle schools in the city. Parents vied to send their children there. Paul was an English and literature teacher and was there as part of an ongoing exchange program that his Bellingham high school had with the Chinese school.

In response to Paul's question about what I was doing, I waxed ecstatic. I described my situation.

"It's a teacher's dream," I concluded.

He said his experience was more like a nightmare. "If there'd been a 747 warming up on the runway out at the Chengdu airport headed for home that first week, I'd have been on it."

When he described his situation, I sympathized.

He was assigned about seven hundred junior middle school students, divided into twelve classes (approximately sixty per class). He was to teach the students oral English. Considering the natural shyness of fifteen-year-old Chinese students, a dozen per class would have been more realistic. Textbook materials were not available, and he had to make up all tests himself.

What made things even more frustrating was that since the exchange program had been going on for some time, there were several people at the school who had taught in the Bellingham school and understood Paul's expectations. The difficulty seemed to be more with the school administration, however, not an exceptional situation in any culture.

What could I say after that? As the year progressed, Paul's outlook seemed to improve, but I think it was because he had resigned himself to doing only what he could in an impossible situation.

A few weeks into the term, the Postgraduate Department sponsored an English speech contest and I was asked by the young president of the English club, Mr. Wang, to be a judge. I was happy to oblige. It sounded like it would provide an interesting insight into another aspect of Chinese college life.

A few days later, when I asked him about the details, I heard that the theme of the speeches was to be about socialism and the Communist Party. I had some doubts. It sounded very political.

"Are you sure I should be doing this?"

Mr. Wang assured me it would not to be too political.

On Saturday afternoon Mr. Wang escorted me to the large lecture hall. The first thing I saw on the blackboard when I entered the room was a large colored chalk drawing of a hammer and sickle, quite professionally executed. Beside it, written in beautiful script, was the specific topic, "Eulogise the Socialist Motherland and the Leadership of the

Communist Party of China." So that was the precise topic of the day. Not too much room for debate there.

There were twelve entrants, some from the postgraduate and some from the doctoral classes. Half of them were my students. I had been asked by three of the entrants ahead of time to critique their written speeches—their grammar and phrasing, not their delivery—so I had had a preview of what I was in for. Some were more political than others, but most attributed the success of New China to the socialist system and the Communist Party. They all heaped much criticism on imperialism and the bureaucratic capitalism that China had suffered under in the past.

About halfway through the program, the import of the word "eulogise" really struck me. Did they know what they were saying? Wasn't this what people did at wakes and funerals? The realization almost undid me for a moment. Suddenly dissolving in smothered laughter would be very hard to explain, however, so I restrained myself. None of the speakers was going for laughs in this contest.

Besides, all I was hearing and reading about in China those days was how they needed to learn science and technology from the West and take part in more joint ventures with other countries. If their system was so good and capitalism was so bad, why did they need the West? I turned my attention back to the contestants. I'd think about that later.

One young man, whose speech was not very intelligible, talked about freedom and democracy and how those as practiced in the West were very appealing to Chinese young people. He went on to say, however, that Americans were not free to speak their minds, whereas in China people were equal and could say whatever they wanted. (I made a mental note to inform our friends and fellow citizens of this in my next letter home.) I was grateful that his was the last speech and also that his pronunciation and intonation were bad so that I could legitimately give him a low mark on grounds other than content.

It turned out that there were six judges for the contest. I was the only waiguoren. We six had been introduced at the beginning, and after the last speaker Mr. Wang, who had been a contestant as well as the emcee, invited one of the college vice-presidents who had acted as a judge to say a few words. Although the audience encouraged him with warm applause, he persisted in his refusal. Then Mr. Wang asked me to speak and I too refused. I thought he would accept my refusal too, but he went on to announce me anyway. I could not really refuse.

I had once again been struck by the lack of quiet during the speeches, particularly in a contest setting. It must have been very distracting to the speakers. I was strongly tempted to comment on that, but realized that would not be polite. Trying to strike a light note, I remarked that I had never had to work so fast as a judge. The scores were collected immediately after a speaker was finished, and I barely got my little ballot marked with a number before someone was there to scoop it up. Only after I had arrived that afternoon and realized that there were no forms on which to record scores, did I ask Mr. Wang what the criteria were for judging. They were not explained or announced. Either everyone else already knew or it was considered irrelevant because I heard no one else ask.

I had painstakingly written each down (content—10%; reading as opposed to memorization—10%; pronunciation—30%; intonation—30%; structure—20%). It was pointless, however, because there was no time to reflect on any of those and give a considered response. One could only judge holistically. Scores also had to be between 8 and 9.5. Why those particular numbers? Who knows?

I played it safe and went on to commend all the speakers for participating and for their courage in facing an audience of their peers. I also commended them for their loyalty and enthusiasm for their country. I had bitten my tongue once again. (Come to think about it, maybe that's why I had been having such a sore tongue—literally!)

I had arrived early, had sat in the front row, and had not turned around. When I stood up and faced the audience to make my remarks, I was amazed to see the large group of students who had turned out for this contest on a beautiful October Saturday afternoon. All of my students were there and, in retrospect, probably all of the rest of the postgrads, even though I didn't know all of them.

Only later did I realize that these kinds of activities were command performances. You had better be there. What I also realized later was that this kind of activity was organized by the Party and was only one of many like it throughout the year. I just happened to have a ringside seat at this one.

When I came to understand a little better how things worked, I realized that the things I found unacceptable in a competitive situation were irrelevant in these events. Real competition, in terms of careful analysis of the things they had listed as criteria, was not the purpose of that event. It was a political exercise, pure and simple. For that reason, too, the fact that the emcee also was a contestant posed no problem. The contest, so-called, was an opportunity to glorify socialism and the Communist Party and to bash capitalism, which they linked with feudalism and equated with imperialism. I later learned that some of the participants were already Party members; some might aspire to be in the future. The contestants were chalking up brownie points, perhaps to be cashed in later.

The following is an excerpt from the speech of one of my students. It didn't merit a prize, but it captures the flavor of the day.

> I remember a story about dark old China. In 1932, when the Tenth Olympic Games was held in Los Angeles in America, the corrupt Kuomintang government had no money to send a sport team to take part in the competition. Later, it was the general Zhang XueLiang himself who subsidized Liu Changchun, who was a famous short-distance race star in old China, so that he could enter the games. An American cameraman asked Liu in Los Angeles if he could take a picture of him with the posture of lifting up his hands, outward the back of it, and hanging his head. And then he wrote the caption under the photo: Look how this little Chinese races!
>
> But decades later, the Chinese Communist party succeeded in leading the Chinese people to overthrow three mountains—imperialism, feudalism, and bureaucratic capitalism—and to set up a new China. It was very lucky that the Twenty-fifth Olympic Games was also held in Los Angeles. This time the Chinese government sent a large sports delegation with more than four hundred athletes, and got good results. No matter where they went, they were welcomed and entertained warmly.
>
> And now, it is well-known that China held the Eleventh Asian Games successfully not long ago. China not only won the most gold medals, but also showed her stability and unity and national power to the whole world.
>
> What did it illustrate? Did it show our country as being rich, strong, and prosperous, day by day?
>
> Yes. In the past forty-one years, China has attained rapid economic development. The standard of living has improved markedly. All the facts have proved there is no new China without the Chinese Communist party, and only socialism can save both China and develop China.
>
> Fellow countrymen! Let's strengthen our victorious conviction! So long as we work together with one heart and struggle with great efforts, we'll surely succeed. We firmly believe that China—the bright red sun —will never set!

The first-place winner was one of my doctoral students, and he deserved it on all counts. His diction was good and he spoke with conviction. I was surprised when he appeared as a contestant because I had thought of him as anything but an idealogue of the Party. His speech did not exhibit quite as much passion or the exaggerated claims of some of the others, but it was a good safe speech. That he won the prize perhaps said something about the judges. Anyway, to my mind the wisdom of the group had prevailed.

And the prizes? Each of the four winners received a book. The books were all different but the subject matter was the same: politics—what else?

When I got home that day, I remembered my astonishment at seeing the word "eulogise" used in that context. Did the word not mean what I thought it meant? I checked my American Heritage dictionary. Sure enough, it said "to praise highly" and it defined "eulogy" as "a public speech or written tribute extolling the virtues of a person or thing; *especially, an oration honoring one recently deceased*" [italics, mine]. Ah, so there it was. That last was the meaning that the word had for me, and I thought that was the general connotation, but perhaps I was wrong.

Melinda stopped in just then and, although she's Canadian, I thought I'd test her understanding. She agreed with me. So there.

But, I remembered that the "s" in the word instead of a "z" indicated an English spelling and that most Chinese had learned British rather than American English, and they used British dictionaries. I thought perhaps that was the key.

Indeed it was. Jilin had lent me his British dictionary before our books arrived and I checked the word out there. Sure enough, it defined the word as "to praise," but there was no reference to "deceased." Another mystery solved.

In a way I was almost disappointed. I had relished a secret but delicious irony during the contest at the thought of all these fervent exhortations in praise of the demise of the Socialist Motherland and the Communist Party.

It was a wonderful story, but I had a very limited audience to appreciate it. There was no point in telling it to Chinese. I didn't think they would have been amused.

12

Generally speaking, Chinese people look very healthy, or maybe that's just my Western assumption that thin people are healthier than the overweight ones so prevalent in the United States. I don't know what the statistics say about the incidence of various diseases in the population, but people look trim and vigorous. From a purely lay point of view it stands to reason that people who walk or ride a bicycle everywhere, five to ten miles, are bound to be trim and have strong heart muscles. And their diet, consisting of much less meat and many more fruits and vegetables, is definitely sensible.

The Chinese put a great deal of stock in exercise, and from the first hour that we were up in the morning we could look out in any direction and see people of varying ages pursuing some kind of physical activity. Xiao Lu, the Foreign Guest House chef, would be out chinning himself and doing handstands on the parallel bars opposite the restaurant, perhaps waiting for the breakfast rice to cook.

Everywhere you could see people of all ages doing Qigong or Tai-chi, the meditation-type exercises. They were usually older people, but not always. And what a contrast they were to the television morning exercise show you might see at home. Whereas Americans would frantically exercise first one set of muscles or one part of the body at a time, to lose weight or trim inches, these exercises embodied slow, highly controlled, yet fluid, graceful movements. It was as if they were trying to tune into, to join, rather than fight nature or the universe.

Once I was walking through the garden, on a path that led to a favorite bench. I stopped short at the sight of a woman ahead—stiff, immobile, eyes closed, arms at side, her serene face thrust upward. Suddenly she thrust her arms upward, threw her head back, and then resumed her first position. I held back, feeling I was intruding on a private moment. While I waited, another couple went around me and on past the woman, neither of whom gave any recognition of the others' presence. I turned and changed my course. It was only I who felt like a transgressor.

One bright Sunday morning, up earlier than usual, I went out in the hall and looked across the street into the garden. A man, perhaps seventy, dressed in blue padded jacket, blue pants, and a blue Mao cap was doing a Qigong type exercise. He seemed oblivious to the little girl behind him, trying to mimic his every move. She was perhaps three or four, and we guessed the man was her grandpa.

When he finished in the garden, he came out in front of the Guest House and began a gentle jogging up and down the short street. His little shadow charged into action. This was something she was a little more adept at. She charged around and way ahead of Grandpa, then looking back and discovering he was headed the other way, scurried back to catch up. When they finally ran down, they sauntered home across the bridge, hand in hand.

Sometimes between classes the young did calisthenics in the garden or on the bars in front of the teaching buildings. The ever-present loudspeaker blared music in the twenty-minute breaks between second and third period, and the music sometimes was obviously meant to accompany a strenuous physical routine. A voice heard over the music called out yi, er, san, su (one, two, three, four).

One morning, while waiting for class to begin in Building 1, I stood at the open window and watched a lithe young man do a series of chin-ups and other equally demanding feats, and then he picked up his books and his still-lit cigarette and sauntered off to class.

Judging from my students' comments, they see a strong physique as helping to make their country stronger. In some cases they see physical exercise as an exercise in patriotism. Most of them tried to participate in some kind of sports activity each day.

Sport or athletics, however, is very different on Chinese college campuses than in the States. While popular and prevalent, athletic events and sports activities in China are strictly intramural. I never read any explanation or discussion of collegiate sports, but I can guess at least a couple of reasons why intercollegiate sports would be a no-no. One, competition in almost any form, unless it can somehow be tied to improving the socialist system, is a bad word; and two, if you've ever read the athletic budget of any American college or university, it is immediately obvious that the Chinese would be foolish to spend scarce dollars toward such ends.

A big event at the college and at most schools is the annual two-day Sports Meet in November. I became aware that my students were practicing and training for this event and that all of them would be involved in some way or another. Then some of our friends also encouraged us to enter some events. That's when we realized this was no ordinary sports meet in which five percent of the student body would be involved and ninety-five percent of the sedentary remainder would be mere spectators.

Professor Zhang persuaded Don to enter the men's shot put, in the over fifty-five class, and I was inveigled into entering a hurling contest of some kind in a similar age class. Anyone who lives or works at the college is eligible to enter events.

Because all classes were cancelled for those days, we had originally planned to go to Xian on Friday to meet American friends who were leading a tour group from the States. But when we realized what we'd be missing, we opted to change our schedule. (We were still too new in China to realize what a foolhardy thing it was not only to actually give up but to try to exchange two airline tickets for two others for a day later.)

In the meantime Don surreptitiously began hefting bricks or anything resembling weights so as not to embarrass himself too badly in the shot put. We didn't realize that these were not events people took too seriously—at least not the older folks. They were just opportunities to have fun.

November 9 dawned sunny, clear and crisp, in itself a good omen, given Chengdu's normal weather. Again, our information about this event or our expected participation in it had not been delivered in any clear or explicit form by the Waiban staff, even though their job was to take care of all arrangements and scheduled activities concerning us. Others hinted, though, that we would be on the reviewing stand. Uhhh, excuse me? Reviewing stand, as in Washington reviewing the troops or the inaugural parade on Pennsylvania Avenue or Mao reviewing the Red Guards in front of the Gate of Heavenly Peace? What did one wear to such an event? We only became aware of the full implications of this when Emily said the night before she would be by about 8:00 to pick us up.

Somehow when I looked at our limited wardrobe I didn't see anything that seemed suitable for such an occasion, and then I came to my senses and realized that the primary concern in dressing for any event was to be warm enough—after all, sunshine or not, it *was* November. It was quite okay in China to wear to tomorrow's event exactly what one had worn today. It made life a lot simpler in many ways. We ended up wearing matching sweatshirts bearing the name of Koenig's Bierhaus, with a picture supposedly of a seventeenth-century Heidelberg Ale Haus. I had bought them through a catalog, mostly as a novelty, although we'd never worn them. Don had stuck them in our luggage unbeknownst to me. When we'd unpacked, I'd been irritated upon finding them, considering how few clothes we'd been able to take with us for an entire year. Anyway, if we were ever to find an appropriate occasion to wear German motif sweatshirts in China, this was probably it. Whether they were appropriate for the reviewing stand is questionable, but the students were captivated.

The reviewing stand at the far side of the sports field was made of wood and painted green. It was not a very substantial or impressive structure, but it was gaily decorated for this occasion with banners and pots of colorful chrysanthemums. Although there were chairs for us to sit on, the area for seating was relatively small, which was a key to the way they perceived such activities. Sports events were not performances by a few for an audience of many. The intent obviously was to get as many people as possible involved. A pretty good idea, really.

We filed across the field and took our places. We foreign teachers and current visiting professors shared the spotlight with the president and other college officials, and after welcoming speeches the troops passed in review. Each department in the college was responsible for participation in the opening ceremonies as well as an entry in various events. Members of each department, sometimes just students, sometimes students and faculty, were dressed alike or in harmonizing colors. Mostly they just passed in review, marching smartly to a certain beat, but occasionally they stopped in front of the reviewing stand and performed. One group, about thirty strong, did a Kung Fu routine. In unison, they did a rapid series of thrusts, jabs, and kicks, then whirled around and did more of the same.

Since the Sports Meet was for the entire college community, children from the college elementary school as well as the middle school also participated, with the Chinese equivalent of pompon girls and flag bearers not unlike those in an American high school. No cheerleaders, though.

And of course it wouldn't have been a parade without a band. The only band on campus was the elementary school drum and bugle corps. In some instances the bugles were as long as the players were tall. The drum and bugle corps is fairly common in China for the same reason that many other things are: the instruments are relatively inexpensive and it fills a need. While I've heard some really crack drum and bugle corps, people can participate in such a group with very little skill. It goes without saying that the results are usually commensurate with the skill. We'd been hearing this group practice in past weeks, and these players were not—I repeat—*not* highly skilled.

On Sports Day, however, the corps was resplendent in red and white uniforms and they played their hearts out. They were so bad they were wonderful. It was the Chinese version of Merideth Wilson's Music Man. The map said we were in Chengdu, Sichuan, China, but it might have been River City, Iowa, USA.

After the ceremonies were over and the flags raised, the games began. While there were the conventional events one might find in the Olympics, like the broad jump and running races, a lot of others were more in the nature of contests you might find at a church picnic or American Legion Fourth of July family outing in River City, Iowa. There was frisbee throwing and running with a Ping-Pong ball balanced on a paddle. Although I entered one of those events, I did not do credit to the red, white, and blue. Don, whose shot put event was scheduled for the next day, was saved similar embarrassment by another activity off campus, the Foreign Experts Day downtown.

13

Foreign expert. Who, me? You must be kidding. We were in China several weeks before I became aware of the term "Foreign Expert" and that I was one. It was an official term, and I saw it used in the *China Daily*. It referred to people who had been invited by the government to provide specialized help, and it was part of China's open policy. There were reportedly four thousand foreign experts and teachers working in over six hundred colleges and schools in 1990. While *expert* is a term I could use only tongue-in-cheek, the Chinese used it quite matter-of-factly.

On Saturday, the second day of the Sports Meet, we were invited to something called Foreign Experts Day, sponsored by the provincial Foreign Affairs Office and held in a large exposition hall downtown. All of us waiguoren were loaded into a small bus and transported downtown. Visiting professors at the college at that time were from the Soviet Union, England, and New Zealand, in addition to us regulars.

I wasn't quite sure of the intent of this gathering. But afterward, I concluded that the intent was to get input from area foreign experts as to how they felt things were going—an opportunity for an informal evaluation, a sharing of views and information, face-to-face conversation. Sounds like a great idea, right? It might have been. But if that really were the intent, the implementation of it fell short.

The day began auspiciously with our arrival in the large square in front of the exposition hall where we parked, alongside other vehicles. Gas-filled balloons with colorful streamers flew high above the building, and huge signs decorating the columned entrance proclaimed a welcome. Dozens of school children in colorful clothes lined the steps waving signs of welcome. Chinese realize that their children are irresistible. We began to sense this was a big deal.

When we got inside, after passing through a reception line, we sat at large square tables, seating about twelve people. On each table were mounds of mandarin oranges, bananas, peanuts, sunflower seeds, and the inevitable covered tea cups. As soon as we were seated, servers wielding large thermoses of hot water appeared, filled our cups that had already been filled with tea leaves. They kept reappearing at frequent intervals. Until you know the location or state of Chinese restroom facilities, or even if there are any, it is always a good idea to limit your intake.

At the front of the huge room was a speaker's table, at which were seated about twenty people. Since there were additional speakers besides those seated at that table, the opening proceedings were lengthy. All welcoming speeches and introductions were made in both Chinese and English; and if a speaker was of another nationality, that added a third dimension. Now, since I was still fairly new in China and being curious by nature, I really wanted to listen and learn. But, fat chance.

Once again, few audience members listened, even though various Sichuan provincial officials spoke, with appropriate responses by many Westerners, including an American vice-consul. If you did want to hear, you were hampered because of the bad manners of the others. Only when the novelty of the American vice-consul, a Canadian official, and a young Harvard Ph.D. student making their speeches in Chinese and having Chinese translators doing the honors in English for the rest of us did the Chinese in the hall cease their chatter for a little while. What truly confounded me was that someone would finish a speech, resume his seat at the speaker's table, and then talk to a seat mate or wander around during the remainder of the speeches.

Bill Miller, from Goshen College, Indiana, gave an informative speech about an exchange program of several years standing that his institution had had with a teachers' college in Chengdu. Having grown up in Ohio and knowing of Goshen college, I was interested in what he had to say. While I have worried in recent years that my hearing was fading, it must not be too bad for despite the hubbub throughout the hall, and people wandering about freely, I managed to hear most of his talk. He waited patiently, surveying the inattentive crowd while his translator caught up with him. He then proceeded little by little to finish his task.

I later sought him out to introduce myself. I conveyed my interest in the Goshen program, and commiserated with him over his reception. He said that while he had been in China long enough not to be too surprised at such behavior, he had never felt so much like sitting down as he had that morning. I commended him on his acting ability and his restraint. If I had faced that situation, I would probably have dressed them all down and stalked out.

When I later expressed to Chinese friends my wonderment at such behavior, as before they excused it by saying people felt they had "heard it all before." One American's theory is that it is a safe way to thumb their noses at authority.

When I talked about it in class as a big difference in social customs, I let students know I was scandalized and they mostly just laughed. But I told them that even if Americans were bored by speeches they either would go to sleep, leave, or if they did talk, would do it quietly. If others talked loudly or moved around, others would glare or in some way censure them.

Besides, what happened to the idea that this Foreign Experts Day was to be an opportunity to exchange ideas? Mid-morning, after the speeches were over, those attending were invited to circulate—what many had been doing already—and talk. But since we hadn't been told the purpose ahead of time, I really wasn't prepared. Besides, I didn't know who was who, and since most of those present did not speak English and were approachable only through a translator, any attempt seemed fruitless.

In talking with the Harvard Ph.D. student who was researching the provincial government's function before Liberation, I learned about her frustrating attempts to get access to the information she needed. Her repeated efforts were met with refusal. When she sought the person there that day who could be helpful, who could cut all the red tape, he merely smiled and advised her to be patient.

Lunch almost made up for the morning fiasco. We were bused to a culinary institute, where young people are trained to create those artistic dishes and aesthetic effects that so characterize high-class Chinese cooking. At the entrance we observed vegetables and fruits being cut in artistic shapes to create dishes and centerpieces that were more in the nature of decorations than something one eats. From there we went to a dining room, where we sampled some of the really fine cuisine and could watch other dishes being prepared on closed circuit TV. In the afternoon it was back to the hall for fancy entertainment: eight-year-olds playing keyboards like sophisticated professionals; dancers whose costumes, makeup, and manners were all very stylized; and scenes from Sichuan opera.

There is an air about Chinese entertainment that seems contradictory to Chinese temperament. In life, Chinese seem demure, rather shy, a little self-conscious. Cosmopolitan and sophisticated are not words I associate with the Chinese. Yet public performances seem so staged, stylized, artificial.

I was particularly bothered by the performance of a young girl who was a whiz on the electric piano. She was probably no more than seven or eight, and she not only had on a fancy sequinned costume but heavy, dramatic makeup. From the beginning of her piece, which lasted about ten minutes, her actions were all highly theatrical, every one done for conscious effect. As she manipulated all the stops and buttons, with the instrument lighting up like a Christmas tree at times, her facial expressions matched her actions. The sophistication of the music, her timing and dramatic effect, so out of character with her age, prompted mixed feelings. One part of me marveled at the perfect execution, but another was made very uncomfortable by this little child performing like a puppet, almost as if someone were behind, pulling strings.

Since there were no stage curtains, or even a stage, I could observe the girl when she had finished. Other children were lined up at one side near where we were sitting, waiting their turn to go on. When the young musician finished and a man carried the piano off, she ran to her mother and in a very childlike action threw herself in her mother's lap. With her arms around her mother's waist, looking up appealingly into her face, it was as if she was asking, "Did I do okay?"

During the remainder of the acts, I watched the little girl who by that time had removed the spangled costume to reveal simple little play clothes. She stayed close to her mother, but clearly was also restless and ready to get on to something else. In those few moments I was relieved and reassured that inside what had appeared to be a sophisticated painted doll was a natural and spontaneous little girl. I liked the little girl much better.

The day had been interesting but much too long. Chinese programs always seem to follow a maxim that if an act is good, two more just like it will be even better. We were finally on our way home.

I couldn't help thinking like an American at that point and how such a meeting would have been handled differently at home. If free exchange of ideas was truly an objective for Foreign Experts Day, why didn't they provide a format that would have facilitated that? Although the physical setting in that large hall was hardly conducive to achieving the purpose, the tables for twelve could each have been provided with a prepared agenda of questions; a discussion leader, translator, and recorder; and a timetable. And, of course, we Americans would have made sure everyone filled in an evaluation blank to register their level of satisfaction with the day's activities, whether or not they felt it had achieved the stated objective and been helpful. Believe me, I would have been glad to have told them. After all, I was a "foreign expert."

14

The next morning, after Foreign Experts Day, we were off to Xian. An historic city, Xian is best known outside China today for those remarkable terra cotta warriors. In the mid-1970's, archaeologists uncovered over seven thousand life-size figures in an emperor's tomb, where they have been for two thousand years. The figures include horses and carts, all seemingly alert and ready to march off into a full-scale military campaign. Even after death the emperor was going to be ready to defend his empire.

Lying north of Chengdu, Xian was on our places-to-see list. When American friends, the Westfalls, who were tour guides, were bringing a group to Xian in November, it seemed an ideal time. We could not only see them, but tour Xian with their group.

On Sunday morning we took off in a prop plane for the ninety-minute flight. We joined up with their group of about thirty, enjoying the sites and activities on their itinerary. They were on the last leg of their tour, and we were especially appreciative of the booty they shared with us when they left—the peanut butter, instant soup, crackers, and cookies they'd been warned to bring along as occasional relief from Chinese cuisine!

So much for the good part. Getting home to Chengdu was another matter. We had gone on November 11, and had hoped to return on the third day, but there were no flights back until November 19. We had known that ahead of time, but saw no problem. We were eager to ride the Chinese trains and assumed we could get a train ticket anytime. Not so, which probably everyone knew but us.

A travel rep stood in line for two days to get us train tickets and finally got them at noon on Wednesday for Wednesday evening—for a sleeper. Whereas the flight had taken an hour and a half, we were on the train for nineteen hours. The Qinling Mountains lie between Xian and Chengdu. They are mostly over six thousand feet, with one peak, Taibai Shan, reaching 11,400 feet, and there are 105 tunnels. The train frequently had to pull off on a siding to let other oncoming trains go by.

Travel in China, by any means, is *not* easy. You cannot book tickets or make reservations for more than one leg of a journey at a time, which is why foreigners usually travel on organized tours.

Our friends had escorted a half dozen groups of Americans to China by that time, and people got their money's worth. However, staying in a four-star hotel and traveling by luxury coach and jet airliner, they were seeing a far different China than we were experiencing, and a world most Chinese didn't even know existed. (A four-star hotel it may have been, but even there the bathroom faucet dripped. One more entry for our faulty bathroom record.)

Don's Class A later asked him where we had stayed in Xian and how much it had cost. When he told them the hotel rate per day, Martin said that was double his monthly salary.

Actually, the cost of the entire tour was quite reasonable. The Chinese government was still slashing prices on food, lodging, and transportation in order to lure tourists back to China after the brutal crackdown in June 1989.

As a result of our Xian experience, we were apprehensive about our proposed travel during Spring Festival in February. We had help each step of the way on the Xian trip and still there were snafus. Did we dare start out on our own for three weeks?

We are big fans of European trains, and we had been anxious to travel by train in China—Paul Theroux had made it sound so exciting in *Riding the Iron Rooster*. But our experience convinced us that given a choice, we would fly. Chinese trains, generally, are nothing like those in Europe. They are dirty, smelly, and crowded. Besides, the night we spent on the train was my birthday. After I hoisted myself up in the upper berth several times, I felt every one of my sixty-three years.

What with sitting around in Xian for two days waiting for tickets, I came down with an honest-to-goodness cold and flu after we got home. I completely lost my voice right before Thanksgiving and decided to try the campus hospital, my first venture.

Xiao Lin from the Waiban went with me, acting as interpreter and relaying my symptoms. I took along a sample of the medications I had taken that day—a Contac and a little vial of Chinese medicine that Professor Zhang had given me that was good for sore throat.

The Contac had come from Zhirong and therefore had Chinese printing on it. The nurses wondered, a bit disapprovingly it seemed to me, where I had gotten it. I told them, but added a little indignantly that Contac was something we took as necessary, that it was an American medicine. One's patriotism—or was it chauvinism—does bubble up at surprising moments.

We had two Thanksgivings in China—first one American and then one Chinese. The American consulate had organized a traditional

Thanksgiving dinner at the Minshan Hotel in the evening, for any waiguoren who cared to attend. A lovelier buffet was never spread, and included a varied and colorful assortment of breads, salads, and desserts, the kinds of dishes we had missed the last few months. Although there was pumpkin pie of sorts, a big roast of pork stood in for Tom turkey.

Because Zhirong had had Thanksgiving in our home two years before, she was determined to entertain us in China. Since she and Jilin had to work on Thursday, we had our Thanksgiving dinner with them and a Chinese couple on Sunday.

There wasn't any turkey or cranberry sauce at the Hu's, either, but a roast chicken in the middle of the table was a good stand-in. The windows were open, and we ate with our coats on and endeavored to keep our sleeves out of the common dishes as we reached across the table with our chopsticks. Nevertheless, a holiday spirit prevailed.

15

"What do you think of China?"

"How do you like Chinese food?"

"How do you like living in China?"

Although it wasn't mandatory, particularly during the first semester, the college encouraged us to have Free Talk with our students occasionally, and I obliged right from the beginning. I wanted to know what they thought, what was on their minds.

Free Talk is a common term that merely meant there was no set discussion agenda and students could ask any questions they wanted. It was an extra opportunity to practice their English. Since the doctoral class was small, those students came to the apartment, which was more convenient for me and more comfortable for them; but I met the postgrads in the classroom. Although there were about fifty-five in all, attendance was optional, so the number could range anywhere from fifteen to thirty.

Because the postgrads' language skills were limited in the beginning, their questions had little variety. A favorite question, in addition to those above, was about what differences I found between China and the United States—although students rarely said "the United States." It was always "America."

How to answer the questions? No matter what our mood was or our latest experience, we always tried to be tactful. Even though students were genuinely curious and really did want to know, no one wants to hear his country trashed even if it's the truth. Don and I both agreed China looks better in pictures, be it our own snapshots or in a National Geographic special, than it does in the flesh.

But one of the topics I could safely talk about, and they could even find some amusement in, was the traffic. We visited in many Chinese cities before coming home, but nowhere was the traffic worse than in Chengdu. Bicycles are, of course, the most common mode of transportation in China. It was not uncommon to see a full-grown hog slung across the back of a bike or a bunch of chickens or ducks tied on each side, being taken to market. In addition there are all sizes of cars, trucks, jeeps, vans, buses, tractors, horse-or-donkey-drawn conveyances, as well as many human-drawn vehicles sharing the road, vying for the same space.

Traffic lights and laws are found only in the center of the city, and there are no lane lines dividing traffic. All drivers beep their horns constantly to warn others to beware. The bicyclers also sound a warning bell, and so the impression is one of complete chaos. The resulting din is muted but constant nonetheless.

The streets were like one perpetual street carnival; and as a passenger, I felt like I was in one big "Dodgem" ring, a ride we saw occasionally in kiddie parks in China. Cars and trucks came within inches of bicyclists and pedestrians, but people seemed either defiant or unperturbed when they heard the beep of a horn. Crossing the street was quite a feat, but miraculously, people escaped unscathed. A UCLA professor there for a few days admitted that California traffic couldn't hold a candle to that.

In class I conveyed my amazement at traffic conditions and that there weren't more accidents. Students would usually just laugh—which is the standard response to anything they don't know much about and have even less control over. Most students would love to be able to drive, but in practical terms, a country with China's population could never cope with private automobiles, so that will have to remain an impossible dream for most.

Given the growing number of joint ventures, Don and I speculated about the potential success of a "driving range," Chinese style: not golf, but cars. For a fee, a driver could spend fifteen minutes behind the wheel of a car of his choice on a set course. But, given the intricacies of Chinese bureaucracy, and acknowledging that we had no influence or connections, we quickly relegated that also to the impossible dream status.

I'd always heard that humor doesn't cross cultural boundaries very well, and I came to appreciate that in China. Once during Free Talk a student led off by asking among other things if I would share an American funny story. Well, it just so happened that a friend had enclosed a couple of stories in a recent letter, so I did have some "material." But I also had had a couple of failures already in telling something so I was a little gun shy.

For example, as a topic from a text we had called *Modern American English*, we had discussed American currency. We compared Chinese currency and remarked about the different colors, shapes, and sizes, and noted that there is not even any consistency in some bills of the same denomination, depending on when they were issued. The one, two, and five fen notes (a fen is comparable to a penny) are different colors and resemble Monopoly money, although they have no numerals on them. They do have pictures: a truck on the one, an airplane on the two, and a ship on the five.

Early on when we were still struggling to understand the money, Don went over to get some bread from a bakery cart that appeared on the bridge every evening. I was always curious when we had made a purchase to see what things cost in "real" money. When he came back with the bread and rolls, I asked him how much he had spent.

He said, "I don't know."

"But you must have some idea," I pressed.

He said in exasperation, "Well, I gave him five yuan, and I got back two trucks, two airplanes, and a ship in change."

That broke me up.

When I went to class the next week, I shared that with each class that had discussed currency. In each of my three classes my joke drew everything from uncomprehending looks to, at best, polite smiles. Even with adult Chinese, the response was not overwhelming.

My explanation for this phenomenon—because it *is* a funny story, right?—is that unless you have traveled outside a country and actually dealt with the experience of confronting a new currency every day or so, you can't really appreciate that idea of "play money."

With that experience fresh in my memory, I was then a little hesitant to share my newest humorous stories. Nevertheless, I decided to have a go. I explained that one of the reasons humor doesn't transfer to another country or culture is that people aren't familiar with the customs or stereotypes or they have had different experiences than those on which a particular joke is based. So I decided I had better set things up a bit.

I first explained that there was a superstition (I made sure they understood *superstition*) that knocking on wood would bring luck. I then told them the story about three elderly sisters who lived together. One decided to go upstairs and take a bath. But when she was halfway out of the tub, she couldn't remember whether she was getting out or getting in. So she called down to her second sister to come up and help her. But when the second sister got halfway up the stairs, she couldn't remember whether she was going up or down. She called down to the third sister who was sitting in her wooden rocking chair to ask if she was going up the stairs or down.

The third sister said, "Thank God I'm not as absentminded as my sisters (she knocks on wood)—Now I wonder if that was the front door or the back door."

The students loved it. I guess older people become absentminded in China, too.

The classes were predominantly male, but one week only men showed up for Free Talk. The first question, surprisingly, was about weddings. A young man asked me to describe an American formal wedding. I explained some of the customs surrounding weddings, that weddings take place in many different situations, and described the simplest to the most elaborate, involving many people and much money. They were particularly interested to learn that traditionally the bride's family bears the major expense because in China it is the groom and his family who pay. The groom has to provide a kind of dowry of a refrigerator, a TV, and other furnishings.

Articles in the *China Daily* recently had recounted the rapid increase in the price of weddings, so I wasn't surprised by the topic. Many young men would like to marry but simply haven't the money. The groom is also expected to provide food, whether simple treats, like candy and cigarettes, or a meal. According to one article, families may save for ten years or go heavily into debt or work an extra job to give a son a nice wedding. The future relations between the bride and her mother-in-law may be affected by what kind of wedding the groom's family provides.

The students clearly thought the situation was abominable—and very unfair. They felt helpless because they have so little control over their finances.

Another young man asked, "Is transportation a factor in whether young people can marry?"

When he saw I was clearly puzzled by the question, he explained, "If young people work a long distance from each other and would have a problem seeing each other, the parents would discourage the marriage and advise them to marry someone who worked close by. Could the same thing happen in the States (although students always say "America")?

I knew that he had a girlfriend near Wuhan, and I wondered if he was describing his own situation.

I explained, "That wouldn't be a problem in the United States because transportation is not the problem it is in China."

After I had been in China awhile, I better understood that his could be a significant concern.

Because of what I had heard about a couple of weddings on campus, I was curious about Chinese weddings. When I asked the doctoral students, all of whom were married, to describe their weddings, I realized that there were fundamental differences between their society and ours. Getting married consists of going to the local authorities and getting a blood test, filling out forms and paying a fee. That's it, for all intents and purposes, assuming the couple is old enough—twenty-three for women, twenty-five for men. They could marry younger only with their unit's permission—that is, their employer. That, incidentally, is happening more and more now in China.

The couple may not be able to live as a married couple until their unit can provide them housing, and so they may not acknowledge their marriage. When they have a place to live, *then* they have a wedding. That can consist simply of telling your friends to come to your room or apartment on a certain day, on a drop-in basis. Some treats or refreshments may be provided, and guests bring gifts. Certain traditional games and jokes are played on the bride and groom as well.

Xiao Lin, on the Waiban staff, had a girlfriend who had graduated with him three years before. She worked in a geological unit north of Chengdu and occasionally came to the college on weekends. Emily learned from someone who worked in the pertinent office that they had gone through the legal formalities recently, and thus were legally married. But Xiao Lin said nothing. Later, when his girlfriend passed the entrance exams for postgraduate study and returned to the college, she lived in the graduate students' dorm. He shared a room with two other staff employees. It would be some time till they could qualify for a room together. Only then would they have a wedding. When he wrote to me after we came home, he made reference to his *girlfriend*.

However, after about a year, they were assigned a room, and they could publicly assume married life. He proudly sent a picture of their room.

One morning, when a large group showed up for postgrads Free Talk, the first question of the day came from Mr. Lu. It was a long one and he had written it out.

"In the past," he said, "when students took and passed the college entrance exam, they had no choice over their major or their school, except to state preferences which were not really honored. Then, when they graduated, they had no choice of job, but went where they were assigned. Now, there are some reforms so that in the future, young people will have more choice over their major, and when they finish college they can make application for jobs themselves and their professors or directors can write recommendations for them. Also, the business or factory can advertise positions and give qualifying tests to the employees. What do you think of the reforms?"

My goodness, I thought, what a novel idea. I think this is what they do in capitalistic countries, though, isn't it? Isn't that a no-no here? I stifled my impulse to make a flippant remark and pondered how to answer the question. Since to me the answer was so obvious, I wondered if I was being set up. I had been told from the beginning that there would be young Communists in the classes ready to bait me. Somehow, because of the student who had asked the question, I thought that was not true in this instance.

To buy a little time, I first attempted to paraphrase the question—it was a long one—not only to make sure that I understood, but to make sure that all the students did, also. Then I did what cagey teachers have always done in that situation: I asked, "What do you think of the reforms?"

He had a hard time answering the question, even though his own question had been detailed and clearly phrased. I wasn't sure how much his difficulty was due to his awkwardness with the language and how much was due to his reluctance to put himself on the line.

Little by little I led him through a discussion. Although he seemed reluctant to say so openly, he did agree that it was a good idea. Others joined the discussion and also seemed to agree. I thought perhaps the students were reluctant to say so openly, so asking me gave them an opportunity to bring the subject up without necessarily being connected with it themselves.

I then asked, "Why do you think it's a good idea?"

The students' reasons were all from the point of view of the student or employee, naturally enough.

I then asked, "Why would it be good for the employer, too?"

That was clearly not something that they had given thought to. I had to ask some very leading questions here, providing a sort of case analysis.

What developed was a very elementary course in economics, with a decided bias toward capitalism, I must confess. We discussed supply and demand, profit and loss, incentives, risk, quality control. My Economics 101 professor might have been pained if he had heard my explanations, but I think they made sense to my students.

Some days, the questions were sticky.

"I've heard that illegal immigrants in America are made to work hard and are cheated of their wages."

"I read that Asian children work in sweatshops in New York City and are paid very little and can't go to school. Is that true?"

Someone said he had heard that American parents encourage their children to be independent, but that Chinese parents encourage dependence. When I asked why he said that, he said a Chinese person had been in a park in the United States and seeing a child fall, had helped him up. The parents had scolded him for doing so, wanting their child to become independent. The observer had said that if that had happened in China, the parents would have thanked the person.

I admitted that American parents probably do value independence in their children, but those parents' reaction would not necessarily be typical. Even if parents didn't think the help was warranted or needed, I said I thought most would say thank you out of politeness.

It's not easy being the spokesperson for 250 million people.

On another day someone prefaced a question with, "I don't know whether this is a rude question or a polite one." I suggested that he ask and let me decide.

He said he had heard that the United States was heaven for children but hell for old people. He seemed uncomfortable asking the question. Again I was puzzled about how to answer. I said that indeed ours was a youth-oriented society and that perhaps because people wanted to stay young, they didn't accord older people the respect they're given in China. I admitted to dreading old age myself.

"What prompts your question?"

It seemed he had read an article in which a reporter had impersonated an old woman for a few days and written about the way she was treated—badly. I said I didn't doubt that the woman had accurately described her treatment, but that that wasn't necessarily the whole story.

By this time, after so many negative stories that session, I was feeling a little testy. I said I wished there were a little more balance used when Chinese publishers chose materials about our country because I thought it gave a misleading impression.

I said, "Most of the people that I've seen in China seem to be happy and well fed and well clothed. But, you know, whenever I go to visit friends over in the staff housing area on campus, no matter what time of day or night, I almost always see someone digging through the trash cans which sit at most intersections. It's usually an old person, a pathetic sight, retrieving bits and pieces and stashing them into a knapsack."

Then I said, "How would you like it if when I went home I told people that Chinese old folks are reduced to digging through garbage cans for fuel and clothing? I would be accurately reporting what I had seen, but would it be fair?"

I think they got my point.

I said, "I wish those things you referred to today about the United States had not happened but unfortunately they did. And as distasteful as I found the information, it's better to know about it than not know about it. Freedom of the press isn't always easy to live with."

But then, how could they know about that, living in China?

16

One Sunday night in September, after we had been gone from home about a month, we talked with son John and his wife, Barbara, by telephone for the first time. They were interested in how we were getting along in our new surroundings. By that time we had tired of our limited diet, had our fill of Chinese food, and were having little luck finding what we thought were some of the staples necessary to existence.

The supplies that we had mailed from home had not arrived. We had not come to China expecting to find Safeway or the A & P down the block, or Baskin-Robbins or Domino's Pizza across town, but we missed having things like milk, bread, meat, and sugar of a quality that we found palatable. Cereal and butter, for example, were nonexistent.

So, warning them not to laugh, we asked them to send us some things just as soon as possible. I'm sure they expected an exotic list, but our requests included such mundane items as mustard, ketchup (I never eat ketchup at home), cereal, cocoa, peanut butter, crackers, mosquito repellant, Kaopectate, and anything chocolate.

They didn't laugh—at least not audibly (we must have sounded pathetic)—and John promised to get on it right away. When he took the box to the post office, he found that the $30 worth of groceries that he had amassed would have cost more than $100 to send airmail. No matter how desperate he knew we were, he had the good sense to send it by surface mail. Fortunately, also, he didn't mention that to us for quite some time. We comforted ourselves for weeks when we were eating plain sandwiches by thinking that John's package ought to be arriving soon. Since it took four months to get there by ship, it was good we no longer needed the Kaopectate and that mosquitoes were not a problem in January.

Immediately after the conversation with John in Tampa, Florida, we also talked with son Doug and family in Dayton, Ohio. Although we reported things were going well, we also mentioned that we missed familiar foods and household items. It was evening in China but morning in the United States, and Doug and Robin attended my sister and brother-in-law's golden wedding celebration later that day. It was a gathering of the clan.

Doug reported to my extended family how we were doing and read some of our letters. In describing our difficulty in getting everything from basic cleaning items to the scarcity of appetizing snacks, we must have sounded more desperate than I realized. They took up a collection and another box was soon on its way.

But that was not all. Because I had commented that there weren't any shortcuts or convenience foods and that cooking in China meant cooking from scratch, beginning in October we began getting small airmail packages of instant soup, instant oatmeal, instant hot chocolate, and instant pudding. Several times a week a college car would have to go downtown to the post office to pick up these packages. Since contents have to be listed on the outside of the package, everyone in the Foreign Affairs Office who could read English could see that these were food packages. Although no one ever said anything, they must have thought we were complaining that China was having a food shortage and we were starving.

It was embarrassing, but we were terribly grateful and I shot off lavish notes of thanks immediately. We had not yet found oatmeal in China, and the packages meant something for breakfast besides toast and fruit. Don's heart disease forbade eggs as a regular menu item, so scrambled eggs were held to one or two days a week. Even then, I used three whites, one whole, my version of Egg Beaters. Jilin became the grateful recipient of our egg yolks. We felt guilty and warned him about cholesterol, but he seemed unconcerned.

Shortly after we arrived in China, Ken Nagy, a biologist from UCLA, was at the college for a week or so. When I commented about the difficulty of getting some of the things we wanted or thought we needed, he said, "Well, just look around you. There are thousands of people here who are doing very well in this environment and living seemingly happy and healthy lives."

He seemed less sanguine about China the morning he left, suffering from a bout of diarrhea brought on by supper the night before in one of the little restaurants in the market. We obliged him with some Chinese remedies we had acquired to cope with similar problems and assured him he would be ready to tackle the Great Wall and Tiananmen Square and other scenic spots in Beijing later that day.

Nevertheless, I had reason to think about his words many times after that. The Chinese sometimes ride a bike for miles to get to work, to school, to shop—and then ride back home again, regardless of weather. If it rains, the ponchos come out. If they go out as a family, Dad may ride the whole family on his bike, if they are not a two-bicycle family.

With little refrigerator space, even if they have a frig, they have to market often. When they get home, they have to cook from scratch. They can, of course, pick up some steamed buns or dumplings on the way home, the Chinese equivalent of fast food—if they can afford it.

There are few efficient cleaning aids or appliances, so cleaning is a chore. Clothes driers are nonexistent, so when they do wash clothes, by whatever method, they must hang them out. When the weather is cold and damp, clothes may hang for days before they're dry.

Yet Chinese people look neat, clean, trim, and cheerful. In spite of a little grumbling and head-shaking over the cold or the perennial cloudiness in Chengdu, they cope very well. They complain about China's poverty, housing shortages, and its overpopulation; but they go about their business in a matter-of-fact way.

So, given the Chinese example, I hesitated to grumble too much about trivial inconveniences. Still, living in contemporary China is not easy to Westerners. We are used to much more convenience and less physical exertion. Cooking continued to be a challenge.

Lunches were the most difficult meal of all, particularly when I struggled up to the third floor at noon after teaching all morning.

That's why the instant soups from home were so welcome. At home we would have had salads, grilled cheese, or quick deli sandwiches, with fresh fruit. The fruit was no problem in China, but there were simply no cold cuts, no heat-'em-up-quick-in-the-microwave foods. The closest thing was a canned Spam-like product. In over forty years of married life, I had never dared bring Spam into the house. It had too many unpleasant associations for my Army veteran husband. But that was before we went to China. I bought a can and fried it, served it on soft Chinese bread, without even mustard or ketchup, and there was nary a complaint. Not exactly a Big Mac but it was a change. B.C. (Before China) became a new benchmark in our lives. We found ourselves doing and accepting things that we would not have B.C.

Soup was especially appealing after the weather got cooler—and it *had* gotten cooler. It was good not only for its own sake, but cooking it warmed the kitchen. Making it could be time-consuming, though— cooking a chicken ahead of time, shopping for all the ingredients. I was grateful for some bouillon cubes I'd stuck in the box from home.

In the market there was a changing variety of vegetables. I learned to plan meals around what was available. There was no preparing a certain favorite menu for company as I might at home. You were limited by what was available that week or even that day. When things were in season, you ate those every day, ad nauseam, and when they were gone, you ate something else ad nauseam. Wonderful apples were available in the fall. Then Don lived off mandarin oranges in the fall and winter. They were cheap, but then *they* were gone, replaced by regular oranges. Where certain foods were concerned, the old saying about feast or famine applied.

We kept hearing little rumors from other Westerners about where someone supposedly had gotten butter. One night at one of the occasional movie nights which were held in the American consulate downtown, one of the announcements preceding the film included a number to call if you needed to know where to get butter and other "necessities." That information was sandwiched between when the serum for a booster shot for hepatitis B would be available and how potential pertinent information about the Gulf situation would be conveyed. I had the same kind of reaction I might have had if someone had sidled up to me during Prohibition and whispered hoarsely where I might get bootleg whiskey.

We heard at one point that a downtown bakery had butter and mentioned it in passing to Jilin, saying we were going to check it out the next time we went downtown. Late the next afternoon he showed up with three kilograms of butter, about six pounds worth, in a large plastic bag. After his classes were over that day, he had ridden his bike to the bakery, about a fourteen-mile round-trip. He was so determined to be helpful and not let anyone outdo him in being helpful that we learned to be careful what we mentioned around Jilin. It was a little like the old adage: be careful what you pray for—you might get it.

Not only is six pounds of butter a lot of butter, but getting it out of a plastic bag is not the most fun I've ever had, either. We shared a kilogram with M & M and still had butter for weeks.

Jilin once asked me if I planned to make apple pie. He knew about apple pie as in "as American as . . . ," and presumed perhaps that it was a daily staple. Because Granny Smith apples or a reasonable facsimile were plentiful then, I said I'd like to but, knowing vegetable shortening wasn't available, said I'd have to have lard. He indicated he knew what I meant.

That conversation took place in the morning. That afternoon he showed up with a quart jar of lard. Surprised, I asked where he'd found it. He said he had bought the fat in the market and gone home and rendered it. In the future, it would probably not be fair to hold my friends to such extreme standards to prove their loyalty and devotion.

In our preliminary reading about China, and whether buildings were heated, I had read that the Yangtze was the dividing line: buildings north of the Yangtze were heated, those south were not. A quick look at the map allayed my apprehension. Chengdu was north of the Yangtze. Ah, but we overlooked some fine print: south of the Yangtze *or* its tributaries. We were in the unheated zone.

Since we were in that zone, buildings were not heated as a general rule, even though the temperature December through February got down almost to freezing. Not only was there no heat in the classrooms, but windows were wide open as well. If I got to the classroom first in the morning, I often closed the windows. It probably wouldn't have made it any warmer—it just seemed like it would. But soon, students would come in and, intending to be helpful, would throw all the windows open again. They believed a closed room was not healthy.

Students from the north of China even complained about Chengdu's weather. They said that they felt much colder in Chengdu than in their home territory, where it snowed all winter and the temperature sank below zero. Not only was the air drier in the north, but at least rooms were heated.

The air in Chengdu was humid, and though the topics in the class might be heated, we still often saw our breath. One of the nicest keepsakes I have is a pair of gloves with half fingers given to me by one of my students. They were knit for her by her mother so that she could write and turn pages and still keep her hands warm. She gave them to me for Christmas.

When I got to the classroom in the morning, I did what any normal Westerner does upon entering a room from outside: I took off my jacket and gloves. I noticed but paid little attention to the quizzical looks of students and their looks of concern when I coughed or blew my nose from time to time. They told me I should put my jacket back on.

At first I kept doing what I was conditioned over a lifetime to do, and then I finally got smart and kept my outdoor clothes on indoors. After all, if there's no difference in the temperature between out and in, why shed any clothes? Why indeed.

As foreigners, we were given one small electric heater, in the shape of a steam radiator, to warm our apartment. We left it in the bedroom, turned it on at night and when Don did school work at his desk, and always kept that door closed when we used it.

On one cold gray day when I had only one class and came home mid-morning, I felt like cooking. Not only would the gas stove warm the house (I didn't feel guilty at using the gas when I was cooking), it would warm my spirit as well. Cold days at the onset of winter always affected me that way. I felt the urge to cook something solid and substantial, something that would stick to the ribs and be a buffer against the cold. I seemed to be answering some primeval call, like a bear getting ready for hibernation.

At home I probably would have made a batch of cornbread and ham and beans or a pot of chili. Here I decided to use the yeast that had arrived in our last box from home, and I mixed up a batch of dough to make dinner and cinnamon rolls. The two bags of flour that Jilin had gotten shortly after we arrived still loomed large, and I decided it was time to use them.

When I said I wanted some flour, Jilin must have thought I was going to compete with the bakery cart that showed up nightly on the bridge. This was also true for the quantity of rice that he brought us—a good fifteen pounds. That was a relatively modest amount for a Chinese consumer, no doubt.

I had earlier seen some suspicious creatures inside the plastic flour bags, but my Scotch tendencies would not allow me to throw out two big bags of flour, particularly when I wasn't sure that what I got to replace it would be any better. I remembered what Don had said about a food processing company that he had worked for. They deliberately made sure they included as much "foreign matter" in their cereal products as the law allowed. I decided that if they could do it, it wouldn't bother me, and that in this case, what Don didn't know wouldn't hurt him. Besides, how could any little creature survive four hundred degree heat?

So, I mixed and kneaded dough and set it to raise beside the warm stove. I had a supply of ground beef from Professor Zhang and decided to mix a meat loaf, using chili powder and onion for seasoning since I didn't have any tomatoes or tomato sauce.

So far, so good, but what I was really hankering for was a different taste. Realizing that I had all the ingredients for a pudding—eggs, sugar, flour, and powdered milk—I yearned to make one, but what to season it with? No vanilla, brown sugar, coconut, nutmeg, chocolate, or lemon . . . lemon? My eyes lit on the little containers of Crystal Light lemonade mix that I had sent from home. It wasn't Real Lemon or a *real* lemon, but the flavor was definitely lemon. I felt inspired.

Three-quarters of a teaspoon did the trick. I mixed in some chunks of canned pineapple, generic quality though it was, and served it over two pieces of a white sponge-like cake. Don was impressed when I brought it to the table that evening. Today lemonade flavoring, tomorrow, Tang. The world seemed infinitely brighter.

I wish that I could say as much for my success as a bread baker. The flour was coarse, I had no sifter, and it definitely had not been presifted. The dough, however, seemed light and responded nicely to kneading. I was encouraged. It raised beautifully, and I was hopeful. The little red Chinese oven, though, was not made with baking bread in mind. The size of a large toaster oven, it accommodated my six-muffin tin nicely, but there was no temperature gauge on the oven. Also, there were only two heat settings available, hot and too hot. To bake both the meat and the bread, I had to turn the heat off and on constantly. The results were not gratifying, but it provided a little variety in our diet.

The lack of everyday conveniences also presented a challenge. We kept coming up with little tricks that enabled us to cope with the exigencies of life in China with a minimum of discomfort. Or at least to make things a little more convenient. Since we did not plan to take anything home with us, neither did we want to spend any more money than necessary to achieve all this, even when things were available.

Because of that, we seldom threw anything away, even if we saw no earthly use for something at the time. We took great pride in improvising or substituting what we had. Starting marriage on a shoestring provided us some valuable experience to fall back on.

We found no salt or pepper shakers among the kitchen stuff that we had inherited and found none in the shops, so Don salvaged a couple of film containers, punched holes in the lids—grey lid for salt, black lid for pepper—and we were in business.

Large plastic Sprite bottles served as boiled water containers for the frig and for tooth brushing in the bathroom. Don fashioned hooks from wire filched from construction sites nearby for hangars for pots and pans and utensils in the kitchen. He suspended them from the gas pipe that ran around two walls near the ceiling in the kitchen. The only things missing were the five-gallon ice cream containers I had salvaged from an ice cream store forty years before. I had wallpapered those and used them for wastebaskets.

For another example, I had an Outback Red shirt I liked very much, the one I later left in Emei. Being white and knit, it went with everything and didn't require ironing. However, the shirt had big shoulder pads. Now shoulder pads were fashionable in the United States, but they looked positively ridiculous in China. I ripped the pads out. But since the shirt was practically new, they seemed too good to throw away. Being a child of the Great Depression, throwing anything away, particularly something that looks *new*, goes against the grain. I had no idea what I could use them for, but they were dutifully stashed away.

Then, I found the perfect use. For weeks I had struggled taking hot pans out of the oven with the little handle that came with it or I used dish towels. Even if I managed not to burn myself, it was awkward. If there were hot pads for sale in China, I hadn't found them. But, hey, I had pads. My shoulder pads immediately became a very useful pair of pot holders.

My kids, particularly my daughters-in-law, have teased me about being frugal. Let's face it, they think I'm tight. And I am. The classic example is Barbara teasing me about washing and all but ironing aluminum foil. Well, they should have seen me in China. Aluminum foil is unheard of in China as a consumer product—at least as far as I know, and I could have used some. Neither did I see any products like wax paper or plastic wrap. There are plastic bags, albeit thin ones.

Our little oven was very small with only about five inches clearance for food and pan. My only baking dish and pans were without lids; and the oven, as I've said, had only those two heats—hot and too hot.

Baking something without bringing a burnt offering to the table each time required switching the oven off and on at significant intervals, learned by trial and error. I tried to cover the food to protect it from the top heating element. Improvising a lid was not easy.

Aluminum foil would have been just the ticket, except where was one to get aluminum foil? When someone sent a large bar of Hershey's chocolate, I grabbed on to the foil inner wrapper as something almost as valuable as the candy itself.

An appeal to my sisters to enclose one piece in their letters each time took care of my needs nicely. I had learned by that time not to make a general request to other relatives and friends. Otherwise I might have had enough foil to cover the Great Wall. I have three sisters, and with careful stewardship I could make a piece serve several uses before a replacement arrived.

The Chinese provided many good examples of making do, but we Americanos were showing that we too had a trick or two up our sleeves.

17

When I broke a molar on a Thanksgiving dinner duck bone and went to the dentist, I became particularly conscious of differences in Chinese and American attitudes toward privacy. When you go to the hospital in China, you first go to a window and get your "ticket," which costs only a few fen. That entitles you to get treatment. Then, depending on what you need, you go to the appropriate office for diagnosis and treatment. There is no appointment desk or any formal waiting room. People crowd right into an office, watch the patient ahead of them being treated, and gather around to listen to the discussion, very interested spectators.

After we got the all-important ticket, we barged into the dentist's office and Mr. He, from the Waiban, explained my problem. The patient in the chair, a middle-aged man, who had just sat down, immediately got out of the chair to give me his place. Although I protested, the dentist, Dr. Yang, and Mr. He also motioned me to sit down. When Dr. Yang examined my mouth and began discussing my case, the patient, who had come around to my left, put on his glasses and peered into my mouth. So did two others who were waiting their turn. When I bit my lip hard afterward, I hoped they would think it was pain I was trying to hide.

When I had a twice-daily series of shots for laryngitis, given in my hip, others who had also come in for a shot crowded around as I lowered my drawers. There were benches in the hall, but no one waits there. Considering the layers of clothes I was wearing and that the shot is given only a few inches below the waist, I wasn't revealing very much. Still, as I turned around to face the onlookers and unzipped my pants, I was suddenly fascinated by the design pattern in the cement floor.

Chinese people think nothing of asking others how old they are, how much money they make, or how much they paid for something. People repeatedly asked our age. Friends asked us how much we had paid for lamps we bought for the apartment and how much I had paid for a sweater. When we discussed some of these differences in customs in class, students found it incredible that we did not know how much money either of our grown children make. Neither do Chinese people feel any hesitation to give advice, whether it be to family, friends, or neighbors. A few of the younger people seemed not to like interference in their lives, though.

Considering the Chinese openness about age, I found it ironic, then, that a headstone on a grave alongside the canal did not indicate the birth or age of the deceased. In the United States, by contrast, the cemetery may be the first time there is public disclosure of someone's age.

One evening Don and I were sitting in one of the college gardens talking with Jack and Napoleon, a couple of his students. An older woman, conservatively dressed, butted in and began to speak with them in animated tones. Both she and they looked at us occasionally. I heard "Meiguo" (American), so I knew they were talking about us. We smiled at her and I asked the men what they were talking about.

They laughed and said she had asked who we were. When she learned we were teachers, she observed that we were paid a lot of money and they assured her we were not (although in truth, for Chinese people, our salaries as foreign teachers did constitute a lot of money). In response to my question, she said that she was a retired worker in an electronics factory nearby.

About seventy years of age herself, she asked how old we were and guessed that we were in our sixties. She said, though, that Don looked healthier than me. I thought that she was speaking euphemistically and really meant "fatter," but on second thought I think she meant it. It may just be that with the Chinese preoccupation with having enough to eat, both at present and in the past, some Chinese people do look admiringly upon someone who is heavier because it means they have had lots of food to eat—particularly a woman of seventy who could well have gone through several periods of starvation in her lifetime. It was my own Western bias which views overweight as unhealthy.

That unself-conscious butting into a conversation happened everywhere. When I shopped at the market, the peasants often carried on a conversation obviously about me with whoever was my shopping escort for the day. They looked at me, sized me up and down like a piece of meat or a big head of cabbage they were bargaining for, and talked excitedly. Or perfect strangers might stop, listen to our comments, and offer their own, before moving on. Others might pause, listen in, trail along behind for a while, I suspect for pure entertainment as much as anything. Some uneducated people might just have been curious about the sound of the language. Once when we were sightseeing near a temple, a few peasants asked our tour guide if they could hear us talk, somewhat as you might ask a pet shop owner to hear a parrot. This wore thin after a while.

While some people stared at us and obviously found us strange looking, and might smile at each other in rather superior fashion, I learned not to let this bother me. I developed a way of looking through people—conscious of their gaze but not really seeing them. Doing that would have bothered me in other times and circumstances—it seemed patronizing and insensitive—but it was the only way to function in such a populous society where you can seldom walk quietly anywhere without being the target of many eyes. If you don't want to turn heads, don't go to China.

What also amazed me was the way everyone entered into these impromptu conversations. Western people do not talk to others as freely, and certainly not to strangers. The differences between the peasant farmers and the staff at the college were light years in terms of education and experience, but they talked freely and casually. When we went into town, Emily or Mr. He, who often accompanied us, talked incessantly with the drivers.

Once when three of us Westerners were sightseeing near a temple, we attracted a group of curious onlookers. We smiled and spoke to them in our limited Chinese. They were startled and broke into laughter and returned our greeting. One man was pointing to Don's hand, and gesturing to his friend. Don held out his hand, gesturing for the man to measure his own against it. His hand was about half the size of Don's and the man was as delighted as a child. For minutes afterward, we saw him pointing to his hand, talking about it with his friends.

When we first arrived in China, it took us a little while to get used to people crowding around when we shopped downtown, leaning over our shoulders to see what we were buying, and literally peering into our billfolds. Except in a few higher-priced shops, there are no dressing rooms, so when you buy clothing you try it on over your clothes in front of an audience.

We noticed that it was the less-educated and less-sophisticated who were more inclined to stare, although "sophisticated" applied to Chinese people, generally, seems supremely incongruous. Nevertheless, after I was there for a while, when I sensed people close by giving me the once-over, I developed my own counter-measures. I would turn in friendly fashion and give them the same treatment, sizing them up from head to foot. They were startled and often looked a little embarrassed and suddenly moved on or looked elsewhere. It was as if they previously thought they had been looking into one of those two-way mirrors where they could see me but I couldn't see them.

College campuses are usually thought of as places of quiet contemplation, but Chengdu College of Geology could be a very noisy place. At seven in the morning, the first campus bell rang—and that continued periodically all day until 11:00 at night when all classroom buildings were locked and presumably all good Chinese young people were in bed. That wasn't all. There was the ubiquitous music—beginning at 7:00 A.M., between periods, evenings, six days a week—whether you wanted to hear it or not. It was the campus alarm clock, exercise drill, news, and entertainment source. No matter if students had their own radios or tapes, or wanted to listen to VOA, the PA system drowned it out for twenty minutes or so at a time. The grad students complained about the large speaker installed right outside their dorm. The term "in loco parentis" is in full force in China, not only as far as education is concerned but in the entire society as well. We visited other campuses in Chengdu and elsewhere and found the practices and some of the music the same. And the music was always at peak volume, whether on campus or where we were shopping.

When Chinese people are "up," meaning awake, they evidently think everyone else is awake. They seemingly have no regard for anyone else's rights in terms of not having to listen to something they don't want to, be it music or conversation. At times, when the Foreign Guest House was full of Chinese conference guests, we could hear TV's blaring away at midnight two floors above us. We could hear the TV in the small café across the canal every night till about 11:00. The young people who congregated in the Guest House lobby sat within six feet of the TV, and it blasted away so loudly that we sometimes could hear it on the third floor.

When students were not in class themselves, they sometimes went running down the hall like children or singing at the top of their lungs. I indicated my astonishment at such behavior and sometimes went out in the hall to look in wonderment, and my students just laughed. They didn't seem to feel it is terrible or at least that it is anything someone can or should do anything about.

Perhaps because they can do nothing about so many things that control their lives, the Chinese are inattentive or undisciplined where other things are concerned. We Americans don't have the outward controls on us, but in a way we are much more self-controlled. We limit ourselves and are irate when others don't, even if we can't do anything about it. I found that curious and surprising because I have not necessarily thought of Americans as self-disciplined people.

One evening as we were making our way home from the Hu's among a throng of people also out for a stroll, Zhirong, who had spent a few months in Chicago visiting her son, spoke of how lonely she had been in the United States. She said no one was ever out so there was no one to talk with. She was overlooking the fact that she had been there during cold weather and that she also spoke almost no English at the time.

Nevertheless, it is easy to see that Chinese may not feel the alienation or loneliness that many Americans feel because they are surrounded by people the moment they step outside their own doors. Perhaps it is because the Chinese world is so limited in scope and they live in such close proximity to each other that they find interest and meaning in others' lives as well as their own. They have little diversion or other stimulation. While most Americans would probably find such an atmosphere claustrophobic, it does have much to recommend it.

In William Least Heat-Moon's book, *PrairyErth*, which is about life in Kansas, he asks one of the women whether lack of privacy isn't the worst thing about a small town and she says, "And also the best: I love going to the post office in the morning and knowing everybody. . . . We can't afford to not care about everybody in a place this small. Our survival, in a way, depends on minimizing privacy because the lack of it draws us into each other's lives, and that's a major resource in a little town where there aren't a thousand entertainments."

She might have been talking about China.

18

Christmas was coming. Early on we decided that it would be a nice time to entertain students and friends, so already in October I'd sent home a request for a tape of Christmas music, party supplies, and decorations to spruce up the apartment.

I also made an appeal to friends and relatives for stamps to give to students. Many of our students were stamp collectors, and it occurred to us that this would be a terrific little gift. We received a wonderful outpouring in time to give each of our 125 students a half dozen stamps for Christmas and even more later as the mail trickled in. We wrapped them in little packages along with some little Shanghai chocolate eggs that Don had scoured the city for. It was like Christmas morning the day we handed those out in class.

We also decided to have a party for friends and colleagues a few days before Christmas, as we might have done at home. Several had entertained us and we wanted to reciprocate. We were granted permission to use the Guest House dining room, and I enlisted Emily's help in making out the guest list. With the aid of computer graphics, I made a fancy little invitation. We did not know the spouses of many of our colleagues, however; and since a woman does not take her husband's name in China, we could not address the invitations Mr. and Mrs. and let it go at that. We needed Emily to supply the missing names. We learned something about social customs in the process.

We just assumed spouses would come and thought we made that clear to Emily. But each time we named someone, she would say, "Do you want to invite his wife?"

We said, "Of course," becoming exasperated after a while. "At home, husbands and wives are always invited to parties (well, almost always). Isn't that true here?"

Evidently not.

Emily might add about someone, "Well, they're not getting along very well right now."

After a while, we left it to her discretion.

On the day of the party, the entire Waiban staff helped decorate the room. A sturdy little potted shrub from the campus greenhouse served as a Christmas tree, and we hung the decorations sent from the States. (Ironically, the strings of Christmas lights, sent from Florida, had been made in China.) The room took on a festive air.

Whether it was due to the appeal of the party itself or that there were few competing activities, the invited guests turned out in full force. I think everyone had a good time—we certainly did. Since not all the guests spoke English, the party was bilingual, even trilingual at times. Entertainment? Home style, mostly. There were songs in Chinese and English and Russian. Refreshments? We shelled peanuts, peeled mandarins, and sampled a variety of cookies and candy. We washed it down with orange soda, Pepsi (of course, there was Pepsi in China), and beer—and of course, tea.

Some of our guests brought cards and gifts. One gift was memorable: a fluffy, bright orange stuffed dog. Breed: Pekinese, perhaps. It was the epitome of kitsch. Given that Chinese seldom have pets, and hardly ever have dogs if they do, we couldn't imagine what prompted the gift, but there it was. We searched valiantly for words of gratitude.

Since the givers were frequent visitors, we thought it important to display this gift in a prominent place. When Melanie and Monique saw the dog for the first time, after a moment of speechlessness, then gales of laughter, they were effusive in their admiration.

Their comments would have been great illustrations of hyperbole to use in class. They outdid each other when they visited thereafter. In the meantime, we were growing fond of the little orange dragon, as we called him. We pretended offense at their thinly disguised ridicule and warned darkly of revenge.

We had been warned that we needed to get to church early for the Christmas services, both on the Sunday before and on Christmas Eve. Presumably many people came in from the countryside who do not come at other times.

Since the temperature was only about forty degrees Fahrenheit on Sunday, we bundled up. We arrived a little before 9:00 and admired the large evergreen wreaths and red bows which decorated the outside walls. Though the service would not start till 10:00, many people were already seated in the courtyard. Even though we did get a seat inside, it was no warmer. We sat wearing four layers plus gloves and could see our breath in the fresh air. There did seem to be some new faces. One little man puffed contentedly on his pipe until someone chided him about it.

By the time the service began, the chairs in the courtyard were filled and people were standing ten-deep at the windows.

The church was decorated extensively and fairly traditionally to my Western eyes. On the windowsills, white candles set amidst greenery were ready to be lighted for Christmas Eve. Greenery and festive red bows also hung from wall lights. A huge tree which brushed the high ceiling stood in a corner of the chancel behind the piano. I doubt if there was room for even one more decoration. Flashing lights spoiled the whole effect somewhat, but perhaps, given their commonness in China, it was only I who was distracted.

The clergy were out in full force that morning. Five people took places in the chancel chairs and I braced for a long service and wished for a battery-operated warmer of some kind. Included in the participants were two retired clergy, one of whom was over ninety years of age. I envisioned frostbite by the end of the service, but they surprised me. In spite of three numbers by the choir, the service was over promptly at 11:00, as usual.

One of the choir numbers was "Deck the Halls," four verses rendered at breakneck speed. The effect was dizzying. The pianist was also choir director. Although he seldom played anything correctly, that one time he never missed a note, despite the fast tempo. He must have practiced for weeks.

At least I thought it was "Deck the Halls" they were singing. I tried to remember all the words and find some religious significance that would justify its being used in a worship service. When I commented about the number to one of the American teachers who sang with the choir, however, she said the song had different lyrics.

But for me, "Deck the Halls" will never be the same. I think that whenever I hear it in the future, I will forever see forty black-haired people in white robes with big red bows singing their hearts out, trying their best to keep up with a runaway piano player.

I woke up about four on Christmas morning and lay awake at least half an hour before deciding I might as well get up. It wasn't excitement about Santa that had me wakeful. I had been lying there awake delivering imaginary lectures to students, college officials, Li Peng, or just anyone who would listen. As if anyone in China would listen.

I was not in a good mood. I was fuming as a result of the previous night's experience, and I needed to get some things off my chest. So I sat down in front of the computer in my long underwear, flannel nightgown, fleecy robe, down jacket, and lined booties, and gave vent to my feelings in my journal. Our whole China experience had been interesting and enlightening but frustrating in a number of ways. The whole non-Christmas season, which was about Christmas but not about Christmas, sort of encapsulated the whole thing.

Several weeks before, I was asked by Mr. Wang, the student head of the English Club, to teach my postgraduate students some Christmas songs to be sung at a "Christmas party." This was the first we had heard about a party. However, we learned little by little from veteran China teachers, plus random comments that were made by the Waiban staff, that there would indeed be a big party for us. The motive was to make us feel better about not being at home on this most important holiday. They even thoughtfully waited for us to tell them when we would not be going to church services, before setting the final date.

I thought it would be fun to teach the songs because the students loved to sing. Because I was often hoarse and had little voice left for singing, I had only taught them a few rounds and some simple folk songs up to this point, but Don had gone all out. He'd attempted to teach his students "I've Been Workin' on the Railroad" and "Old McDonald Had a Farm," among others. When I mentioned this in a letter home along with the news that already they were asking at the college if we would stay another year, a friend wrote back to say that perhaps we would have to stay another year if Don were going to teach his students all the verses to "Old MacDonald's Farm."

I set about choosing the music for our little chorus and enlisted Professor Zhang to help direct the students. He had a wonderful tenor voice, the kind that church choir directors pray for. The Zhang family had a piano, and we had spent many enjoyable evenings in sing-alongs around the piano to my reluctant accompaniment. (Reluctant because my piano playing up to that period of my life was a very private matter. There were only a few people in the world who'd ever heard me play, for reasons that are obvious to anyone who has heard me play. But there was no one else available, so I was stuck—and so were they.)

Since he had a book of Christmas songs and carols, brought from the United States, we were singing Christmas music already in September. Professor Zhang particularly liked "Silent Night." When it came time to choose the three numbers for the choral group, that seemed a natural choice for one. It wasn't difficult, it was the quintessential Christmas carol, and it was a favorite of his.

However, he turned thumbs down on it. He feared it "might get the Waiban staff in trouble," since they were one of the sponsors of the party. I thought that was curious, but didn't question his judgement. I assumed that it was considered too religious. So, we settled for "Silver Bells," "We Wish You a Merry Christmas," and . . . "Bicycle Built For Two." Surprised? So was I. Actually, it was all Don's fault.

While Professor Zhang, Don, and I were considering other Christmas songs, Don happened to mention that he'd taught his students "Bicycle Built For Two" the previous week and that they had loved it. Since Professor Zhang didn't know the song, Don sang it for him and he loved it. Since practically everyone in the country rides a bicycle, he thought the students would have a great time with the song.

So, "Bicycle Built For Two" it was, which of course has nothing to do with Christmas, but . . . he was right, they loved it. I not only spent a few minutes on the songs in class each week, but we practiced on three Sunday evenings as well.

We elected to go to church on Sunday, December 23, and to bypass the Christmas Eve service a day later, so we told the Waiban we would be free on Christmas Eve. Therefore, after all this, we were expecting a Christmas party, no?

The party was to be held in the main student dining hall where the twice-weekly dances are held. Hundreds of invitations were distributed. When we finally got our printed invitation a few days before the party, we noticed that it said "new year Party [sic]." A new year party on December 24 at which, as it turned out, there was a Christmas tree, two performances of "Jingle Bells," and Santa Claus—both a poster and a live Santa in a red suit delivering gifts. The colored lights didn't count as Christmas decorations because Chinese use colored lights for everything. There were colored lights in the students' dining room the year around for the dances.

The students were excited about Christmas, asked questions about it beforehand, and began giving us cards, some of them homemade. I lectured about Christmas, explaining the biblical and historical foundations of Christmas, and discussed a lot of the secular traditions. Ironically, Don, feeling unsure of his knowledge, made no formal presentation but was besieged with questions about the Bible and the Christmas story.

So came Christmas Eve and the "new year Party." Since we couldn't be at home, it sounded like fun. We were escorted to the hall by Emily and ushered to our seats. The hall is a barn of a place, with all the acoustical problems of a gymnasium. About six hundred people attended. The seating was cabaret style, with tables set in a big U-shape around the edge and a few screens that formed the backdrop for the performers. We were seated in a front row at the bottom of the U, facing the performance area. The usual peanuts, sunflower seeds, and mandarin oranges were piled in front of each place. The noise level was high as people continued to file in, even after the program started half an hour late.

The first act on the program was a little play by the doctoral students. I had written it as an introduction to the postgrads' carol singing, or what started out as carol singing. In the play the students were sitting around trying to think of something they could do to cheer up all the foreigners in their midst who were so far from home at Christmas. They keep coming up with ideas but then having them shot down. For example, when someone mentions he's heard that people decorate live evergreen trees in their homes at Christmas, Mr. Hu is ready to go cut down a nice little evergreen in front of the campus museum. But others warn that he would get them all in trouble. Miss Jia has read that people bake Christmas cookies and take them to friends, so why don't they do that? Someone sarcastically reminds her that Chinese people don't have ovens, and you can't bake Christmas cookies in a wok. Mr. Chen and Mr. Jiang both remember that Santa Claus, a jolly fat man in a red suit, is very much a part of Christmas, so why don't they find someone to play Santa? The group really shoots down that idea. They shout scornfully, "Just where are you going to find a *fat* Chinese?"

And so it goes until someone brings up the idea of singing carols. They could get a bunch of students together and go caroling, serenading the teachers in their homes. Well, everyone thinks that's a terrific idea and they call all the students up on stage to have a little practice. Voila: the introduction to the postgrads' chorus. The students had fun doing it and it worked well in rehearsal, but well-laid plans do go awry, especially in China.

The little play was drowned in the hub-bub and the nonattention of the audience. Its purpose was defeated and the point lost. I couldn't even hear or understand the dialogue, and I had written it. I could only console myself that the students had had a good time rehearsing it—and, of course, more practice in English.

The three songs by the postgrads went off pretty well, what we could hear, anyway. The sound system was a fiasco. Sound systems are always iffy, but this was the worst ever. If someone had written a comedy sketch in which everything that could go wrong would, they could not have done better. We cringed as feedback assailed our ears, microphones squealed, and the volume fluctuated drastically. The little fellow in charge, wearing a visored wool cap and athletic shoes, ran from one microphone to another and to the amplifier and back again as everything that could go wrong did. He needed those athletic shoes to get traction. Melinda and Monique and I rued the fact that we wouldn't have a video tape of just his performance to show as a party film back home.

The program was a kind of variety show. I sat for the first half hour trying to listen to the various acts: songs, instrumental numbers, and dances from various student groups on campus. I fumed at the circus atmosphere and people's obvious inattention. Even when there were several acts deserving of attention or at least polite semblance of it, hardly anyone applauded. If we had not started the applause some-times, I'm not sure there would have been any.

I leaned over to Emily at one point and asked why people came to something to which they paid absolutely no attention. She didn't answer. What could she say.

Mr. Wang, the emcee, had asked Don and me to contribute some-thing for the program and I was glad we had decided not to recite "Twas the Night Before Christmas." M & M, who'd also been asked, had suggested that the four of us combine our talents and do the four numbers we had done at our own Christmas party the week before. We had discovered on our various travels that we harmonized well together and had wowed our Chinese audiences. Chinese music does not use the harmonies that are so common to Western music, and Chinese people seemed awed by our ability to do that.

As the evening wore on, we four North Americanos resolved that we were not going to perform the three carols we planned in such a circus atmosphere. It was not only the constant feedback or that the microphones weren't working, but the band that was to play for the dance to follow was warming up on the stage behind. It was competing with continuing performances down front.

When Mr. Wang came to tell us we were up next, we told him we would not sing unless the band amplifiers were turned off. I also asked Emily to translate a little announcement for us. Taking the microphone in hand, I asked first if the audience could hear me. Not hearing much lessening in the din, I waited. (It didn't occur to me till later that proba-bly at least two-thirds of the audience did not understand English.) Emily took the microphone and said something in Chinese, which had some effect. I decided it was probably as quiet as it was going to get.

I said, "While you may be celebrating the New Year, it is Christmas Eve for us, and the songs we are about to sing tell the real meaning of Christmas. These songs are very important to us and will be sung in churches all over the world this Christmas eve."

I would have liked to say more, but it was neither the time nor the place—and it would have fallen on deaf ears. We sang three traditional carols, in harmony, and ended with "We Wish You a Merry Christmas." Although we could hardly hear ourselves, at least they applauded when we finished.

We left soon after the dancing started, and managed to get away without any visitors. Once alone at home, we post-mortemed the evening. We had little good to say about it. The experience reminded me of how frustrated I'd felt after Commencement at my own college the previous spring. The college had decided for the first time to ask a teacher to deliver the commencement address, and since I was retiring, I got the bid. I was flattered and worked hard on my speech. It was held in the college gymnasium with a makeshift sound system. When people told me they'd been unable to hear my address, I felt hours of work had been wasted.

I was experiencing similar feelings about the play that the students had performed.

I remembered China's constant refrain, whether from the *China Daily* or from college officials or students, that they need to learn English and the advanced technology of the West. We remarked that they needed to learn a lot more from the West than just technology if they are going to be accepted and respected by the rest of the world. Chinese habits and manners seemed crude in many ways. Their actions, to Western eyes, are often lacking in common courtesy and respect for others. They do not seem to compliment or offer reassurance to others as a matter of course. You don't get any sense of how you're doing. At such times I mused that that evidently was purely a cultural value, but when you have come to expect such behavior, its absence is distressing. Every culture has a right to maintain the integrity of its own character; however, when you want cultural interaction, those differences can get in the way of satisfactory relations.

I thought, too, of a Bertrand Russell article that we had just recently read in the doctoral class—"How To Avoid Foolish Opinions"—and decided I might reprise it as a way of making some pertinent points. Russell offered several rules, obvious but profound in their simplicity. One of them was to get to know other countries and other kinds of people, that that would help us avoid dogmatism. Another was, when we are unable to meet people with different opinions, we should at least imagine a dialogue with them. Another was that we should be wary of any opinion that flatters our self-esteem. Chinese people were constantly asking what we thought of their schools, their country, their food. They were asking for confirmation rather than information or an appraisal; and since we were guests in their country and basically thoughtful and considerate people, we were not going to trash their society. But if they really wanted to know, if they really were seeking suggestions for improvement or alternatives to other ways of doing things, they could have asked their questions a different way.

I was often reminded of the articles I had read about the experiences of people who visited China twenty years ago and their descriptions of the people they met. Chinese people have traditionally felt that they were a superior people, inhabitants of the Middle Kingdom, and had nothing to learn from others. That was even more blatant after the Revolution. But though they now espouse a policy of openness, the openness is still a narrowly defined one. We all have cultural blinders and theirs limit their comprehension of what it means to be open and seeking truth.

When we had come to China, I hadn't expected any acknowledgment or recognition of Christmas at all. Imagine my surprise, then, when early in November we saw beautiful Christmas cards and a wide selection of Western Christmas tapes for sale at the Foreign Language Bookstore. As December approached, we saw Santa Claus and Christmas tree pictures here and there. A Foreign Language Middle School nearby invited us and the Canadians to come and tell them about Christmas traditions, although when we got there and listened to their prepared program, they seemed to have all the bases covered. They even had one short skit in which a very pregnant Mary was featured.

I ended the season feeling very frustrated with the Chinese approach to Christmas. They seem to have just taken the trappings of Christmas—sending cards, buying gifts for children, and singing "Jingle Bells" and other songs—and totally rejected the rest. I resented it. I felt they had no right to it, which is why I insisted on telling the history of Christmas. I was determined that they were at least going to hear it, even if it didn't mean anything.

I was surprised at my own reaction. Perhaps it began when Professor Zhang, who loved "Silent Night," discouraged including it in the students' performance. I guess he thought it too "political." How could you begin to capture the essence of Christmas without hearing any of the carols. When I stop to think about it, I guess "Bicycle Built For Two" was probably not a bad choice after all for a Chinese Christmas.

19

Christmas was over and we had only a few weeks left in the semester. By then we had gotten to know our students a lot better and, through them and their experiences, gained a better understanding of the educational system in China.

We had met Chinese students in the United States a couple of years before we went to China, and I still remember how incredible I found the information that students have little control over their choice of academic major when they go to college.

One year at Thanksgiving, we hosted two young couples. Both husbands and both wives had received bachelor's degrees in China before coming to the United States. Of the four, however, only one of the women had been able to study what she preferred—Russian language and Russian literature. The other woman wanted to study Western medicine, but was sent to a Chinese traditional medical college instead. One of the men who had hoped to study civil engineering was assigned to mechanical engineering, and the other, who wanted to major in Chinese literature, was required to study paleontology. He had no interest in paleontology at all. Yet, both of those men have now finished their doctoral studies in those fields. I find it mind-boggling to think of expending that much time, energy, and emotion on something you have less than an all-consuming interest in.

Up till now, students have had to select five majors and the schools where they wanted to study *before* taking the college entrance exams at the end of middle school. They also ranked them according to preference. Since some colleges have higher standards than others, students had to play a little Russian roulette in guessing what their scores were going to be. If they were too pessimistic about their scores and chose a lower-ranked school, they were stuck with the lesser school.

The three-day college entrance exam is given at the end of middle school in July. Students then have to wait until September, when they receive a letter telling them what their scores were, what their major is, and where they are to study. They have only a short time to get to school before the start of the new term.

The government calls the shots in China, even in the choice of careers. When it is determined that a certain number of people are needed in a particular profession, *voila*, x number of people become instant accountants, electrical engineers, chemists, or whatever.

When I had asked our four young visitors in the United States about the system, they said they suspected that other reasons may enter in career appointments, too. The one young man has relatives who had fled to Taiwan. The other's parents had taken part in the Hundred Flowers campaign in the mid-fifties, when Mao had invited intellectuals to assess how the Revolution was proceeding. Along with many others who had taken Mao seriously, the parents had had to pay for their naïveté. The sons thought perhaps their university assignments amounted to censure for their family connections.

When I met my students in Chengdu, I learned that very few of them had listed geology as a top career choice. A handful had not even listed it at all.

One young woman said, "I'd never even heard of geology until I was assigned to this college."

Mr. Han was one of those who had no interest in geology. He wanted to be an architect, but he was getting his doctorate in petroleum geology. His heart was still not in geology. He had pursued further degrees only as a possible means of advancement. Even though all my students were then pursuing graduate degrees in geology, many still hoped somehow to pursue other interests in the future, and they believed that knowing English might provide a means of doing that.

Reforms are currently underway in the selection process for higher education, but it remains to be seen how extensive they will be.

Just as I was curious about Chinese education, students were very interested in American education and what went on in American schools.

One Tuesday evening, as part of a regular English lecture series, I spoke about American education, generally, and higher education, specifically. Some 250 students showed up. Because most Chinese students dream of going abroad to study, they frequently asked about available scholarships, how to apply, which are the best schools, and what their chances were of being accepted. They wanted to know the difference between public and private schools and which were best. They also had questions about simpler, more mundane matters.

One night during Free Talk with the postgrads, someone asked if it were true that American students did not rise when the teacher entered and left the room, did not say "good morning," and did not rise to recite. Did it bother me that they did not do those things?

I said yes, it was true, but it didn't bother me. I explained that students used to follow those customs in our country but no longer. Americans just aren't that formal.

(I thought to myself, however, that many American teachers would probably find such customs appealing, given the atmosphere in many schools today. I did not have the stomach for confessing some of the major problems that American teachers confront these days: drug use, violence in the classroom, verbal abuse, and personal attacks by students. I find such occurrences so unbelievable myself, I could not imagine how preposterous the Chinese would find them.)

I told them another difference that I had noticed was that Chinese students do not challenge or disagree with their teachers as much as American students do. We try to encourage students to question from the beginning of their education, I explained. We want them to learn not only what, but why, to question and explore for themselves whether something is right or wrong.

"I'm frustrated when students don't ask questions," I said.

One of my Chinese students spoke up immediately, saying that Chinese teachers only lecture students and leave no opportunity to ask questions.

I told them about one of my doctoral students' observations when he was at Cambridge for a semester. Mr. Liu, the student, had explained the differences in Chinese education and that of the West by saying that the Chinese approach is to teach facts, that Chinese education stresses memorization but spends little time on application. He observed that he and other Chinese students had a great deal more knowledge on some subjects than their fellow Cambridge students, but they had not been trained to explore and question and analyze—in short, to think— the way Western students had. They were at a disadvantage because of it, he said.

From the nodding heads, I could see that many of my students agreed. I then asked why it was important that students learn to analyze and question.

They had no answer, and did not attempt one.

I asked if they had heard of Socrates. None had. (I was in the East, right?)

I explained a little about Socrates (which was really all I knew!)— that Socrates taught by asking his students questions that led them to discover their own answers.

"What advantage would that have for the student?" I asked.

Silence.

I tried again. "You're all scientists. Why is it better for you to discover your own answers instead of merely learning facts from a text or memorizing data from your professors' lectures?"

They looked at each other and back at me, obviously puzzled and a little uncomfortable.

"What if someone challenges a statement or your conclusions, pointing out discrepancies?" I said.

More awkward silences followed, but finally we struggled through to some answers. (The Socratic method is never quick or easy!)

I pointed out that educators at home had long been saying that with the "knowledge explosion," not only can knowledge expand quickly but it can also become obsolete very quickly. Therefore, it is important to teach people *how to learn* and *how to think*. With those kinds of intellectual skills, students are better equipped to deal with a changing world and to solve problems they may have in the future.

As I spoke, students again were nodding their heads in agreement. One student talked about changes in the middle school examination system in China that put more emphasis on practice and said he thought that would be good. I had just recently read something similar in the *China Daily*. Graduation from middle school would now be based on a separate exam from the college entrance exam.

The students seemed to agree that Chinese education needed to be reformed. Mr. Shen commented that too few students are able to go to a university.

I cited a *China Daily* report that only a little over one percent of China's students attend college or university simply because there aren't facilities for any more.

"That means much talent is being lost," I said. "Those whose scores are not high enough, but who still are above-average students, also represent a natural resource."

Mr. Deng, sitting in the front row, had not entered into the discussion. He looked serious and disapproving, even agitated. He was class monitor and co-president of the English Club. He was very cooperative and friendly, but he wouldn't have that position if he weren't acceptable to the powers that be. I learned later that all of the class monitors and others in similar student positions were Party members, so I assumed that was a necessary qualification.

He claimed what Mr. Shen had said about Chinese education was not true. When he went on, I stopped him and told him what the statistics were, culled from the *China Daily*. How, then, could he say that wasn't true?

He replied, "I know many scientists who are accomplished and successful and they don't have higher degrees."

I pointed out that that may have been true in the past but that seldom was possible anymore. We were in a different age. It is very difficult for anyone to go very far without formal education, particularly in a developed country as China aspired to be. Again, most students were murmuring or nodding their agreement.

It was as if Mr. Deng didn't like what he was hearing and therefore it couldn't be true.

Students generally seemed to agree that change was needed. Most of my doctoral students were teachers.

"Are you teaching differently?" I asked.

They said, "We're trying, but it's hard to change the system."

The system of testing, which includes many entrance examinations, demands that they "teach for the test."

These discussions reminded me of an observation that a doctoral student had made shortly after I arrived. He said that he thought it was easier to get into American colleges but also easier to fail, whereas it was harder to get into Chinese colleges but harder to fail once you're in.

That baffled me at first. But then I began to understand. If students pass all those difficult entrance exams along the way, the system deems them capable and goes to great lengths to help them succeed in college. For example, teachers commonly give make-up tests, and I don't just mean because of sickness. Fail once, well, just try it again. How many times one can take a make-up exam was not clear to me.

That college or university degree is, perhaps, more important in China than in the United States, or at least more important than in the United States in the past. In China the kind of job you got upon graduation usually was determined by grades and the recommendation of one's adviser. And since in China that first job assignment usually meant getting locked into a career path, the degree takes on even greater importance.

Knowing that should make students apply themselves diligently at all times, but from the complaints of some Chinese teachers, that was not necessarily the case. Because flunking out is so rare, students may get the idea it is impossible and therefore they become complacent and slack off.

At the same time I was writing home saying how fortunate American students were to have the educational choices they do, I was telling Chinese students how fortunate *they* were to have their college education paid for, and to receive a stipend besides. It was a minuscule amount and they were always complaining about it, but I reminded them many American students had to work part-time to pay their tuition. The idea of being able to hold a part-time job, however, was very appealing to the Chinese. Many of them envy Western young people their independence. Being able to earn your own money is a big part of that appeal.

Chinese students seem to regard their teachers highly and consider someone who has been their teacher always their teacher. But, as in most societies, Chinese teachers are not paid well. Few young people aspire to teach. Few of my doctoral students who were teaching had chosen to teach; they had been drafted.

The government recognizes the teacher shortage and acknowledges that better salaries and living conditions are necessary to change the situation. Although China had professorships, there were no formal advanced degrees among the older professors. China did not adopt a degree-conferring system until the early 1980's. Highly qualified, full professors at the college received a monthly salary of only two hundred yuan—forty-seven dollars in 1991 American dollars. Granted, living expenses in China are minimal, but it is still pathetically low.

China is also facing a crucial problem in higher education in the next five years. Many of her senior professors will be retiring. Because colleges were closed for ten years during the Cultural Revolution, from 1966 to 1976, there are no professors in the middle years ready to take their places.

20

One Sunday, shortly after we had come to Chengdu, we were sitting in the sunshine in the little garden at the side of the Jinjiang Hotel, waiting for the car to pick us up. Since we had half an hour to wait and it was warm, Don went into the hotel to get some cold drinks. While I waited on a bench, a young man sauntered my way. He pretended to admire the flowers, but he was transparent in his hope to engage this foreigner in conversation.

As he got nearer, I thought I would make it easier and said hello. That was all it took. He told me he had an interior decorating office in the hotel and worked for a private enterprise based on Hainan Island, an area off the southern coast of China, where the government has established enterprise zones. In these zones the government relaxes restrictions that businesses have to abide by in other areas.

He spoke glowingly about his job and his employers, told us how much money he made, and said that his company even provided him a housing allowance. He had a master's degree in math and had been a college math teacher, earning only 150 yuan ($30) a month. That was only about fifteen percent of what he was making at present. He praised capitalism and spoke bitterly and strongly about socialism and the Communist Party. He made no attempt to keep his voice down.

He said, rather forcefully, "I hate the Communist Party. They are ruining this country," and added that the employees in his company often criticize the government.

I hid my surprise, but glanced around to see if anyone were within earshot, wondering if it was safe for people to talk so frankly, particularly to strangers, or for us to be seen talking with someone who was so open and vocal. Fleetingly, and perhaps naïvely, because we were still relatively new to China, I wondered if someone was checking us out to see if we encouraged such associations or would capitalize on them in any way.

I relaxed, however, as he went on to admit that he had no security in his job but felt it was much better to have cut himself loose from his former job, which he saw as a dead end.

The phrase "cut himself loose" was mine, but that is exactly what he did. When you had a job within the system, you had coupons or tickets for rice and oil and other staples. Those enabled you to buy those items at greatly reduced prices. When you got a job outside the system, you no longer had access to the coupons, and had to buy things on the open market. That could be scary.

According to the *China Daily*, subsidies made up one-third of the nation's budget: for housing, food, cooking oil, transportation, and the like. For urban dwellers, their employer units provide medical care as well, with little or no co-payment required. That caused problems in that people had gotten so used to subsidized prices they resisted higher prices when they became necessary. The unfortunate part is that many of those benefits were available to city-dwellers, but not to the country as a whole. Eighty percent of the people live in the countryside.

I was trying to find an example of a metaphor one day when I was talking with Xiao Lin, who worked in the Waiban. We were in the small bus on the way home from a picnic. He was explaining how frustrated his girlfriend was in her job.

She liked her job, but many of the people in her unit were political appointees. They didn't necessarily have any training nor did they do anything. They were uncooperative when she needed help. Even if there was no work, she was not allowed to leave.

He said that it was very risky to quit a job, cut yourself loose from all the benefits, and go to work for a private firm. You would have to make sure it was a very good, dependable job because if it didn't last, you could be left high and dry.

I said that going out on your own to get a job in China is a little like going out into deep water in a small boat without a life preserver. He had a terrible time understanding that until I wrote it out. I said at first it was a metaphor but decided it was a simile—a distinction that probably matters only to English teachers.

When M & M and I were talking about the difference and trying to come up with an example, Xiao Lin said, "Isn't the 'iron rice bowl' a metaphor?" Of course. It was perfect.

The "iron rice bowl" in China was a guaranteed meal ticket—everyone was assured of a job and an income. That's what you got as long as you worked for any government agency or approved enterprise. The iron bowl couldn't be broken.

I had been reading, however, that some factories were doing away with the iron rice bowl. They started contracting with workers for a certain time period and providing some health insurance and other benefits. The worker was trading that security for the possibility of higher pay. Those instances, however, were still very much in the minority.

Since we have returned to the States, though, the government has pursued development of a market economy with even greater energy, and is eliminating the iron rice bowl.

Learning to speak English is one way for students to change jobs, and several of Don's Class A students who finished their study in January were able to do just that. One student went to Nigeria, another went to work for a Swedish-Chinese joint venture, and another also dealt with foreign business representatives.

Chinese people's attempts to learn and practice English was sometimes wearing, but it was also a way that we learned a great deal about China. It was an Open Sesame into people's experience, expectations, and perceptions.

21

That package that son John sent in September finally arrived at the end of January. Its arrival was a memorable event for more than just his parents.

Letters were delivered to the college post office twice daily, but packages, big or small, had to be picked up at the main post office downtown. The Waiban staff picked up our mail each day at the campus post office; and when they received notice that there was a package for someone in care of their department, they sent a car downtown to pick it up.

They delivered to our door a large beat-up cardboard box, handling it very gingerly. Not only was it open on one side, but the aroma of vinegar permeated the air. We were delighted to finally get the package, but apprehensive about what was inside. Surely this child of ours wasn't dumb enough to have sent a jar of pickles over the Pacific Ocean, not to mention China Railways.

We finished tearing open the box and surveyed the contents. All the packages and boxes inside were dusted lightly with pancake mix from a torn package. But the vinegar smell? I had forgotten that ketchup contains vinegar and for whatever reason, the bottom had come out of a large plastic bottle of ketchup—that's right, not a glass bottle, but plastic, which one would expect to be unbreakable, right? What wasn't dusted with pancake flour was smeared with ketchup. It was not an appetizing sight, but after washing off the remaining packages with a little soap and water, we oohed and aahed over each find: chocolate pudding mix, Parmesan cheese, pizza mix, a Kellogg's variety pack of cereals, and a big container of mustard to make up for the ketchup.

One part of Don mourned the missing ketchup, but another part of him gloated over what he inferred to be his son's inadequate packing. Don has taken a lot of kidding in the family over the years about his over-enthusiasm when it comes to packing. It sometimes takes major tools and appliances to open his packages.

Needless to say, the next trans-Pacific phone call included some offers to provide packing lessons when we got home.

More boxes arrived from other family members and friends. Intended to arrive before Christmas, perhaps even by Thanksgiving, in addition to foodstuffs, they contained Christmas decorations, some of which had been made in China.

Package contents also revealed interesting perceptions of China. Among all the largess we received was a supply of Lipton tea bags, Uncle Ben's rice, and a can of peas at a time when every farmer in the market had a mound of fresh peas for sale. I must confess, though, that when I had my first cup of Lipton tea, I put my feet up and said, "Now, *that's* a cup of tea." Chinese tea isn't for every day, either.

And when we had Chinese people for dinner, I enjoyed being able to serve them Uncle Ben's brown rice. It was a change for both of us. Along with the canned peas came some Boston baked beans. I confess half the can never made it to the table. They took an inordinate amount of tasting during the heating process just to make sure they were table-right. Don just thought it was a small can.

Those packages from home also contained cleaning supplies, responding to my earlier complaints. We put them to good use, Don especially.

I'm married to Mr. Clean. There is no physical likeness to that fellow you saw on television years ago, but Don abhors dirt and seems to get an abiding sense of satisfaction in seeing things sparkle. Disorder offends him. Although I don't consider myself a slob, given a choice between tidying up the apartment and reading a book, I'd compromise by giving things a quick swipe and curl up with a clear conscience. Not so my husband.

Our bathroom had a huge bathtub, the kind even a six-foot husband could stretch out in comfortably. But stretching out in the tub was not very enticing. It was not only that we were shower people but also that the tub, doubtlessly a gleaming white once, was a pale gray, as in grime. We climbed in, turned on the shower, and ignored the discolored tub. Since the portable shower head was lying in the tub bottom after the housekeepers came each Friday, we assumed there was an attempt at cleaning and that was the best they could do.

After cans of Comet and a box of Brillo pads arrived, Don on a whim—and maybe out of boredom—started in on the tub one evening. He was almost finished before he called me to see what he'd been doing. The tub was transformed. It was gleaming white. It sparkled—all but one portion about a foot square which he had left so I could appreciate the before and after. I ooohhed and aaahhed—it *was* remarkable.

Then he decided to leave it that way to see what the housecleaner, due the next morning, would do. He wished he could be a mouse and see her reaction.

Whatever the reaction was, it didn't produce any visible result.

When we got home from class that day, the tub was just as he had left it. If she thought he had somehow performed a miracle, she must have decided she couldn't improve on it or compete, so left him to his own devices. He finished the job later, but as far as we could tell the housekeepers made no attempt to maintain the new, white look.

The arrival of another small package about that time pleased me as well. It contained the white turtleneck I had left at Emei Mountain in the fall. The next time Mr. He escorted a group to Emei, he retrieved my shirt, which had been saved for me. Regardless of whether someone was motivated by commitment to socialist principle or just basic honesty, I was grateful.

By this time, first-semester final exams were almost over and we had had farewell parties with two of our classes who were finished with their study.

The doctoral students wanted to have a party at the end of the term, so they all came to the apartment on a Saturday night. I fixed spaghetti and pasta salad and provided wine, beer, and Pepsi, and each student brought a dish. The students obviously had coordinated the menu very well because there was a nice variety and the food was also very attractive. There were several meats: rabbit, pork, liver, duck; also, jiaozi; cold salads. The men had prepared their own dishes in most cases, cooked over little coal burners outside their rooms. I marveled to think what masterpieces they could turn out in a real kitchen.

They seemed to like the spaghetti—a meat sauce over fine Chinese noodles—and pasta salad. Because the table was full and the pans were hot (I had made the sauce in the wok), I left it in the kitchen and when we started to eat, I invited them to try some spaghetti. Knowing that my tentativeness about trying Chinese food in the beginning was often a matter of not knowing how to eat something, I demonstrated, then fixed a plate and asked Mr. Chen if he'd like to try. The others watched him curiously, as he mixed the sauce in well, tasted, and pronounced it good. He urged the others to try, and they eagerly followed suit.

When everyone seemingly had had their fill, I asked if they'd like to sing, play games, or . . . they immediately opted for games. We played a couple of games that they chose.

They imposed a rule that if anyone goofed that person had to be "punished." The punishment could be volunteered by the person or selected by the group. Everyone responded cheerfully, either performing some silly action, reciting a poem, singing a song, or dancing. I told them if I had known about this Chinese custom before I came to China, I would have taken singing and dancing lessons, learned some card tricks, or memorized a selection of poetry instead of spending so much time preparing teaching materials, selecting books and filmstrips and the like.

Not only were students glad that the semester ended, they were excited about the coming holiday, and we were catching their excitement. One thing Chinese students understood before we arrived was that Christmas is for us what Spring Festival is for them. To my knowledge, there's no such song as "I'll Be Home For Spring Festival," but if there were, it would be most appropriate. Although traveling isn't easy, all Chinese go home during Spring Festival if they possibly can. That goes especially for students, as there are no classes for about six weeks.

We had our own travel plans for the holiday. Accompanied by Barbara Stover, a friend and former Danville teaching colleague, we would spend two weeks journeying cross country by train, boat and plane, ending up in Hong Kong, where we would stay for another week. We had been planning our itinerary with Emily for some time, but we were going to have to manage on this trip without the "buffering" that the Waiban staff provided. We'd been in China long enough to know this venture was not without certain risks.

22

Somewhere out there through the darkness and drizzle a boat was waiting for us. It was where the spotlight was coming from. At least, that's what our guides said as they led us through the grim, desolate docks of Chongqing and out on foot along a makeshift bridge of teetering wooden planks. They said the riverboat lay just a couple of hundred yards across the mud flats. Of course, since the spotlight was shining in our eyes, we were blind to everything before us, so we had to take their word for it. I was not exactly at ease. Nor were Don and Barbara Stover, judging from their nervous laughter as we sought a firm footing, at the same time juggling luggage for our three week sojourn. I felt as if we were being smuggled out of the country, rather than starting a three-day, sight-seeing trip down the Yangtze River. Perhaps it *was* a mistake to attempt this holiday journey on our own, unaccompanied by someone from the college Waiban.

Emily had seen us off just that morning, helping us get settled into our six-person compartment aboard the train before saying goodbye. The two-hundred-mile ride southeast from Chengdu to Chongqing had gone relatively smoothly. We shared the compartment with two Chinese—a woman who appeared to be in her sixties and a young man. Judging from her nail polish and jewelry, I figured the woman was from Shanghai or maybe even Hong Kong.

There was a moment of excitement after lunch. First, a man and a small child claimed the leftover seat in our compartment. Then, a short time later, another man attempted to squeeze in. This sparked a shouting and shoving match between the two original Chinese inhabitants and the interloper, who eventually withdrew. I was glad we hadn't gone to the dining car for lunch. The train was crowded and we might not have had seats when we came back.

Later in the afternoon, I engaged the Chinese woman in limited conversation, which was the best we could manage since I spoke little Chinese and she spoke little English. (It was then that I discovered I had once again left behind our *Chinese for Travelers* phrase book.) Imagine my surprise when I learned that the woman was from neither Hong Kong nor Shanghai, but rather from the New York borough of Queens, where she had lived since 1978. Now, she was touring mainland China with her nephew from Taiwan.

During the rest of the train ride, we had plenty of time to contemplate the rain-swept scenery. I was reminded again that Sichuan province is ringed, and thereby protected, by mountains. Indeed, Chiang Kai Shek had moved his capital to Chongqing to be safe from the Japanese. We had time, too, to review our ambitious itinerary. At Chongqing that night we would sleep aboard the boat, before starting down the Yangtze early the next morning. Three days hence, we would disembark in Wuhan, where, after a stint of sight-seeing, we would catch a flight to the city of Hangzhou, on the coast south of Shanghai. After a few days of sight-seeing there, we would fly southwest to Guilin. And if all went well, our zigzag, 2,500-mile course would land us in Hong Kong two weeks from now.

If all went well. . . . At the moment, I feared our journey might come to an abrupt halt, with one or all of us losing our footing in the dark, tumbling off this makeshift plank bridge and sinking waist-deep into the Yangtze mud.

I probably should have had more confidence in the man and woman who were acting as our guides. After all, these were people from the

Waiban at the Chongqing Institute of Architecture and Engineering. Emily had arranged for them to meet us at the train station and deliver us to the boat. In fact, she had used her connections with colleges in all the cities along our route, so that even as we traveled alone from point A to point B, we would find someone to assist us at each stop. The Chinese accomplish things, big and little, by using *guanxi*, which means, loosely translated, cashing in on your relationships. Emily was proving herself to be a master of the art. At each city, someone from a college Waiban would meet us and provide on-campus housing. They also would provide local tour guides and buy our tickets for our next destination. The latter was critical for us, since tickets could be reserved but none could be bought prior to our arrival in each city. All in all, the plan seemed to be foolproof, but this was China and we were still apprehensive, just as we were apprehensive groping in the dark along this makeshift bridge.

We were relieved, then, when at last we came upon a proper metal gangplank that led up to the boat, whose silhouette now stood out prominently in the night. We stopped to pay fees and for our night's lodging. Don had to disrobe enough to get our white cards out of the moneybelt he wore under his clothes. The white cards certified that we were employed in the country and therefore qualified to use RMB, the local currency or literally, "the people's money." From there we boarded the boat and Don again had to drop his pants to retrieve our passports from the moneybelt. He's a cautious traveler.

We were assigned cabins in second class; we had Cabin #21, and Barb, #22, with a Chinese roommate. The Chinese have no first class accommodations. That would be too bourgeois.

We settled up with the Waiban staff and expressed appreciation for their meeting us and providing assistance. We counted ourselves lucky to be able to stay overnight on the boat, thus avoiding a rush to make it aboard in time for tomorrow's 7:00 A.M. departure.

Our accommodations were not luxurious, but comfortable and acceptable, and the price was certainly right. We unpacked the necessary items and then took a little tour of the ship. We'd become inured by many things in China, but the sight of dressed ducks, chickens, slabs of pork—and yes, dogs—hanging in the gangways outside our cabin was a surprise and caused us to momentarily reconsider our intention to eat our meals on board. We had laid in a good supply of breakfast food, but we didn't really want to eat instant oatmeal three times a day. So when the cabin attendant came around later to inquire, we reluctantly made reservations for the dining room. We weren't going to have steak and baked potato and apple cobbler for dessert, but you couldn't beat the price—15 yuan ($3) per meal. Besides, baked lasagna and Caesar salad is hardly appropriate when you're floating down the Yangtze.

I'd like to say Sunday dawned bright and clear, but it didn't. Nonetheless, we were up and dressed by 6:30. When Barb knocked we were ready for a simple breakfast of oatmeal, nut cake, and coffee or tea. The young attendant knocked on the door, retrieved our thermos, and brought us a hot refill just in time. Not wanting to miss any of the departure activity, we hurried through the meal.

We needn't have hurried. Departure time came, and people kept boarding, making the same long trek across the sand and narrow gangplank that we had crossed the night before. The line was a steady stream; many of the passengers appeared to be students heading for home.

Chongqing presented an interesting picture in early morning light. Through the haze the city rose steeply on the hills on either side of the river, with several enormous buildings punctuating the skyline. The twinkling lights sprinkled all over the landscape made a pretty sight and we were sorry not to see it in nicer weather. Our guidebook noted that bicycles were forbidden because of the steep hills, and even our brief ride through the city the night before showed me why.

We finally shoved off about 8:00. Not exactly on time, but on the other hand I wouldn't want to have left anyone behind. Even the captain seemed to be making sure everyone got home for Spring Festival.

The ride was smooth all day and the scenery a fascinating display, as we passed through hilly terrain where villages clung to the hillsides. The ship's horn, which sounded intermittently, was deep and thrilling, warning upcoming traffic. Although we wished for sunshine, we still enjoyed the misty appearance. It made everything seem even more Chinese, an expression I fell back on frequently. The boat traffic was varied, from the cruisers like the one we were on, to huge barges lashed two and three together and pushed by a towboat, to junks and tiny two-person sampans of the kind found on this river three hundred or more years ago.

Lunch, at 11:30 in the dining room, was typical Chinese cuisine with a variety of dishes made from pork, mushrooms, eggs, rice, cooked cabbage with peppers, and some unknown but tasty items, and, as always, an ample supply of rice over which we ladled soup. Coke and beer were offered, and, of course, tea.

There were several brief stops during the day, at which passengers and freight were taken aboard or off-loaded. We planned to go ashore when we got to Wanxian, the first port-of-call, to buy fruit in the market. Our arrival was scheduled for 9:00 that night. On deck we met a young man from Hangzhou, and we asked him to accompany us. Since he was eager to speak English, he was delighted. However, the ship didn't dock until eleven, and we decided against disembarking. Many of our fellow passengers streamed ashore. But to us the long walk up the dark path to the market looked dangerous, and a few apples and oranges hardly seemed worth it. The idea of carrying passports and a huge sum of cash in such circumstances, even in the relative security of a moneybelt, made me nervous.

We watched freight being loaded and unloaded: sacks of rice being taken off and vegetables, fruit, live chickens, and many dead dogs being taken aboard. Observing the latter, we thought back to the two meals we'd had so far and wondered if what we had thought was duck was really duck.

Barb and I turned in early, but Don remained on deck until the early hours of the morning watching the proceedings. When he finally came into our cabin, he reported that new passengers were sprawled all over the decks. Their tickets evidently entitled them to board the ship, but not to beds. It was up to them to find a spot to sleep. At 2:00 in the morning, the boat set out again.

We were up by 6:30. This was to be the big day on the Yangtze, the reason we were making this water journey. We would be passing through the breathtaking gorges of the Yangtze. By 8:00, we already were entering the first gorge, so we rushed through breakfast in the lounge and out to the bow. The temperature was icy and the wind biting, but we braved the weather as long as we could, for the view was spectacular.

The region of the three Sanxia Gorges stretches over 120 miles. Each gorge is progressively longer: the first covering five miles; the second, twenty-five; and the third, fifty. The walls of the gorges, too, rise progressively higher and steeper, reaching skyscraper altitudes. Their rock formations seemed in turn solid and protective, then stark and overpowering, but always impressive. From our vantage point, we could see on either side of the river mountain peaks that went on, sometimes six or seven after the other, before they faded into infinity. And whenever our boat whistle sounded, the noise echoed back to us from a half dozen different locations.

We fled to the stern whenever the wind on the bow got the best of us. But we discovered we could not remain back there without becoming part of the show. Always, there was some Chinese traveler who wanted to practice his English with us. And the minute one started a conversation, dozens of others crowded around. Barb felt a little claustrophobic in the crush of attention, but I guess I'd gotten used to it.

(Having witnessed the beauty of the gorges, we were saddened when in 1993 China decided to flood them as part of a huge hydroelectric project. The project, which would supply electricity for half the country, had been under debate for years. Interestingly, it was overwhelmingly opposed by our students, some of whom, as geologists, would end up being employed by it. As negatives, they cited the forced relocations of millions of people, the loss of millions of acres of farm land, and the potential danger if the dam were sabotaged. For our part, we mourn the loss of one of the world's scenic wonders.)

Soon after we emerged from the last gorge, we entered the one-hundred-thirty-foot locks of the Gezhouba Dam, a structure that rivals in impressiveness the natural wonders we had just observed. Barb and I went aft to see our boat secured. The lock keepers did not immediately close the gates behind us, but waited instead until two other vessels—one our twin and the second only a little smaller—had wedged in with us. Then, when they started lowering the water level, it was like someone had pulled the plug in a bathtub. We scurried back to the bow so as not to miss the show in front. Millions of gallons flowed out, and in less than half an hour we descended the height of a three-story building.

The region just east of the dam appeared to be much more industrial and much less interesting visually. It was just as well, since fog soon set in and we could hardly see anyway. We returned to the second-class lounge, glad to be sheltered from the wind.

Compared to most accommodations in China, conditions on the boat were far superior. While hardly luxurious by Western standards, our quarters were clean and comfortable. The workers also seemed industrious and certainly were accommodating. The food, on the other hand, I found wanting. As Chinese food went, it was acceptable. But we already were getting tired of Chinese meals, day after day. In Chengdu, we could at least alternate between Chinese and American cooking. Some of the dishes served on board might have been more palatable if we hadn't seen them so often. We had eggs in some form at each meal, sometimes in two different dishes. We had about four different kinds of bread for breakfast, but none the rest of the day. And dessert did not exist. So we often returned to our cabin for fruit, cookies, and maybe hot chocolate if we needed to warm up.

There was little to see on the third day. The river widened and rain started even before we had breakfast. As the day progressed, it got worse, with thick fog also enshrouding us. Ideally, spring is the best season to travel the Yangtze, given weather patterns, but we couldn't go then. We were grateful just to have had relatively clear conditions when we passed through the gorges.

We spent the day in the lounge, reading and talking, and getting better acquainted with the Chinese and Japanese travelers who had been our dining room companions. These included a Japanese couple, who speak Chinese and were studying calligraphy at Beijing University, and their four-year-old son; two young Japanese men, recent graduates in psychology having a last fling before settling down to jobs; and a Chinese father and daughter from Hong Kong. Initially, I had assumed that since the daughter spoke to the Japanese couple, she and her father were Japanese. To be honest, I didn't expect to find any Chinese traveling second class. I forgot that some Chinese people live outside the People's Republic.

Despite not having any heat, we had a cozy little gathering in the lounge. We listened to the shortwave radio and Barbara offered a big piece of notebook paper to the father to make a paper airplane for his son. The mother offered each of us a glass of tea made with her own tea bags. We found it to be definitely better than the tea we'd had in the dining room. Meanwhile, Don and the man from Hong Kong conversed, with the daughter acting as interpreter. Don learned that the man had gone to Hong Kong from Guangzhou in 1947. He and his daughter promised to call us when we arrived in Hong Kong, in a couple of weeks.

I could not help but be struck by the friendliness and camaraderie among the Chinese and Japanese aboard. The two young Chinese boat attendants doted on the little Japanese boy. And while I read in one corner of the lounge, the Japanese woman and the Chinese woman who was Barb's roommate engaged in animated conversation in another. I think their conversation amounted to a Chinese language lesson, but they had a good time. Thinking about the fact that their parents had probably been enemies, I was gratified to see such intimate little exchanges. Then, again the warm interactions among all three nationalities made for an interesting spectacle, given the history of this century.

Although it was dark by 5:30, we kept a lookout for the big double-decker Yangtze bridge. When we caught a glimpse of it far ahead, we turned out the lights in the lounge so we could see better. Built in 1957, with Russian help, the bridge is a landmark in transportation for China, for it linked north and south by rail for the first time. Extending nearly a mile, the bridge carries automotive, bicycle, and pedestrian traffic on its upper deck and trains below.

For us, the bridge marked our arrival at Wuhan. Shortly after we passed under the lighted span, our ship docked.

Once again, Emily's *guanxi* came through for us. Waiting for us on the bank were a man and woman from the Waiban at the Wuhan College of Geosciences. Emily had arranged for us to stay at the college guest house and for the Waiban staff to take us sight-seeing for a couple of days, while they obtained our plane tickets to Hangzhou. They had already made reservations, but they had to take our passports to the provincial Foreign Affairs Department, which in turn would take them to the airport to get the tickets. Such is the way things are done in China.

Wuhan doesn't make the scenic tour circuit. In fact, our only real reason for being there was to switch from boat to plane. Nevertheless, we made the most of what the city had to offer. Among the attractions we visited was the provincial museum, which houses relics from a tomb dating back to 400 B.C. It also contains some military displays, with photos of Mao and other Communist leaders. Until I asked questions about people such as Dr. Sun Yat Sen, our young woman guide offered no explanations at all about who was in the photographs. She seemed almost embarrassed when she explained some photos depicting Communist heroes and events. I asked if Chiang Kai Shek's picture was there since it was only later that he and Mao were on opposite sides. She said no, because Chiang is not considered a Revolutionary hero. Nevertheless, when I asked her to identify other military figures in pictures dating from the 1930's, she said they were Kuomintang members who fought the Japanese, and that they are not considered heroes.

At one stop, we had a taste of Chinese intransigence. We had decided to have a snack in the revolving restaurant atop Wuhan's giant television tower, our appetites being whetted by the sight of our favorite, rarely obtainable soda crackers on display in glass cases. Yet, when we tried to buy the crackers, the clerks told us that the cases were locked and that they didn't have the key. They didn't bother to try to find it, so we took our business elsewhere. Obviously, we were not in a service economy.

We had to be ready at 6:40 the next morning for pick-up to go to the airport. We could have slept longer but Don's motto is, "It's better to be an hour early than five minutes late." Thus, we always are an hour early. As it turned out, we could have slept in for several more hours.

The scene inside the airport was bedlam. Our guide was indispensable since there were no signs in English. That surprised me, since a number of foreign businesses had established joint ventures in Wuhan. Once the young woman from the Waiban had helped us with boarding passes and we were in line, however, she and the driver bade us goodbye. We had prepared a note of thanks and enclosed forty yuan for the young woman. We handed the folded paper to her and told her that our names and addresses were written on it. She was suspicious, however, and kept refusing to take it.

"If there is money in it I don't want it," she said.

We offered again, but again she refused. In the end, Don shoved the folded paper into her hand and we turned away.

Taking tips, even a small amount, is illegal in China, and the woman was clearly nervous to have this scene taking place in front of the driver. We didn't want to get her in trouble, but we appreciated her taking time away from her family during Spring Festival and we wanted to express our gratitude.

As our departure time neared, we thought we heard an announcement of our flight. Seeing people line up, we joined them at the gate. But when we got to the door, the attendant waved us away. What we thought was "Hangzhou" must have been "Wangzhou" or something like that. Airport speakers everywhere are notoriously bad, but these were barely audible.

The next time the attendant announced a flight, which was a half hour later, we again got in line. But again, she waved us away at the door. The same thing happened several more times.

We were becoming worried. We approached several different young attendants, pointing to the number on the flight board and saying, "Hangzhou," and asking "when?" All we got back were shakes of the head or shrugs or the clipped phrase, "no time."

All of this was done with a surly, almost defiant or hostile attitude. At a time when China is opening to the outside world and trying to attract tourist dollars, her service personnel could use a few lessons in politeness and consideration.

It was mid-morning by this time. The weather turned grayer and a light rain began to fall, diminishing visibility. We could see no sign of a plane being prepared and we wondered whether our flight had been delayed or canceled because of weather conditions either in Hangzhou or somewhere along the route. Yet, the board still read Hangzhou —8:10.

During this entire time, only one young man came up to us. Don told him about our plight, thinking perhaps the young man could help us get some information. But then the fellow had to rush off to reboard his plane, which made only a brief stop in Wuhan. Where were all those people who want to practice their English when we really needed them?

I was feeling more depressed all the time, knowing that if the flight was canceled, we might be stuck in the city for several more days. There wasn't anything left in Wuhan I wanted to see.

Suddenly the door attendant motioned to Don. It was time to board. Everyone else rushed to get in line, too. She pointed to a plane a hundred yards from the terminal. There was no sign of activity around it. Nevertheless, we all headed toward the plane and about the same time as the first passengers arrived, someone opened a door and let down the boarding steps.

Our aircraft was an old, two-engine Russian prop plane, rather decrepit. For instance, Don's seat was in a permanent half-reclining position. As we thought, the plane had not been serviced. So we had to wait onboard for another forty-five minutes before we finally were ready to take off. At that point, we didn't really care. We were just glad to be going.

23

After the rainy morning in Wuhan, we were pleased to emerge into sunshine on the airfield at Hangzhou. Don collected the luggage and we stood in front of the terminal, soaking up the warmth and waiting for someone from Zheijiang University to meet us. A young Chinese businessman from Hong Kong joined us in conversation. We had been comparing notes on the service we had received from China Air personnel that day—the stewardesses who did little more than pass out biscuits and cans of orange drink during the two-hour flight and the three male gate attendants who looked on with indifferent, if not hostile, expressions as I struggled unaided down the steep, wobbly steps from the plane to the tarmac, leaning on my cane, loaded down with luggage. I suggested that a big problem was our inability to speak Chinese. But the Hong Kong businessman shook his head, saying that he spoke Chinese and still encountered ill-treatment. His accent gave him away. He said, for instance, that taxi drivers became irate if he refused to pay inflated, exorbitant fares; they thought anyone from Hong Kong or Taiwan was rich and should be willing to spend money freely.

The businessman spoke longingly of the treatment he'd received in China ten years earlier. The Chinese were just then opening their markets and were much more anxious to do business.

All the time we were talking, taxi drivers besieged us, offering us rides into the city. Finally, giving up hope that anyone from the university was coming to meet us, we decided we might as well hire a cab. The man from Hong Kong negotiated a price for us and we set off.

The ride to the university took about half an hour in a small Japanese car that sputtered all the way. When the engine died, the battery sounded as if it had spent all its energy, but then miraculously it came to life.

The architecture in Hangzhou was different than we had seen so far. The apartment buildings, constructed of unadorned cement, were not so large as those elsewhere in China and were in the style of Western townhouses, complete with gables. Although there was a sameness about them, they still looked neater and more substantial than any we had seen in other cities. The shopping area we went through, though not downtown, was more modern, and the whole city seemed cleaner and somehow more civilized.

When the taxi driver stopped at the university gates, which were closed to automobile traffic, the guard pointed down the street. The Foreign Guest House and all staff housing, we learned later, are outside the campus. When we drove up to the entrance to the Guest House, a young woman from the Waiban was sitting out front, reading a book, waiting for us. She assumed we'd be along eventually, having learned by calling the airport that our plane had finally arrived. Thank goodness we hadn't waited at the airport any longer.

She helped us register and we made arrangements to eat each evening in the dining room, which would be open only for us since all the other foreign teachers were gone on holiday. Once again, we handed over our passports and the necessary cash for our tickets to Guilin, our next stop.

Our accommodations at the Guest House were pleasant enough,

though we had still another faulty bathroom story to add to the list we were compiling. The water in the stool ran continuously, so after using it, we had to close the valve each time.

We had barely gotten settled in when there was a knock at the door. A mutual friend in Chengdu had arranged for a young woman student, Hui Xi, and her brother-in-law, Xiao Yin, a teacher at the university, to be our guides for the next three days. Neither had very good command of English, but they seemed serious about helping us, and we recognized that we would need help. We arranged to start the next morning at 8:00.

Zheijiang University has many foreign teachers, and our dinner showed their influence. Our food was served on individual side plates: a chicken leg, hot greens in a vinaigrette dressing, tomato in cream sauce soup. Other dishes we had later included something like a meatball (probably made of fish or bean curd) in tomato sauce and a breaded pork (tasty but spicy). We decided the cook knew what she was doing. The third night, after we'd brought forks the previous two nights, the table was set with a knife and fork at each place. That's personalized service.

Our do-it-yourself breakfasts also became a little more interesting in Hangzhou. We discovered a little bakery on the corner where we could buy delicious breads, New Zealand butter, and scrumptious desserts. We tried something new every day. Even the fruit market on the street was more attractive. The vendors had digital cash registers that displayed the weight and price. Our cut-and-dried purchases from them were a nice change after months of haggling with the farmers in Chengdu.

Promptly at 8:00 the next morning, we started out with our guides. In spite of a steady drizzle, we walked to the botanical gardens nearby and found them lovely and extensive. They had a mystical beauty in the morning mist; and while we regretted the inability to take good pictures, the effect was enchanting. The plantings, the architecture, the numerous pools, and rock formations added to the enchantment. Some flowers were already blooming, and we could imagine the lushness that another two months would bring.

From there, we wound our way to West Lake. Hangzhou is dubbed the paradise of China. The area we saw that day certainly qualified the city for that title. While the fog which hung over the lake was frustrating in one sense, in another it created a sense of mystery. The humpbacked bridges, the islands and the trees on the horizon, just barely visible through the mist, added to the overall effect. Even the names of places in the area delighted us: Yellow Dragon Spring, Jade Fountain, Purple Cloud Cave, Three Pools Mirroring the Moon. Legends surround each one, and our guides knew them all.

We spent the day visiting temples, pagodas, and climbing the low hills, which give another perspective on West Lake. We told our guides we wanted a small, simple lunch, so we stopped at a tea house along the lake and ate a bread roll, bean curd, and peanuts, and drank a cup of tea. It was truly a lovely spot, and it was made all the more beautiful by the sun's attempts to break through the clouds.

While we were sitting in our lakeside pavilion, a wedding party came along. The group had gotten out of a boat down the way and were walking along the shore. Since a photographer was preceding them, capturing the event on video camera, we didn't think they would mind our joining in the picture taking. The bride and her attendant wore street-length red suits, adorned with corsages. The groom and his attendant wore well-tailored, navy-blue suits.

When we learned that the Bao Shu Pagoda, next on our agenda, was quite far, we decided to patronize one of the water taxis. The ride was lovely and relaxing and certainly beat walking—and cost us all of sixty cents.

The pagoda, a brick octagonal monument surmounted by a metal spire, stood atop a tall hill and could be reached only by a stiff climb. Don decided to sit this one out, but Barbara and I attacked the long flight of steps. Since the pagoda is visible from many parts of the city, we knew it would provide a worthwhile vista. Indeed, it did.

We went on, climbing still more steep, rocky steps to some huge boulders which rested in precarious positions. You could crawl under or through many and hope they didn't collapse or start sliding on you. The landscape was wild and craggy in this spot, but it offered a spectacular view of peaceful, unchanging West Lake on one side and the new, bustling city on the other—a stark contrast.

We bused home to the Guest House after that.

We had hoped to take a boat ride on West Lake the next day, but the sky was overcast, so we postponed it. Instead, we boarded a bus and headed to the Yellow Dragon Cave.

The entrance was a long tree-lined lane, the trees forming a canopy overhead. The staff at the cave gardens wore ancient-style costumes, and when we first arrived, elaborately costumed and heavily made-up actors were performing scenes from a Chinese opera. Their movements and mannerisms were exaggerated and highly stylized. Elsewhere on the grounds costumed musicians performed on traditional Chinese instruments.

We left the cave grounds and went downtown to board a bus to Dragon Well, an area famous for its tea. There we would eat lunch at a restaurant our guides had recommended. We never got there. While we were waiting for the bus, a Chinese woman struck up a conversation with our guides. She asked who we were, commenting about how young we looked and how tall we are—the Chinese were always telling Don (at six feet) he's too tall! The woman and a female companion, who we later learned was her sister-in-law, joined us on the bus, which headed up a mountain, past fields of tea bushes. When we got off in a village at the end of the line, we intended to catch another bus and go on to the restaurant. But the woman asked if we would like to come home with her to see a tea farmer's house and how tea is dried. We eagerly followed her and her companion up the hill.

The woman's house was a plain, one-story, white stucco building. She led us into an L-shaped room with concrete floors. The only furniture was a square table with stools around it, but in one corner there was a large electric kettle, resembling a giant wok. We learned that this was used to dry tea. After tea is picked, it is first air dried, then put into the big heated kettle and stirred by hand. When it is thoroughly dried, the tea is packed with limestone in air-tight containers.

After the brief tour, the three women—a neighbor had come in to see the waiguoren—made glasses of tea for us, pouring off the first water and refilling the glasses before serving us. (I learned after being served tea countless times in glass in China that I have very heat-sensitive hands. I much prefer hot tea in a cup!) The woman brought out pictures of her family and other relatives and also showed us business cards from people who had bought tea from them. I asked if they were better off under the more liberal economic policies promoted by Deng Xiao Ping. They said yes, that they were able to keep more of their tea to sell for themselves.

Although Chinese farmers can own their houses, the land is held by the government. For the use of the land, tea growers are required to sell part of their crop to the government at a predetermined price. Any surplus they may sell on the open market, although they must get licenses from the government to do so.

Feeling some obligation to repay the women for their hospitality, we asked if we could buy some tea. They were more than ready to sell. They asked which quality. During our brief tour, we had learned that the quality of tea depends on the time it is picked. The best quality tea is that picked before April 1. That picked between April 1 and April 10 is considered second quality, and the April 11 to April 15 harvest is considered third quality. All tea picked after that is considered fourth quality. Well, how could we choose anything but the best? Then, we worked out the quantity we would buy with vague hand gestures. The women made up three plastic-wrapped packages of tea—constituting a sale for each of the women's families.

We were shocked, however, when the women announced that the tea would cost one hundred yuan, or roughly twenty dollars. Having become accustomed to three-dollar dinners, we thought the price was exorbitant. Still, we couldn't back out of the deal without appearing ungracious. So Don dipped into his moneybelt, slipping off to a side room to partially disrobe, and paid up.

Considering the enjoyment we had talking with the women, the experience was probably worth the price. Still, we were certain we were paying far too much—a conclusion confirmed by our guides' embarrassed expressions. And later, we even speculated that the women might have had a lucrative racket going, luring tourists into their house just so they could sell them overpriced tea. Causing us even more chagrin was the fact that neither Don nor I even like Chinese tea. Chengdu friends were pleased to get a memento from our trip to Hangzhou, however.

We ended up having lunch that day at Tiger Spring, an old temple that has been turned into a tearoom. Like many of the Chinese eating there, we brought a picnic lunch and bought only beverages. Most of the tearooms at historic sites in China are owned by the state. If they don't turn a profit, no matter. Their operation is subsidized to make sure "the people" have access to all their cultural relics, their heritage.

Having seen enough temples, we elected to go that afternoon to the zoo to see its one giant panda. We were assured the panda would not be sleeping, and indeed she was not. It wasn't nap time, it was snack time—or was it early supper? The floor of the cage was strewn with shoots of bamboo and the panda was seated with her back to us, chomping away. When she finished one pile, she ambled over to a new pile and again seated herself with her back to the audience. Maybe she thought it impolite to eat in front of others.

The zoo was in a pleasant setting, taking advantage of the hills and valleys and rocky terrain, but the Society for the Prevention of Cruelty to Animals probably would have looked askance at the concrete-and-iron-bar cages in which the animals were housed.

On our last day in Hangzhou, we visited the silk market and finally took that scenic boat ride on West Lake. We had lunch at an island tea house.

Later, our boatman landed us in front of the Hangzhou Shangri-La Hotel. The hotel is impressive, and its entrance on the lake side, through a bower of fine old trees, is imposing. Inside, we found a spacious, elegant lobby, with deep, comfortable sofas complemented by flowering potted trees and striking woven hangings strategically placed wherever there was a large expanse of wall. Although Barb and I had been setting endurance records for not going to the W.C. during the day, despite drinking two cups of tea at lunch, we decided to break our self-imposed limit. (We were up to nine hours the two previous days.) We thought the Shangri La probably would have decent accommodations, a few cuts above the standard Chinese W.C.'s. Besides, checking out the W.C. could also give us an excuse to see more of the hotel. The rest was as plush as the lobby.

The W.C. did have elegant appointments: fine oak doors and frames on the stalls, shiny chrome fixtures, soft lighting. I thought at last I had found one restroom in China where everything worked and was kept in neat order. But it was not to be; the hand dryer on the wall was broken and white linen towels lay scattered about the counter surrounding the lavatories.

The next morning Barb and I took a last walk over to West Lake and sat on a bench for a while. A brisk wind ruffled the water and made us keep our coats buttoned up, but the setting was idyllic. I could go back to Hangzhou one day and, perhaps, stay at the Shangri La. Yet, I know, too, that anyone who visits China and stays only at such places would not truly have seen China.

Our flight to Guilin left promptly at 4:20, with only nine passengers aboard the thirty-seat aircraft. This was by far the newest and nicest China Air plane we had ever taken. We were even served a nice meal —shrimp salad, presented in generous portions. Since Don doesn't care for shrimp, I lucked out. Between eating and reading that day's edition of *China Daily* (in Chengdu, it was always four days late), the 650-mile flight went quickly.

As we came in to land we got our first glimpse of Guilin's unusual karst mountains, those water-scarred, limestone peaks that dot the countryside like solitary sentries. Indeed, there were some right off the runway.

Once off the plane, we were met by a man and a young woman from a travel agency. They had arranged a full schedule of sight-seeing for us in a package deal whose price included meals and delivery to the Grand Hotel, which was considered a two-star facility. It didn't deserve the rating, but we thought it would probably do. Besides, who could argue with the price: one hundred yuan ($20) per night—the same amount we had paid for our three packets of tea. Guilin has only become a major tourist attraction since 1982 and most of the city's hotels are new.

Since bathrooms had become our *bêtes noires* and an indication of whether a place was acceptable, Barb and I immediately checked out the facilities in our respective rooms. She remarked on how new and modern the fixtures were, and I noted that the floor was dry and that I couldn't hear any water running. We thought we were home free. But then, I drew some water to wash a shirt in the sink. It sounded as if the water were running out on the floor below. When I peered behind the pedestal base, sure enough, the drain pipe was cut off about four inches above the floor and the water was splashing out and racing over to a crude drain. I discovered, too, that the bathtub had a hole cut in the side so that it drained by the same method. Later, Barb informed us that she had no hot water in her room. So much for our assumption that at last we had found good hotel bathrooms.

It rained during the night and the temperature outside and inside became quite chilly. There was no heat in the rooms; we guessed the thermostat on the wall was there only for appearances.

The next morning it was still raining, and our wish for warmer weather hadn't been fulfilled either. But our tour guide from the travel agency, who introduced herself as Janet Li, took us to a Holiday Inn, a three-star hotel, where we enjoyed the heat, the flowers, and the clean white table cloth as much we did the good breakfast of juice, toast, and poached eggs. We learned that the hotel was a joint Japanese-Chinese venture and that the manager was Australian. The hotel setting was beautiful and we would have been tempted to relocate there had not the room rate been four times what we were paying at the Grand.

From there, we began our day of sight-seeing. The Reed Pipe Cave, which we saw first, was spectacular. Its huge grotto and attractively lit stalactites and stalagmites reminded me of a long-ago visit to Carlsbad Caverns in New Mexico. Another cave we visited, Wind Cave, was a baby by comparison.

We stopped for lunch at a Chinese restaurant, a place, evidently, where tour guides often brought foreign tourists. We were seated at the one table in the room that had a white table cloth, albeit very stained. Near the door was a wire pen occupied by a live chicken (a Rhode Island Red?).

I asked Miss Li, "Is that going to be someone's dinner?"

"Yes," she said. "Do you want it?"

I quickly assured her I did not.

Moments before I had observed someone catching a fish from a tank beside the chicken pen and taking it back to the kitchen. Apparently, it was intended for us, because when we informed Miss Li that we also did not want fish, she seemed surprised and immediately called for the manager. After much negotiating, which included an offer of dog, we finally persuaded Miss Li and the manager that we wanted very little to eat and settled for soup, cooked vegetables, and some peanuts.

We resumed our sight-seeing with a stop at the Flower Bridge, which afforded us a beautiful view of a pagoda, high atop a hill. We also went to the zoo for a brief look at Guilin's panda. The zoo grounds provided a wonderful view of Camel Hill, whose shape bears a remarkable resemblance to the animal.

Late in the day, Miss Li took us to a government store selling Oriental rugs and rocks gathered from caves around Guilin. The handmade rugs seemed reasonably priced, starting at about $130. The prices on the rocks, however, astounded me. One, for example, cost three thousand, five hundred yuan, or $700.

"Do you think they're expensive?" Janet asked, observing my flabbergasted expression.

"Don't you think they're expensive?" I replied. When she didn't respond, I asked, "Who buys them?"

"The Japanese, Taiwanese, and Hong Kong Chinese," she answered.

As we walked around the shop, sales clerks followed us like vultures. They were young and dressed in tacky, mod garb. I couldn't help thinking of the sophisticated setting in which such high-end merchandise would be displayed had it been in the United States.

Earlier in the day we had told Miss Li that we wanted to have western food for dinner. She seemed surprised. Furthermore, she ignored our request, taking us instead to another Chinese restaurant that night. At least, we were able to get jiaozi, the meat dumpling that we'd grown so fond of in Chengdu.

While we were waiting for the food to arrive, she told us we would have a Chinese breakfast in the morning. Again, we told her we were ready for Western fare. I was becoming impatient with Miss Li. For one thing, her English was very poor. (She had told us earlier that she normally guided Japanese tourists, and that we were an experiment for her.) But beyond that, she seemed to turn a deaf ear to any and all of our requests.

At the dinner table, I asked, "How would you feel if you couldn't have rice or other Chinese food for a few months?"

She said, "I'd miss it, but if I were in a different country I would eat that country's food."

"Have you ever been in a different country?" I asked.

"No," she replied.

I said, "It's one thing to talk about it and it's another to do it."

I fear I was turning into the Ugly American.

The tour manager came to our hotel at 9:00 that night with our passports and our tickets to Hong Kong. It was a relief to know everything was taken care of in that department.

At 10:00 that night, there was loud hammering and the sound of an electric drill or saw from somewhere in the hotel. I wondered what could be so pressing that it had to be done at that hour. I remarked to Don that I would bet nothing like this was happening at the Holiday Inn.

We had breakfast the next morning at the Osmanthus Hotel, a Chinese inn. Again, Miss Li hadn't heeded our request. The menu was strictly Chinese: assorted steamed bread, a kind of noodle, rice gruel, some vegetables and, of course, tea. Don looked grim.

I couldn't help comparing the personnel at the Osmanthus with those at the Holiday Inn (both were three-star hotels). Both had all-Chinese personnel, with the exception of the manager at the Holiday Inn. From the doorman to the dining room attendants, all the employees at the Holiday Inn were smiling, polite, and self assured, while the staff at the Osmanthus was stiff and stern-faced. What conclusion could I draw from this?

After breakfast, we drove about thirty minutes to a dock, where we boarded a boat for a four-hour ride down the River Li. The scenery was spectacular and, due to the nature of the karst mountains, unique. But we probably would have been more excited had we not just spent three days on the Yangtze.

That night we returned to the same restaurant where we had had dinner previously. When Miss Li picked us up, she announced that she had ordered jiaozi. We stressed our approval. Our food was slow in arriving, however. Several times, Miss Li left us in our private dining room, then came back apologizing for the delay. When finally the jiaozi was served, it was cold. It was then Miss Li confessed that the jiaozi had come from another restaurant. No wonder our food was cold. It had just come across town on the back of a bicycle.

Of course, had we been thinking, we would have realized that it would be hard to get jiaozi in Guilin. Jiaozi is a regional specialty of North China. We were in the South.

The number of firecracker explosions had been increasing all week in anticipation of the Chinese New Year. By evening, it seemed as if we were in a war zone. At both the restaurant and our hotel, the noise was incessant and deafening. It continued all through the night.

(Because of a rising death and accident rate associated with firecrackers, in 1993 the Chinese government banned their use in urban areas throughout the country. Considering how pervasive a role fireworks play in Chinese culture, it will be interesting to see if the government can make the ban stick. One enterprising audio studio has already rushed to fill the void by offering for sale "firecracker tapes" for those who want to scare away demons.)

The next morning, we checked out of the Grand Hotel, glad to be leaving the place, and stowed our bags. We had insisted on a Western breakfast this last morning, agreeing to pay extra if the cost exceeded what our package deal with the travel agency allowed.

On our way to the Holiday Inn, we found the back streets and doorways littered with red paper, the remains of fireworks. Inside, we relished the warmth as well as our coffee and eggs and orange juice. We finished eating just in time to see a mini-New Year's parade and a little ceremony taking place out front. Several "dragons" were charging the hotel, accompanied by a band and dancers. Hotel employees threw whole strings of lighted firecrackers at their feet, and we Westerners rushed out to take pictures of the colorful spectacle.

I asked the Holiday Inn manager, who was standing nearby, who these performers were, if they were professionals or members of organizations, and if the hotels hired them to come around. She dodged the question, saying only that the hotel guests, and particularly those from Hong Kong and Taiwan, wanted to be blessed for the New Year.

The dragons' objective was to knock down a packet that was held high up in the air. The packet contained money and other goodies. It reminded me of a Mexican piñata. After a certain amount of mock battle, one succeeded. As I spoke with the manager, I noticed Chinese hotel guests also were throwing money to the "beasts."

We went to more caves and temples that morning. Miss Li herself said prayers for the New Year in one of the temples. For lunch, she took us to a restaurant where she said we could get American food. It was a fast food place next door to the Around the World Hotel. Our supposedly American "meat sandwiches with vegetable" turned out to be the worst, most unappetizing food either Don, Barbara, or I had ever eaten. It was not good PR for American food.

From there, we went to a park where there was a Japanese permanent exhibition beside the Guilin Museum, both built in 1989. Guilin has a Japanese sister city, and the Japanese pavilion was part of the exchange program between them. The Japanese and Chinese buildings provided an interesting contrast. The Japanese exhibit and its surrounding gardens represented a large and distinctive home, as might be found in Japan. Among the displays inside, there were lovely flower arrangements and a display of wood sculptures of animals. Outside, the gardens, with rocks, a bridge, and a cascading waterfall, were beautifully designed and well tended. I found it lovely and restful.

The Guilin Museum, although a large building with several wings, was typical of Chinese buildings everywhere. It was less than two years old, and already it looked drab and dingy. The walls had not been painted. The floors had not been waxed. Everything was scuffed, marked, or dirty.

The gardens provided an even greater contrast. There was a courtyard in the middle of the Guilin Museum building with many shrubs and trees. But it appeared that no one had touched it since the initial planting. Some deciduous trees looked dead, rather than dormant. Shrubs were untrimmed, and weeds all but choked the few clumps of overgrown grass.

The Chinese museum housed ceramic pieces from various dynasties and some terra cotta soldiers, a cart, and horses from the amazing excavation at Xian, which we'd visited in the fall.

Overall, I looked at the two exhibits as illustrating the different natures of these two nations, their people, and cultures. They stood as simple, yet significant, symbols that explained why these two countries have such different status in the world today.

Ironically this last day was the first we'd seen sunshine in Guilin, but by this time, we had no desire to visit still more temples and museums. Even though we had hours to spare, we decided to go right to the airport. Along the road out of the city, we photographed a herd of grazing water buffalo, tended by a young woman. We also passed numerous graves, with small upright doors set into mounds. People in

rural areas still bury their dead in this way, even though the government has tried to outlaw it. With no surplus land for burial, China
promotes cremation.

We spent two hours waiting in an upstairs restaurant at the airport.
While Don made conversation with a young Frenchman, Barb tried
communicating further with Miss Li. By that time, I had run out of
patience with our guide. I had just spent five months teaching students
English, and I didn't feel like doing it during my vacation for someone
who was supposed to be competent in the language.

Suffice it to say I was more than ready for Hong Kong.

24

The first thing that struck us as we landed in Hong Kong was the bright
lights. Not since we left Chicago had we seen so much glitter. Then,
we were left wide-eyed by the modern, wide-windowed shuttle bus
that carried us from the plane to the terminal. And the terminal: it was
clean and spacious, and staffed by courteous personnel in smart uniforms.

Over the past six months, we had forgotten what the rest of the
world was like.

Ever since we began planning our itinerary, our fellow waiguoren
kept saying things like, "By all means include Hong Kong on your
trip," or, "Oh, you'll love Hong Kong. You'll be able to get Western
food and stock up on items you haven't seen since leaving home, and
everybody speaks English!"

That had sounded very appealing. And the city seemed even more
appealing now that we had arrived.

By 8:00 that evening, we were settled into our small hotel on the
island of Kowloon. It was much warmer in Hong Kong, so the first
thing we did was shed our long underwear. The second thing was set
out to look for Western food.

At the hotel, we learned that we were in a strictly Chinese part of
Kowloon and that it would be best to look elsewhere for the kind of
restaurant we were seeking. Furthermore, we were reminded that it
was Chinese New Year, equivalent to Christmas Day night in the
West, and that many restaurants would be closed.

We decided our best bet was to take a cab to another part of the city.
But at what kind of restaurant did we want to eat? It is embarrassing to
write this now, but we settled on a McDonald's. We'd heard they were

thick in Hong Kong, so it seemed one would be easy to find. Besides, the very thought of burgers and fries made our mouths water.

We hailed a cab and Don told the driver to take us to McDonald's, thinking that he surely would know where one was. To our chagrin, however, our Chinese-speaking driver didn't understand. He kept shoving his microphone in Don's face so Don could tell the dispatcher where we wanted to go. When we kept hearing the reply in "Chinglish," we realized the dispatcher hadn't heard of McDonald's, either.

It was at that moment that Barb leaned over and whispered, "It's so nice to be in Hong Kong where *everyone* speaks English."

Finally, we said, "Take us to a hotel." At last, the driver understood. He let us off in front of a posh place, where a doorman rushed to open the car door for me. One look and I knew the hotel restaurant would not suit our clothes, wallets, or our appetites.

We set out on foot. Finally, we caught a glimpse of a Holiday Inn and figured it would have an eatery that would do. But as we got closer, I spied off to the left a glowing set of golden arches. It was like a mirage in the desert, but in this case it actually materialized.

At home, we're Wendy's patrons. But I must admit, no hamburgers and French fries ever tasted so good as those we had that night. We even splurged on chocolate sundaes. Don considered a second, but feared the recriminating looks from his dinner companions.

The warmth we'd experienced that first night in Hong Kong turned out to be a temporary phenomenon. The next few days were cold, windy, and overcast. Back on with our overcoats, if not our long johns.

Since Barb was staying in Hong Kong only three days, we let her set our itinerary. That first morning we took the bus down to the Star Ferry, crossed over to Hong Kong, and took another bus to Stanley Market. The ride up was as interesting as the market. Peeking behind residential walls from the top of our double-decker bus, we caught glimpses not only of palatial homes, but also of creatively designed swimming pools and multi-car garages, whose doors, when open, often revealed Mercedes and Rolls Royces. Again, we were struck by the contrast between this place and the country in which we'd been living these past months.

Stanley Market was an interesting, but confusing, maze of shops, selling everything from inexpensive costume jewelry to fine art, T-shirts to high fashion. It was a shopper's mecca. Supposedly there were bargains to be had, but I left them for someone else.

We got lunch at a British-style pub in the market. We were amused to see a Westerner from a restaurant next door bring three rice lunches to the pub's Chinese waitresses, and then later to witness a Western waitress from that same, next-door restaurant ducking in for a foaming pint. Clearly, we were in a multicultural city.

Out of Hong Kong's six million residents, we knew only three people. The first two were the father and daughter from the Yangtze ferry. The third was Chris, a young German we had met in November on the train from Xian to Chengdu. That afternoon, as we negotiated our way along one of downtown Hong Kong's jam-packed sidewalks, we found ourselves face-to-face with Chris. After recovering from the shock of this one-in-two-million chance encounter, we gleaned from Chris several restaurant recommendations and arranged for a more leisurely conversation later by phone.

Dinner that night was Barb's treat. We had chosen the Chalet, a restaurant on the ninth floor of the Royal Pacific Hotel, which afforded a view over the harbor. It was a good night to have a view, because Hong Kong put on an incredible fireworks display in celebration of Chinese New Year. The food was pretty good, too: veal cordon bleu for Barb and me, and steak for Don, followed by chocolate mousse and chocolate fondue. We were almost afraid to leave the table for a better look at the fireworks for fear that our waiters would clear our plates before we'd cleaned up every morsel.

We left the restaurant shortly after the fireworks ended and dawdled in the hotel lobby among the shops and boutiques. Later, when we went out to hail a cab, we found throngs of people still pouring along the sidewalks. Trying to go in the opposite direction was like bucking the tide.

The next day's itinerary included a short cruise out of the Hong Kong harbor. It gave us an overall look at some of the city's buildings and the airport. When we saw how short the runways were, we immediately understood why Hong Kong was planning a new airport.

After lunch at a Burger Chef, where I had the first chocolate milk shake in six months (pretty good), we took the tram up to Victoria Peak. The view of the city was marred by haze, but it was enjoyable nonetheless.

After Barb left for home, Don and I browsed and shopped for the next few days. While we bought little, we marveled at the array of recognizable brands available. We saw beautifully tailored clothes bearing price tags of hundreds of dollars, and store after store selling glittery jewelry, leather goods, electronic gadgets, cameras, tape players and video equipment in endless profusion. In the drugstores there seemed little we couldn't find in the way of personal toiletries and over-the-counter drugs. In fact, there seemed little you couldn't buy in Hong Kong.

We stocked up on things to take back to Chengdu. We were glad to get them, but I also felt a little sad. I wondered about the fate that made such over-abundance available in this place, while only a few miles away were people who had so little. China was near and yet so far.

We felt no regrets, however, while enjoying access to real news. Both CNN and CBS TV News were available, and we kept them on whenever we were in our hotel room. We also bought Hong Kong newspapers, which practice the openness toward public affairs we consider "normal." In the local papers we read news about China that we couldn't read *in* China.

Another one of the contrasts that struck us was the abundance of telephones in Hong Kong. Store windows were full of telephones of all descriptions, from sleek designer models to fit any decor, to business "communications systems" with more buttons than my laptop computer. Whereas hardly anyone in China has his or her own phone, in Hong Kong we saw people, young and old, in cars, restaurants, walking along the streets, talking on hand-held cellular models. Here the authorities encouraged, rather than discouraged, communication.

One evening we took our cameras downtown to photograph the fantastic New Year lighting displays on many of the buildings. The sides of skyscrapers were graced with colorful, neon-outlined scenes ten stories high. Since 1991 was the year of the sheep, lots of sheep and Chinese shepherds were featured. Considering how little electricity is available in China, the spectacular light show seemed even more amazing, particularly when we learned that entirely different displays had been up at Christmas.

Later that evening we made our way to Ned Kelly's, an Australian pub that Chris had recommended. It was crowded, but we found a table next to the stage. We ordered a meal (Don, stew; for me, bangers and mash) and stayed for a couple of hours, enthralled by the band that was performing. It was truly an international ensemble. A Texan who sat at our table said the leader, a piano-tuba player, was Australian. The drummer was Indian, and the other four musicians were Filipinos. Their style of music: Dixieland jazz.

The Texan was in marketing for IBM. He held a master's degree in English literature and used to teach until he decided about twenty-six years ago that he wanted to make a decent living. The teaching profession loses a lot of good people that way.

In the course of our conversation he gave me what he called his McDonald's theory of economics. He cited the cost of Big Macs in Moscow, New York, Tokyo, and Hong Kong. The differences were startling, and he said he thought they provided a quick indicator of the cost of living and told something about the economy of each country. All this was said tongue-in-cheek and I'm not sure his theory has any validity. Nevertheless, I had to check. A Big Mac in Hong Kong cost us the equivalent of $1.15 in U.S. currency. When I got home, I found a Danville Big Mac cost $1.98.

One afternoon we sat along the wharf in the sunshine, along with hundreds of others. At last, it was warmer. Twice we were approached by students seeking interviews. They'd been assigned to get information from foreigners: why they had come to Hong Kong, what they thought about it, what they'd purchased, and how long they were staying. We saw other foreigners submitting to the same thing. The clincher was having a picture taken with the subject. I guess that was the teacher's way of insuring the interviews weren't a lazy student's fabrication.

On Thursday, after we'd been in Hong Kong nearly a week, we went to dinner with the Lous, the father and daughter we'd met on the Yangtze. Kawi Fong (Loretta), the daughter, came to our hotel to collect us. We took the subway over to Hong Kong. She apologized because it was crowded, but it didn't seem so after living in China for six months. It appeared new, clean, and efficient.

We ate in an Indonesian restaurant, where we were joined by another daughter, Elaine, and Elaine's boyfriend, Alex. Both worked in banking—she at Barclay's and he at an institution from New Zealand.

Most of our discussion centered on 1997, when the People's Republic is to assume control of Hong Kong. The Lous told us that some of their friends, colleagues, and neighbors already were emigrating. Canada was the most popular choice, with Australia and New Zealand next, and Great Britain fourth.

The Lous, themselves, were not very confident over what might happen after the takeover. All of them had visited China, and they all voiced the same complaints we had over inefficiency and endless bureaucracy, the bad service, and the lack of cleanliness and courtesy. They envied the citizens of Macao who have been granted dual citizenship by Portugal, and seemed bitter about Britain's failure to do the same for them. Yet, none of our dinner companions were ready to flee the country. In fact, Mr. Lou told us that another of his daughters, who married a Scotsman and lived in England, actually wanted to return.

After we finished our meal, which consisted of many intriguingly spiced dishes, the Lous offered to see us back to Kowloon. In the end, we persuaded them that was unnecessary. We'd gotten around just fine by ourselves all week.

Our last full day in Hong Kong was the sunniest yet. We ate a light lunch downtown, then sat out on the pier by the clock tower, soaking up sunshine and reading the newspaper. We watched the Queen Elizabeth II sail into port.

We were relaxed and comfortable. Yet, I found myself becoming restless. Much as I enjoy travel and exotic places, I get satiated very quickly. I could never be one of the idle rich, let alone the idle poor. I need to get back to normal every once in a while, to do something productive, and build up to the next getaway. And in Hong Kong, I felt guilty among such opulence, after our experience in China.

That night we went to City Hall to hear the Hong Kong Philharmonic. The orchestra had a wonderful sound—crisp, brilliant, yet smooth and harmonious. The evening seemed to epitomize the Hong Kong experience. The conductor, David Atherton, was a Caucasian, as was the guest soloist, British pianist Martin Roscoe, yet the orchestra musicians were a multiethnic, multinational group. And the night's program was devoted to works by Russian-born composers: Moussorgsky, Rachmaninoff, and Stravinsky. We may have been in the East, but Hong Kong's true orientation is West.

On Saturday, departure day, we were up early and taxied to the airport by 8:15. While waiting for our check-in counter to open, we talked with a man from Arizona who was going to Chengdu as a consultant. His client was a Chinese man, born in Guanzhou but now an American citizen, who owned an electronics firm and was attempting to do business in China.

Our traveling companion told us half in disgust about what he'd seen of business in China—under the table deals and money slipped to someone in a back alley in order to get plane tickets in a hurry. He mentioned his qualms about giving someone his passport even temporarily in order to get tickets home. We told him we knew the feeling.

Our flight back to Chengdu was comfortable, and on a Boeing 737, comforting. Anything would be better than those Russian relics. The lunch, however, was vintage Chinese: hot rice, with three or four pieces of meat, a cold serving of four different kinds of meat, a hot dog bread roll, a boiled egg, a plastic-encased vegetable vaguely resembling shredded dill pickles (one bite was enough), a little chocolate bar (a far cry from Hershey's or Toblerone), and an orange (thank goodness, something tasty and juicy). My cup of black coffee was so strong it could have served two, if suitably diluted. So much for food on China Airlines. Oh, I forgot the cold boiled peanuts. I was sorry Barb wasn't along to experience the cold boiled peanuts.

25

It was good to be back in Chengdu. But we no sooner got the laundry done from our previous travels than the Waiban whisked us off again. We were going to Zigong, in southern Sichuan, to a Lantern Festival. I vaguely knew about Chinese lanterns, but we had just seen a light spectacle in Hong Kong. What could China have to offer to compete with that. We had committed to the trip weeks ago, however, so off we went. Eight of us, including Emily and Mr. Chen, the driver, piled into the blue Toyota van. In addition to a professor from the University of Geneva, three professors from the college, all women who were long-time friends, joined us. Two of them spoke English and they were genial traveling companions.

Normally I wouldn't have relished just getting home from one trip and then taking off again, but this time we could leave all the details to someone else. Besides, this was only for three days. We would be back before the start of classes on Monday.

Ever since we had arrived in China, I had been amused by what often seemed to us, rightly or wrongly, Chinese tendencies to talk endlessly about things. When Emily went with us to the market, she didn't just ask the price of the fruits and vegetables, she had good-natured verbal sparring matches with the farmers and other customers. The pitch and tone of Chinese voices even in the most commonplace conversations often suggested they were angry with each other, but that may be true of any language. After all, Americans can sound pretty excitable too.

Nevertheless, I had an experience on our way to Zigong that gave me another view of that talkativeness. Midmorning, we stopped at a Chinese guest house, one not likely to get more than a one-star rating, for a toilet break. We five women all went inside. The restroom was typically Chinese. The interior walls were covered entirely with the ubiquitous white ceramic tile. The only thing in the room was a partition, approximately three feet high, dividing the room into two stalls. Two slit trenches in each stall meant four people could be accommodated.

Since there were no doors, and we were all considerably taller than three feet, any semblance of privacy was impossible. Emily courteously bade me go before her.

I joined Mrs. Li in one of the stalls. I had had no compelling need to go in the first place, and even in more accommodating circumstances I sometimes have what has been delicately referred to in Ann Lander's columns as a bashful kidney. But there I was, a woman with arthritic joints trying to maintain a squatting position within two feet of another human being, albeit female; struggling to keep pantyhose, long underwear, and flannel pants from dragging on the floor, while not dropping the toilet tissue I had fished out of my pocket for later use, since there was, of course, none available.

These difficulties alone might have been enough to prevent me from relaxing sufficiently. But to make matters worse, my toilet mates maintained a steady chatter, just as they might if they were meeting on the street, throughout the entire ordeal.

No circumstance, it seems, can silence the loquacious Chinese.

Although Zigong was only about 160 miles from Chengdu, the trip took almost seven hours. Less than an hour out of Chengdu we got into the first of several ranges of mountains, which made for spectacular scenery. The road wound along the edge of deep gorges and alongside the banks of sometimes rushing, sometimes meandering rivers. Sometimes a train whizzed by on tracks that in places ran parallel to the road. The tracks were in better condition than the road.

Although we had been in China long enough to have become a little blasé about traffic, the trip produced some white knuckles and quickly drawn breaths. A light rain was falling and we saw seven traffic mishaps along the way, coming and going, although no injuries to anyone as far as we could tell. Too narrow roads, too much speed for the conditions, and drivers who were a little too macho were probably the cause.

One time we went around a truck parked in the middle of the road and we saw that the driver and passenger were both asleep. It was 12:30—sushi time, of course.

One of the stops on our agenda was the Zigong Dinosaur Museum. The impressive building, fairly new, was constructed over the site where dozens of dinosaurs had been excavated, and it has many magnificent, well-preserved fossils on display.

The director of the museum is an alumnus of the college and had studied under the three professors in our group. That rated us VIP treatment. We were ushered into a separate lounge, asked to sign the guest book, and served tea.

While others socialized, I scanned the English-language museum brochure we were provided. Jean Sesiano, the Swiss professor, was bothered by a technical term in the brochure that he thought was incorrect. I was bothered by grammatical and usage errors and the overall verbosity of the piece. For instance, one sentence read: "The vari-colored fossils tell people: It is the remains fossil and uesfige (sic) and fossil things left behind by the deceased preserved in the stratum through the effect of nature that proved the existence of the ancient living things and provided us with much information for understanding the secret of the life in ancient times."

I mentioned to Emily in an aside that I found it difficult to read such pamphlets for content because I was mentally making corrections. I was distracted by the errors in language, generally, and had this urge to rewrite them.

Although that was not my intent, Emily repeated my comment to the museum director, sitting on her left, and he said he would be happy if I would do a rewrite. I wasn't sure I wanted the opportunity. I wasn't looking for work. Although I had read that lanterns were traditional in China, first appearing dynasties ago, we hadn't realized what a festival would be like. We underestimated it to the extent that we didn't even take a camera to the main display on the second evening we were there. It was spectacular, a light show hard to describe. An entire park, with lakes and ponds, had displays consisting of animated, lighted life-sized figures that portrayed characters in Chinese folklore, plus a few from Western literature: Cinderella, and the emperor who wore no clothes. There were two-story buildings totally lighted from within, covered with silk or other materials. It was sort of a Chinese Disneyland.

Reluctant travelers though we had been, the trip to Zigong turned out to be a pleasant surprise and topped off our winter holiday.

Even though I was busy with the start of a new semester, I kept thinking about the museum brochures at Zigong. I was intrigued by the Chinese use of language. Our discussion at Zigong had raised the subject, but I had made mental notes ever since we had arrived in China. I was only aware of the way they used English, but I assumed their expression in the Chinese language was similar.

China was opening to the outside world and wanted to put its best foot forward, but the face it was presenting to the world was oftentimes not a very effective one. I wondered why the Chinese who produced English language publications didn't enlist professional help. The country was full of native English speakers. People on campus occasionally asked me to critique articles or papers that they were going to submit for publication or to a conference. Sometimes they were going to send a promotional brochure abroad.

The problems of grammar and syntax were relatively easy to fix. It was the other flaws that were hard to address. In the bluntest of terms: the Chinese over-write. They're effusive. They glorify everything and wallow in self-congratulation. Repeated exposure could cause biliousness in the reader.

A children's art group, for example, hoped to travel abroad, demonstrating its technique as well as showing off the accomplishments of its protégés. The leaders put together a brochure that was full of inflated praise and prose. Their claims were doubtful—so obviously so that their brochure would not have been effective or convincing.

I could seldom listen to or read the content of public announcements in China and concentrate on the content because the grammar and style were so deplorable.

Examples were everywhere. We had particularly noted them when we traveled. In Hangzhou we had seen numerous signs along the street admonishing people about their habits. Often there was a message on each side of the sign:

> Do well in hygeine (sic)
> Build up socialist civilization

> Forever carry oneself with civilization
> Pay attention to hygeine (sic)
> Do luster to the landscape

> Don't litter
> Fruit Pe-
> eels (sic) and Paper

> Honoue (sic) Those Who Pay
> Attention to Hygeine (sic)
> Disgrace Those Who Do Not

> Everyone is committed to the promotion
> of Public Health

Ohhhhh? Everyone? Then why do I see orange and banana peels and sugar cane peel everywhere?

The word *warmly* is a favorite among Chinese, as in signs or printed programs which read, "Warmly welcome you."

The most painful to read are the tourist pamphlets or promotional booklets. The four-page brochure given to English speakers at the Zigong Dinosaur Museum was typical.

The brochure was titled "A Brief Display Introduction of the Zigong Dinosaur Museum." The short paragraph that followed was then interrupted by another heading that read, "A Succinct Introduction of the Main Contents." Succinct it was not. The diction and grammar and even facts were ill chosen and often incorrect.

The museum was unique and had a fine collection. A more professional brochure would enhance the stature and credibility of the institution and the scientific work that was still going on there.

That week after we got home I started to do some editing. I enlisted Professor Sesiano's assistance as a geologist to make sure the scientific information was accurate and well organized. The two of us completed a tighter, leaner version and handed it over to Foreign Affairs to ship off to the museum. Whether they ever used it, I don't know. At least we had the satisfaction of trimming a lot of fat.

When Emily went to the market or downtown shopping with me, she often jokingly said she was going into some kind of business. Prompted by the editing project, I proposed that she and I go into business together as consultants to people who use English in any form. We would establish branches all over China. She would procure the clients, and I would provide the composition and editing skills. She thought it a great idea, but we decided getting it launched might be the equivalent of building another Great Wall.

26

Since 1949 China has undergone many spasmodic political movements, but none so prolonged or devastating or with such lasting effects as the Cultural Revolution. From most accounts, by 1966 Mao had become dissatisfied with the progress of his Revolution. He did not like or trust the direction the leaders were taking, even though he had chosen them; or certainly none had assumed leadership without his acquiescence. Many were veterans of the Long March, some comrades in arms of even longer standing.

Supposedly there were people who pretended to support the Party and the Government but who secretly were plotting its downfall. Mao felt he could not trust even the army, and turned to the youth to cleanse the Party and the country. What followed plunged the nation into chaos. During those years, China suffered a nearly bankrupt economy, failures in agriculture, disastrous experiments in education, destruction of rich cultural relics, to mention only a few catastrophes. The country was not to be rescued from this mayhem until Mao's death in 1976.

I had heard and read a lot about the Cultural Revolution, but I was surprised when I got to China to read in the *China Daily* an acknowledgment that it had been a terrible time and clearly a mistake. If the *China Daily* said so, then it was okay to speak about it openly. I remembered the pictures I had seen of gangs of Red Guards roaming the country freely, and I'd read about Nien Cheng's ordeal in *Life and Death in Shanghai*. The Chinese students and visiting scholars we had met in the States had told about their experiences and how their careers, their families, and their institutions had been affected. I knew that schools, colleges, and universities had been shut down. Our students also referred to the Cultural Revolution as a mistake.

But still, for some reason, it did not occur to me for weeks to ask about what had happened in Chengdu and, specifically, at the college during those years. Perhaps it was because the campus seemed such a quiet, friendly place and all the staff so civil that upheaval there seemed unlikely. But appearances are deceiving, as we learned from some staff members. They, too, were not untouched, nor were our students, wherever they had been at that time.

Mao literally gave students license to question, harass, and even torture teachers during that time, and reportedly students did just that at the Chengdu College of Geology. Students and other young people berated and taunted teachers at times. Some professors were required to wear dunce caps, were beaten with sticks, or ridden like a horse, all publicly. Some staff members also made accusations of others, often senior to them. People were paraded before crowds and mocked. Some faculty members were held in house arrest, separated from their families, and forced to live in separate quarters on campus. Day after day they were questioned and had to rewrite their stories till they satisfied the questioners.

We were horrified. We asked, "Who were those people? Where are they today?"

"They're still here," was the reply.

We sensed that we should not press for further information about what had occurred there on campus. Those we talked with were reluctant to identify who had been involved and what they had done. Nevertheless, thinking of the people I knew on campus, I wondered what their role had been.

The college was actually closed for six years, the orders to close all colleges coming from the government. The students did not necessarily leave the campus, however. They divided into two camps, each vying for the title of the most revolutionary. Armed with guns, the students' conflicts resulted in several deaths. Students were buried on or near campus and families came later to claim the bodies.

Staff members, some of whom were already teachers at the time, and some who were still students, told of riding the trains to Beijing. Some of them went to make posters. The railroads were directed to allow young people, from teenagers on up, to ride the trains free. Supposedly they were going to Beijing in hopes of seeing Chairman Mao. For many it was a big lark, a chance to travel that they would never have had in their lives.

Although many young people thought they were obeying Chairman Mao's command to cleanse the Revolution of these selfish elements, stories abound of young people who looted and burglarized and destroyed property and lives indiscriminately. When that became common, a new tack was called for. Young people and their teachers were sent to the countryside to work alongside and to learn from the peasants.

Some said a whole generation of students who were caught in middle school at that time lost out on their chance for higher education. Some of my students had been in junior middle school then. One such student, Mr. Luo, and his class had lived in two rooms built for students in the countryside. They not only lived there but had lessons in the morning. Then they helped the peasants in the afternoon. Others, a little older, finished middle school; and since the colleges and universities were closed, they had to go to the countryside for long periods. The peasants had to house and feed them, whether they wanted to or not. When I think of how useful teenagers, many of them from the cities, would be without much adult supervision other than illiterate peasants, I am sympathetic to the peasants. Many students from the cities looked down on the peasants and did as little as possible.

Most of our students who had had this experience spoke of always being hungry. The peasants undoubtedly had little to eat themselves, given the state of agriculture at that time. Teens, no matter where they live, have notoriously big appetites. One male student told about how the boys put the girls up to drawing the peasants into conversation in the evening. While the peasants were distracted, the boys stole food. The laughter among the rest of the class indicated that was not an uncommon or at least unlikely occurrence.

Students had mixed reactions to their experience in the countryside. Although they hated it at the time, and felt it was pointless in most cases, as adults they can empathize with the peasants. Some feel that young people have become so materialistic that some kind of national service would be good for many of today's young people. But others feel it was a complete waste of human resources. Remember that these were the views of twenty-seven to thirty-year-old doctoral students.

The Cultural Revolution became more than an enigmatic historical phenomenon when friends at the college told us of their experiences. Jilin, for example, and other teachers and students had to go to the countryside for "reeducation," to work alongside the peasants and take turns in criticizing the bad politician of the week. Jilin was also in a group of teachers who were assigned to an army unit some distance from Chengdu. For several months, their duty was to collect night soil (human waste) from the army latrines and carry it to the peasants' fields. Borrowing the feminist barb of past years, I said to him, "And for this you went to college?" It was admittedly a pretty sick joke, but he is able to laugh at the experience now.

As a medical student and doctor, Zhirong saw much suffering and had great sympathy for people. She, too, along with her classmates was sent to the countryside to help the peasants. They were also commanded to attend meetings in the evening. People were regularly hauled in front of the local party bigwigs at these meetings and accused of stealing a little food. Even though they had stolen only because they were hungry, they were severely beaten. She told of a particular beating she witnessed. In that period in China, people were all organized into communes and ate all their meals in a communal kitchen. Because a man did not feel well, his wife had cooked him a small amount of food over an open fire. When it was discovered, he was beaten.

Professor Zhang was sent to the countryside even before the Cultural Revolution. Food production was down, partly as a result of drought and other natural disasters, but mostly because of stupid mistakes made in the Great Leap Forward and other political miscalculations. Because of that, around 1965, many professors were sent to the countryside for a year. Professor Zhang was assigned to two different families. Since he was a scientist, we assumed he went to help the peasants improve their farming methods. But no. It was to drill them in correct political thought. By more fully understanding socialism and Maoist principles, the Party thought the farmers could improve their production.

He lived for six months in a shed which he shared with a pig on the other side of a waist-high partition. With the second family, he had one room in a two-room house. The room contained a very nice desk, which he was certain had come from a landlord's house. He used this desk not only to store his political books but also books in his scientific field. He was always fearful, however, that someone would find them when he was gone. To pursue academic or intellectual pursuits during those times was considered counterrevolutionary.

He came home from that year-long assignment just as the Cultural Revolution began. He was then sent off to the countryside for three more years. He was gone when HuiXin gave birth to their daughter. Life was so hard that some of his colleagues committed suicide.

We heard countless tragic stories. Wei Juming, a chemistry professor in Shanghai, told us she had to wait for ten years until after the Cultural Revolution was over to find out that her husband had been murdered. He simply disappeared one day, leaving her with their three-year-old daughter. He had earlier been a visiting scholar in France and that made him suspect. She was finally able to get the police to go through the files and piece together information based on dental and other records. There was no question that he had been killed, perhaps tortured.

The brother of a friend at the college, Yu Ming, herself a retired professor, was also murdered at that time. He too had foreign academic connections, which were damning, no matter how innocent. Not only was that period full of immeasurable personal tragedy, but it was a terrible waste of talent as well, since these were some of China's best and brightest.

Perhaps the most impassioned story we heard was that of the Yangs, whom we had learned to know through mutual friends and from attendance at church. They are Stephen and Ruth to their Western friends. Both physicians and now more than eighty years old, they had recently retired from Hua Xie (West China Medical and Science University). He was a chest surgeon, she a pediatrician. They are Quaker Christians and received their education at that university in the 1920's and 1930's. Ruth's father was the first Chinese president of the university.

In 1945, during World War II, Stephen received one of twenty United States State Department fellowships to study in the United States. The fellowships, a one-time deal, were established by President

Roosevelt shortly before his death. The American experience in wartime China had convinced Roosevelt that China needed more highly trained medical personnel. Stephen went to the United States in 1946 and received a master's degree in surgery from the University of Michigan in 1949. He then worked for a year in Toronto, where Ruth had been studying pediatrics since 1947. They returned to China in 1950, one year after the Revolution.

How did these two people who were indisputably loyal Chinese, trained to serve, fare after they returned? Their lives were inextricably bound up with foreigners, and they paid dearly for those associations in "New China," the term used when referring to the post-revolutionary country.

The Yangs have three children. A son and daughter were born before they went abroad to study and were cared for by grandparents. They had another son while they were in Canada. Their daughter had to go to the countryside for eight years and lost the opportunity to go to college because of the Cultural Revolution. Their youngest son, who was barely into junior middle school, also had to go. Because he was too old when the Cultural Revolution was over, he missed out on even a middle school (secondary) education. The Yang children were treated so badly because Stephen was suspected of being an American spy since he had received a State Department scholarship.

Stephen was under house arrest and isolated for months, confined to the pathology lab, where he was watched by four doctors. Every morning he had to answer questions, writing down the answers, and then returning them. The upholders of the Revolution were suspicious because he came from a Christian family, had many foreign contacts, and became a staff person in Canada. He had also become the director of the hospital at Huaxie, which had been founded and supported by missionaries.

All of that was too much for a paranoid political system. Their house was ransacked and most things destroyed, including pictures and mementoes from the past.

When I said, "That must have tested your Quaker faith," he laughed the hearty laugh that was his characteristic response to everything. He said, "My faith is what saved me." His is an indomitable spirit.

During part of that period, Ruth was at a military camp along with other staff members getting military training. Although she received her full salary during that time, Stephen did not. He was confined the first time in a teaching building, for six months in 1968–1969. Ruth was confined for three months. There were repeated attempts to brainwash them and demands that they constantly rewrite their biographies. There were, of course, no classes at the university during this time.

After six years, students began to be enrolled again at the College of Geology, but only young military people who were sent to the college for a political education. Often they were not only not intellectually qualified but they were arrogant, thinking they knew more than the teachers and professors.

We were amazed when people told us what they had done or the lies they had told to get something they needed or wanted. Oftentimes it was to cope with or circumvent some stupid law or some senseless bureaucratic rule, but they seemed to feel absolutely no compunction about doing so.

In a rather frivolous example, Jilin and Zhirong told of how they avoided a traffic fine one time. Within the city it was illegal for a person to ride another on a bicycle, even though it is done all the time, especially in outlying areas away from the city center. When Jilin and Zhirong were going home from the hospital one time, after work, she on the back of the bike, they were stopped. They told the policeman that she had just had an abortion and her husband was taking her home. They laughed merrily in telling it. They were just as guilt free about other more serious prevarications. Far be it from me to deny that Westerners also prevaricate and attempt to thwart authority, but it was the sheer cavalier attitude that impressed me.

Maybe living in a totalitarian society does that to you, but I wonder if it's possible to keep a clear sense of right and wrong or sensitivity to ethical issues when you have violated the truth so often.

The stories shared by these people of drought, near starvation, and physical abuse are heart-wrenching. What came to light were stupid policies adopted by the government and of how certain local officials carried them out and abused and exploited their fellow citizens.

Zhirong and Jilin love China and though they clearly have no love for the Party or the government, like many others, they have learned to do what is necessary to get along. Given that experience, who can say what one would do. The Chinese, unlike us, haven't the luxury of calling an official and venting our wrath or expressing our opposition to what we see as stupid policies.

When we said we couldn't imagine such a horrible plight or people treating their fellows that way, Jilin said, "But most of the people in your country believe in God."

Whether that is relevant, he seemed to be implying that if people don't believe in something to provide them a standard of behavior, that is what can happen.

In one serious way, Chinese higher education is still experiencing the consequences of the Mao-led Revolution. It was an exultation of the peasant and a suspicion and rejection of the intellectual. China suffered and is still suffering because of a lack of trust in educated people. Those with education were thought to be against the Revolution and were not put in positions of leadership. China now has a dearth of professors in the middle ranks because none were trained during those years of the Cultural Revolution.

According to author Han Suyin, who has written extensively about China, Mao admitted to Lord Mountbatten after the Communists had gained control of the country, "We know how to fight, and we know how to run small villages, but we don't know how to develop socialism. We will have to learn."

According to any number of objective criteria, it's questionable whether they have yet learned. They continue to fine-tune and to adopt more and more market policies, all the while insisting that theirs is a socialist system. The people have survived in spite of them.

27

One of the joys of teaching in China was that I could do almost anything and discuss almost any topic I wanted in class as long as we used English as a medium of expression. Whatever news or topic I heard about on one of the world radio services or that I read in the *China Daily*—who would dare criticize using a selection from an approved newspaper—or any article from an available source that struck my fancy could be the topic for the day. Either out of genuine interest or just that they would latch on to any reason to speak English, students usually rose to the occasion. Sometimes something bombed and I never repeated it, but that was rare.

Our class periods were two hours long, so if we had serious, substantive discussion for the first hour or more, I usually introduced something of a lighter nature to close out the session. Games were fun; Twenty Questions, for example, usually worked well.

Some of the simplest things worked surprisingly well. One, a variation of Show and Tell, was to gather up a bag of common items from our apartment and ask students the English names for them. They had a lot of fun with that and thought it very useful. Don came up with an even neater variation.

He had a student reach into the bag and pull out an item and immediately try to sell it to another student. Since the student may not have known the English word for it or in some cases not even known what the item was, it produced some ludicrous situations. For instance, a fellow who drew dental floss tried to sell it to a fellow student as thread to mend his clothes. A deodorant stick was foreign to all students. A flashlight that turned on by rotating the end confounded a student who was futilely trying to find the switch. Her "customer" further rattled her by accusing her of selling something that didn't work. Once again we had accomplished the objective: having fun while learning.

Because my doctoral students thought learning the English names of common items was practical, I decided once when we had class at the apartment to have a little identification quiz. They had to identify items of furniture, kitchen utensils, dishes, and foods. They had to learn *gas meter* and *faucet*, *curtain* and *door knob*. On succeeding visits, they checked each other to see if they still remembered.

As another change of pace, I started Free Talk off one night by reading a couple of poems. One of them was "Digging for China." I had to prep them first but it paid off.

I first drew a circle on the board and asked them what it was. They guessed a circle, a ball, a balloon, the moon—and then I rather scornfully told them it was the world, as if it should have been obvious. They giggled.

Then I put an *x* on one side of the "world" and said that was China. Then I pointed to the opposite side and asked them what that would be. Although I heard different answers, someone finally said the United States. I asked them if they had ever realized that if they would dig straight through the earth, they'd come out in the United States. They hadn't. (I guess that shouldn't have been surprising since I had always read that the Chinese had traditionally had no interest in the outside world, thinking themselves superior, with nothing worthwhile to learn from others.)

I told them, however, that we Americans had thought about it. I told them about growing up on a farm that had lots of livestock and how fence building was a regular chore. Digging post holes or other kind of holes was a fairly common activity. When I was very little and my dad dug a hole, I was curious and peered in the hole now and then, checking his progress. Dad always said he was digging for China, and when he got about as deep as he was going to go, he would ask if I could see a "Chinaman" down there. I always took the bait and peered in. Of course I never did. But my students' delight in the idea set them up nicely for Richard Wilbur's poem.

Digging for China

"Far enough down is China," somebody said.
"Dig deep enough and you might see the sky
As clear as at the bottom of a well.
Except it would be real—a different sky.
Then you could burrow down until you came
To China! Oh, it's nothing like New Jersey.
There's people, trees, and houses, and all that,
But much, much different. Nothing looks the same."

I went and got the trowel out of the shed
And sweated like a coolie all that morning,
Digging a hole beside the lilac-bush,
Down on my hands and knees. It was a sort
Of praying, I suspect. I watched my hand
Dig deeper and darker, and I tried and tried
To dream a place where nothing was the same.
The trowel never did break through to blue.

Before the dream could weary of itself
My eyes were tired of looking into darkness,
My sunbaked head of hanging down a hole.
I stood up in a place I had forgotten,
Blinking and staggering while the earth went round
And showed me silver barns, the fields dozing
In palls of brightness, patens growing and gone
In the tides of leaves, and the whole sky china blue.
Until I got my balance back again
All I saw was China, China, China.

They loved it.

Another poem about basketball, "Foul Shot," by Edwin Hoey, also tickled their fancy. Basketball is big in China, and I had a room full of basketball players. The poem visually captures the drama that permeates the scene when the score is tied and there are two seconds to play.

Lest it seem we spent all our time with students in the classroom, there were many informal occasions as well. Sometimes it was just conversations along the way when we went for a walk in the evening. Except when the weather was very cold, students often sat in the gardens preparing lessons for the next day. A great deal of Chinese education, even at that level, amounted to memorizing passages of English prose and spouting it back to the teacher upon command. So you could stroll along the pool by the new library and hear several voices around you reciting in great concentration. If our students spied us strolling by, they were relieved to stop and practice English with a live English speaker.

Don's A class, which left at the end of the first semester, became regulars one afternoon a week throughout the fall for tea and conversation at our apartment. And at Christmas they introduced us to jiaozi, or, I should say, to our first jiaozi party in China. We had been served jiaozi at people's homes, but never had we made them from scratch in our own apartment.

You don't have to be in China long before you hear those who are from the North and those from the South ridicule each other's taste in food. The rice-eaters of the South disparage the grain-eaters of the North who relish noodles and jiaozi, and vice-versa. I had further confirmation of what I had long suspected: that Don and I are by temperament Northerners. We fell for jiaozi in a big way.

About fifteen students brought all the fixings for jiaozi, a meat and vegetable dumpling, which can be boiled, fried, or steamed. We especially like it fried. It became our favorite Chinese food. I had often ordered wontons in American Chinese restaurants, but now they seem like a pale imitation.

When jiaozi is being made, everyone is a player. There can be no spectators; and students told about how at Spring Festival or other special occasions family members gather around and make jiaozi and talk all night. In the North, families make hundreds and put them outside to freeze and then they eat them all week.

The wraps, a pastry square made of flour and water and sometimes an egg, can be bought in the market in China and also in the produce department of your local vegetable market in the States. But those tend to be dry. If you're having a dinner, half the fun is the guests helping to mix or roll the dough or stuff the little dumplings.

Our round dining table was moved into the middle of the living room and became a work station. Another crew was in the kitchen wielding cleavers, cutting the vegetables, and mixing them with the seasonings and the finely ground pork. When the first batch was ready, another crew started cooking.

I was warned sternly that the water in the pot must be boiling when the jiaozi go in, and as soon as it comes to a boil again, cold water must be added. The water must be brought to a boil three times before the jiaozi are ready to eat. Soy sauce, minced garlic, pepper sauce, and other ingredients are ready for people to combine their own sauce when it's time to eat.

With upwards of twenty people in the apartment by the time the evening was over, the cleanup was a huge task, but even that was a cooperative affair. Making jiaozi is an occasion, a festive affair. That was only the first of several jiaozi parties. A group of my students came to cook jiaozi for us on New Year's Eve and then in farewell, and we always felt honored when they did.

I had taken some games with us: simple card games like UNO and word games like Boggle, which were a big hit with students. I wished for Scrabble. When conversation got heavy or the topics depressing, a quick game could always save the day.

We had sent a supply of popcorn to China. When we served it to students the first time, they were amazed. They laughed at first and said that only children ate popcorn in China. But they loved it. When we later bought some Chinese popcorn, I could see why they thought our American imported corn was so good. The Chinese corn was almost impossible to pop without burning. Students were fascinated by how we made it and were disappointed that Don had fixed it in the kitchen without calling them to watch. Nothing would do, but he had to pop another batch. We explained that popcorn and movies go together in the States and usually tried to have a big bowl on hand when we had a movie night. We were always a little surprised at how little they ate. Don and I together could put away a big bowl. While they were appreciative, they ate only rather dainty portions.

One hot summer evening I took a basket of popcorn to the postgrad Free Talk. Those students too were surprised that we could make it ourselves. They ate freely at first, but then I realized I was chomping away alone. They politely declined when I offered more. Since only a half dozen students came that night—the fewest ever—I thought I would have to take half of the popcorn home. But when I got up to go and said Don would think they didn't like his popcorn, they fell to again and when I suggested they could wrap up the remainder in the paper towels, they scrambled to take me up on it. They evidently were just bashful before, although we also realized Chinese people do not eat as much as we. No wonder we're fat, by their standards.

Our social circle on campus was necessarily limited to those who spoke English, but that was a good number. Excluding those who taught English, many of the faculty have studied or traveled abroad. Many of those, in their mid-fifties and above, studied English in middle school before 1949, particularly if they had grown up in Eastern cities. Professor Liu, who grew up in Chongqing, shamed us one evening when he talked about American books and movies he had seen.

He ticked off old movie greats from the 1930's and 1940's— Randolph Scott, Errol Flynn, Carole Lombard, Clark Gable, Olivia de Haviland. Then he started singing pop songs from the era as well as Stephen Foster songs—"My Old Kentucky Home," "Swanee River," "Old Black Joe." He apologized for forgetting the words, but he still knew them as well as we.

We were entertained in Chinese homes and enjoyed some fine cuisine. One of the most exquisite meals we had the entire year, including hotel banquets, was at Professor Liu's. It was cooked in one of those little balcony kitchens, about four by ten feet. Mrs. Liu prepared all the dishes in a wok on a two-burner gas stove. The room in which we ate, not much bigger than the square table in the middle, was little more than an entry way.

What a dinner it was—sixteen courses. There would have been seventeen except that the fish burned. That was no great loss to us, except that they were small fish fried whole. We had not been served that before so I was curious about what they might have tasted like. Each dish was colorful and attractively served. Mrs. Liu would have rated an A+ from me for "presentation." She did not join us until the last dish was served. Although there were a half dozen cold dishes on the table when we sat down, the others were cooked and served consecutively. That's why the hostess never can join the guests at the table. She is busy cooking one dish at a time until the very end. Professor Liu warned us from the very beginning that his wife would not be able to serve us very good dishes because she was coming down with a cold. He kept apologizing all the way through. That, we'd learned, is the Chinese way. We, in turn, had learned that we were expected to say how good everything was—and indeed it was. That was one time when our effusiveness was more than mere courtesy.

When we entertained Chinese people for a meal, there was no way that I could compete with that profusion, nor did I want to. When we had discussed American customs in class, I had taken a place setting of dinnerware to class with the appropriate cutlery and napkin and described a dinner party and a menu that I might serve. While my guests at home would have been pleased and complimentary over such a dinner, it probably seemed quite ordinary to Chinese. Only six or seven dishes at most. In China it would be thought insulting to your guests to serve such a paltry meal. Many of the younger generation, however, find such traditional practices excessive.

I tried to serve as American a meal as I could muster when we invited Chinese for dinner, but that depended to a certain extent on what the market had to offer. When I could get canned tomato sauce and round cabbage and ground beef, all at the same time, I could serve cabbage rolls. I could make french fries in my little oven when I could get potatoes. When celery and green pepper were available, I could serve pasta salad, or potato salad with my homemade mayonnaise. In strawberry season we had shortcake or strawberries with chocolate sauce. But there was no barbecuing of steaks or chops on the grill; and while I could serve baked potatoes, there wasn't any sour cream—and even if there were, I don't think it would have appealed to Chinese tastes. I tried, but authentic American cooking, it wasn't.

28

One day, after listening for the nth time to the doctoral students complaining that they didn't have enough time for housework or their families or leisure, I had an idea. Why not a reduced work week in China? There are too many people assigned to a unit, having too little work to do, but still having to be on the job six days a week. We could see the Waiban staff of seven doing the work of two or maybe three people, at most. Countless people, including the students themselves, had told me that many Chinese people did not have enough to do on their jobs and sat around reading the newspaper or drinking tea.

So I was ready to suggest a system of flex-time: allow people to work fewer hours or days, assuring that someone is always on duty. No cut in pay would be necessary because the money was already allocated. Since people were not really working on the job anyway, what difference would it make at work? People could have more time to do housework and to be with spouses and children. It would give families a real boost and significantly improve the quality of life.

It seemed a bright idea—and practical. The next morning, with considerable enthusiasm, I made my modest proposal in class. Light did not break forth, however. The only excitement shown for the idea was mine. I explained that this concept of "flex-time" had been used with considerable success in the United States in a variety of circumstances.

When I asked for reaction, I got mostly silence.

Mr. Yao said, "The surplus labor is only a temporary phenomenon. It's because the economy is bad right now."

I knew that was not true, but decided not to challenge it and dropped the subject.

It could be they would think a little bit about it and come back to it later. I was also noticing that when students brought something up that was critical or contrary to the status quo it was okay to talk about it, but if I introduced it arbitrarily it didn't necessarily get agreement or even a response.

I didn't think the students needed to be persuaded of the surplus of labor. They themselves had mentioned there were more teachers than necessary at the college and that some of them didn't do anything. Seldom did a teacher have more than two classes.

Besides, I had in mind a very fresh example. Two of Don's students who had finished in January had stopped in a few nights before to visit. One of them, Martin, had come to Chengdu on business with five colleagues. He said his unit had a surplus of workers now and many, including his wife, had been laid off (my expression, not his) at seventy percent pay. He was still "working," but there was nothing to do and he often sat in the office and listened to the Voice of America. His boss would tell him to read the newspaper and he would say, I am *listening* to news.

He was unhappy with his job and asked to be transferred to Yanyuan, a small town where a new paper pulp mill was being built. His parents, both engineers, worked there, having moved a year or so before. His father is a chemical engineer whose specialty is the papermaking process. Martin didn't even know what he would do at the Yanyuan plant; he just wanted a change and to be with his parents.

Martin's boss said he couldn't release him because they had just paid for him to learn English, so he just sat. One thing in his favor is that in China special effort is made for children, particularly sons, to live near or with their parents so they can look after them. (In times past, even during the Cultural Revolution, there was always concern that one child be allowed to stay at home to look after parents.) It is also easier to move to a small town than to a large city, since most people want to do just the reverse.

This story has a happy development. In a letter we received a few months after we were home, Martin reported that he indeed had been transferred to the new plant and had been translating the equipment installation manuals from English into Chinese.

One afternoon when a couple of students came to the apartment, I noticed Mr. Dong was absorbed in studying the huge map of the United States which decorated one wall of the living room.

He finally said, "Is it true people can live anywhere they want to in your country?" I nodded my head.

He shook his head in wonderment. "If that were possible in China, almost everyone would move to the cities. But there isn't enough housing or electricity or water."

I qualified my answer. "Well, the American people can live anywhere they can afford to live—if they have a job, in other words."

His comment provided still another example of how decisions determined by the marketplace in the United States are made by the government in China. Considering all the social implications—that some American cities are running out of water and growing populations place too much strain on the existing infrastructure—I wondered if we would always have that luxury.

It was time for another writing assignment for the doctoral students, so next day I asked them to write a reaction to my modest proposal for flexible scheduling and tell me three reasons, with solid support, why they agreed or disagreed with it. I asked them to give logical arguments (was that asking too much?) and gave them a week to complete the assignment. I wasn't very optimistic about the results.

When the eight papers came in I was surprised. Only two were opposed and a third said he thought it a good idea but detailed why the government would find it unacceptable. The opponents' concern was that if people had too much free time they would just get into trouble by gambling or drinking excessively and society would be damaged. One said people have enough time and, besides, they wouldn't have any money to do anything in their extra time off. That was that.

The other five found the flex time idea beneficial and feasible. Such responses give me hope. Either they were afraid initially to endorse the idea or they had to think about it. One of the students mentioned such a proposal had been discussed in the country earlier. Evidently, it had been rejected.

One student who thought the idea quite workable ended with, "But the government would never allow it." He realized that the bottom line seems to be, "Keep them at work where we can keep an eye on them." Idle hands and minds cause problems for totalitarian governments.

It did seem to be okay for the students to be critical if they initiated the topic. One night during Free Talk the topic veered around to economic systems, and students were in a mood to be frank. Someone commented that Jilin and Zhirong's son was studying in the United States. I explained that although he had a master's degree in physics, he was now studying for a doctorate in business. Someone else told of several Chinese who had received doctorates in business about five years ago, but who had not been able to get jobs in China when they returned from abroad. The economic systems are so different that their knowledge was not applicable. (With all China's expressed concern for opening up to Western business, I would have thought there would be many places for these grads.)

Another student told about a government decision to increase production of color TV's the past year, which consequently flooded the shops with TV's that people could not afford to buy. They were priced at two thousand yuan ($400), which is a year's salary for teachers as well as many other people. I expressed my surprise. Supposedly the advantage of a planned economy is that it could accurately determine what the potential market was, use resources more efficiently, and thus avoid such bloopers. In our system, I said, someone who made that much of a gaffe would have to reduce the price and still might be driven out of business, thus allowing the more efficient business to survive. We the consumer would be better served because of it. The students had no comment.

Electronic goods, both domestic and imported, are very expensive in China. When I asked who bought the expensive items, students said that many government leaders and business people and that many business people are very rich. I asked if they meant that someone could start a business, hire whomever he wanted, pay them whatever he wanted. They said yes. I asked how that could be in a socialist society. Didn't that create a double standard? They said that yes, capitalism did exist along with socialism; but I never read the word "capitalism" in any but a negative way in publications in China. The approved term is "market economy." Business people were often referred to in pejorative terms, in tones of suspicion and disapproval. When I learned it was legal to start a business, I asked the students why they didn't do a little moonlighting on weekends. They told me teachers were forbidden to work anywhere else. It was impossible to make any more money in any way.

There could be only so many professors and associate professors in the college, also. That again was dictated by government. Unless professors retired or died, there was no way for the young ones to move up. Considering that full professors at the college made less than fifty dollars a month, these young teachers were not excited about their futures.

One student's question in the postgrads' Free Talk session about that time also led to a discussion about economics.

He asked, "Why is it that when Chinese students go abroad they study harder than American students who spend more time in recreation (and may also have jobs, I could have added), but American students make more contribution to their country? Why?"

"Why do you assume they make more contribution?" I responded.

The student said, "Because your country is more technologically advanced."

Where does one start? I said there were many reasons for that and, seeing there was serious interest in the question, waded in.

I started with the Industrial Revolution and went on to say that when people pursue their own interests and well-being, it usually contributes to the development of the whole country.

When I finished, I asked if they understood me and all said yes. I hoped they did, even the four students in the group that I knew were Party members. I wondered if it would raise any questions in their minds about their own system.

Whenever we had a class discussion in which students seemed to refuse to entertain a new idea or look at something a different way, I was reminded of a conversation we had had with a visiting Western professor. Since he had considerable experience in China, I asked if he thought the Chinese really did want advice and to learn to improve. After all, the country was full of "foreign experts" there at the invitation of the government. He said they want the benefit of Western technology, but they don't really want to change their way of doing things. They want a formula or "a little black box," as if you could somehow divorce the results from the method of achieving it. They want advancement and improved technology and all the rest, but only on their terms.

He was speaking specifically as a scientist, but even so it characterizes what I think is generally China's misconception of what opening up and learning from the West is all about. The students who want to go to the United States or elsewhere in the West to study always say they want to learn technology and scientific development. They seem uninterested in learning anything else or making any other changes. But it seemed to me that they need to learn a lot more than those things if they are truly to catch up to the rest of the world. Maybe that's because the government has implied that lack of technology is the only reason China is behind.

One time when Don's students, who had job experience, came to the apartment for Free Talk, they were feeling rather discouraged about China's present state and her future. One man in particular, Mr. Li, affirmed his belief that Chinese were just as smart as the Japanese, for example, and wondered why China was so far behind the developed nations.

I stifled the impulse to tell him and instead asked, "What do you consider to be the developed nations?"

They all chimed in, "Japan, the United States, Germany, Canada, England. . . ."

I asked, "What do all those nations have in common?"

Mr. Li was silent and seemed at a loss for an answer, as were the others.

I asked again. Others waited for Mr. Li to answer.

Finally, he said, rather tentatively, "Maybe the social system . . . ?" He meant, of course, the type of government.

I bit my tongue and waited a decent interval before saying, "That's right. It's a system that provides incentives and rewards people for working hard."

This very nice man was class monitor, a Party member, and one who did not rock the boat. He felt uncomfortable saying anything that might remotely question the status quo.

What Chinese people do not seem to question, at least not openly, is why the developed nations *are* developed and progressive, and what made that development possible. If they do wonder or know, at least they don't say so openly. It is that tendency to accept, that lack of questioning, that is at the base of their problems. Chinese people are too tolerant for their own good. But, on the other hand, they know what can happen to people in China who do question.

Although our students were scientists and most had rather narrow interests, some surprised me every now and then. When I polled my doctoral students early in the semester about what they'd like to discuss or learn about, Mr. Jiang said he'd like me to compare Chinese and American literature. Since I know nothing at all about Chinese literature, and said so, that left American lit. I didn't really feel adequate to discuss that either without doing a tremendous amount of work, for which I had neither time nor resources.

Mr. Jiang had discussed Victor Hugo when I assigned students to speak about a famous person they admired.

He said he "appreciated Hugo's ideas very much and was moved by them." He particularly liked his characterizations and his ability to present opposite views. He spoke about how Hugo frequently wrote on the theme of loneliness. He also knew that he had written about the French Revolution.

He mentioned reading several of Hugo's works. I asked if he had read *Les Misérables*. Neither he nor anyone else was familiar with it. I told them the story—of how students demonstrated in the middle of Paris against injustice and the corruption of the government. I told them I had seen a musical production based on the story in Chicago in mid-June 1989, and how moved I had been by it.

That is all I said and I don't know whether they understood my implication or not, but I thought I should perhaps not say more.

The parallels to the events in Beijing and the student demonstrations in Tiananmen Square were striking. In Hugo's story, the students in Paris are convinced that since their cause is just and they are fighting for the rights of all people, the citizens of Paris will rise up and join them. But in the end they are isolated and abandoned, with no food. Soldiers eventually storm their barricade and kill everyone, with the exception of a young man who escapes into the sewers. Hugo could have been writing about students in Beijing.

While I was not ready to develop a course in American literature, I did spend a few classes on poetry. Teachers tend to impose their own preferences on students and I chose two poems of Robert Frost. I thought his themes, too, would be more easily understood. The first, "The Road Not Taken," was not particularly successful, for a reason I should have anticipated. The poem discusses a fork in the road and the narrator's puzzlement over which of two paths to travel. I thought that poem spoke to universal human experience, but in reality, Chinese people do not have the choices open to some of the rest of us.

By contrast, another of Frost's poems, "Mending Wall," turned out even better than I anticipated. It was a veritable mine, yielding up rich nuggets.

Something there is that doesn't love a wall,
That sends the frozen-ground-swell under it,
And spills the upper boulders in the sun;
And makes gaps even two can pass abreast.
The work of hunters is another thing:
I have come after them and made repair
Where they have left not one stone on a stone,
But they would have the rabbit out of hiding,
To please the yelping dogs. The gaps I mean,
No one has seen them made or heard them made,
But at spring mending-time we find them there.
I let my neighbor know beyond the hill;
And on a day we meet to walk the line
And set the wall between us once again.
We keep the wall between us as we go.
To each the boulders that have fallen to each.
And some are loaves and some so nearly balls
We have to use a spell to make them balance:
"Stay where you are until our backs are turned!"
We wear our fingers rough with handling them.
Oh, just another kind of outdoor game,
One on a side. It comes to little more:
There where it is we do not need the wall:
He is all pine and I am apple orchard.
My apple trees will never get across
And eat the cones under his pines, I tell him.
He only says, "Good fences make good neighbors."
Spring is the mischief in me, and I wonder
If I could put a notion in his head:
"*Why* do they make good neighbors? Isn't it
Where there are cows? But here there are no cows.
Before I built a wall I'd ask to know
What I was walling in or walling out,
And to whom I was like to give offense.
Something there is that doesn't love a wall,
That wants it down." I could say "Elves" to him,
But it's not elves exactly, and I'd rather
He said it for himself. I see him there
Bringing a stone grasped firmly by the top
In each hand, like an old-stone savage armed.
He moves in darkness as it seems to me,

Not of woods only and the shade of trees.
He will not go behind his father's saying,
And he likes having thought of it so well
He says again; "Good fences make good neighbors."

After we had discussed the literal meaning of the poem, we began discussing its implications, its symbolism. Then, we turned to the wall of all walls, China's Great Wall.

China had officially adopted a policy of openness in 1979, changing a long tradition that predated the Communists. Supposedly walls and fences were coming down.

I asked why people or nations build walls.

My students answered, "For security." . . . "To be safe from enemies."

That wasn't too hard. They thought at the time the wall was built it probably was a good idea.

I referred to the line, "Before I built a wall I'd ask to know what I was walling in or walling out, and to whom I was like to give offense."

"What did China wall in?"

Someone said in a little voice, "The people."

"Was that a good idea?" I asked.

A few people imperceptibly shook their heads, a little embarrassed, but didn't answer.

"What was walled 'out'?"

After a little pause, there were a number of answers.

"People" . . . "News". . ."Ideas". . ."Technology."

"Does there come a time when walls outlive their usefulness?" I asked. "When it's time for them to come down? When they may even make people less secure?"

They were thoughtful but silent.

"Can you think of any other walls in the world?" I asked.

Finally someone mentioned the Berlin Wall. And someone else pointed out that it had come down.

"Was it good for Germany that it came down?" I asked.

We had earlier discussed the problems that beset a unified Germany. I acknowledged that tearing down walls involved risk. I asked how the Berlin Wall was different from China's wall.

There was no response.

I said, "In addition to physical walls, what other kinds of walls are there between nations—or within nations—or even between friends and families?"

They were familiar with the term "generation gap," and that was an obvious answer.

The discussion that flowed from considering this poem was cautious and tentative, but thoughtful. Seeing all sorts of symbolism and relevance in our discussion myself, I was frustrated at the lack of response, but I knew when to quit. I didn't know whether they were unaccustomed to considering poetry in this way, exploring symbolic implications, or if they were inhibited by the topic's strong political overtones. The consensus, incidentally, seemed to be that while there was a big hole in the wall, the wall was still intact.

The one-family, one-child policy was an issue of both political and personal interest and stimulated a lively discussion in all of our classes. Most of my doctoral students were already married and some had a child. Most came from big families and wished they could have more children. Even though our students and people, generally, support the policy, they do see bad side-effects. In class we discussed numerous newspaper columns on this topic and I saw a TV program in English.

I asked students if they agreed with the conclusions set forth in the articles: that these "only" children are catered to and nurtured to fulfill the expectations of parents who put all their hopes and their resources on this one child. People who really can't afford it nonetheless sacrifice to pay for lessons in music, dance, or art. I told them about two college families I knew that had bought new pianos for their daughters, one six, the other eleven. All four parents are teachers. When I learned new pianos cost approximately $4,000, I thought I must have misunderstood.

I said, "How can they afford that, teachers' salaries being what they are?"

They just laughed, shrugged, and said, "Maybe the grandparents bought the piano."

All young parents want their child to be a scholar or excel in some way. It's the Chinese version of the American dream, that your child will have a better life than you. Many of the generation who are now parents were children of the Cultural Revolution and suffered because of it. They want to be sure their children have what they did not. This only child is often dubbed "The Little Emperor" or "King."

Even though they acknowledged the need for the policy, most of our students said they would like to have more than one child. They were very envious of our family snapshots displayed in the apartment showing not only two children but several grandchildren. Four doting grandparents per Chinese child add to the problem, also. I read complaints from parents saying they had a hard time disciplining or restraining or denying their own children something because of over-lenient grandparents. And, of course, every child learns how to play off one loving adult against another. Thus, the "little emperor."

29

We Americans have a saying about "barking at the moon." But in Chengdu there is a saying about dogs barking at the sun, implying it's a rare phenomenon to *see* the sun in Chengdu.

That may be an exaggeration, but sunshiny days and blue skies are not common. Weather has always affected my moods and I had been apprehensive about Chengdu's notorious gray skies. Perhaps forewarned was forearmed. The weather did not bother me, or perhaps I was determined that nothing was going to spoil our stay in China.

Spring arrived and new little green leaves appeared on the trees, shoving the old dusty leaves aside. Since it never freezes in Chengdu, trees do not shed their leaves in that autumn ritual we Midwesterners are used to. It rained fairly frequently, but seldom did it rain hard enough to cleanse the foliage or clean the streets.

We were looking forward to warmer temperatures and shedding our longies. One of the things that made it easier to adjust to less comfort and convenience was that we were so much better off than anyone else on campus, particularly in our living conditions.

Housing is in short supply all over China and a bone of contention for most people at the college. Undergraduate students lived eight to a room, and postgrads, two or three. Since I had daily contact with the doctoral students, almost all of whom were young teachers at the college, I particularly heard their complaints. Even though they were married, oftentimes with a child, most of them lived in only one room and shared toilets and a laundry room down the hall with everyone else who lived on that floor.

Officially the students were not even allowed to cook in their buildings, but everyone did and the college turned a blind eye. They could not afford to eat in the dining halls on their meager salaries. But when I say cooking, that meant they cooked in the hall in a wok on a little coal burner.

One morning after class, I went to the market and ran into Li Yong, whom I had just left in class. He too had been shopping. In fact he was on his way back to his room with his purchase, a live chicken tied on the back of his bicycle. He was taking it home to kill and cook for his pregnant wife. She was due in a few weeks and feeling a great deal of discomfort, but she was still working. By killing the chicken himself, he could save a few cents. This was a couple who lived in one of those multi-storied buildings where you cooked in the hall and went down the hall even for water. Now there was an equal opportunity husband.

Frank, one of Don's students, whose wife was a teacher at the college, invited us for supper one Sunday evening. They were in their early thirties and had a six-year-old son. They lived across the canal in one of the oldest buildings. It was not even an apartment building but a converted dormitory. A five-story building, it housed fifty families per floor. We climbed littered stairs to the third floor, past bicycles on landings, and went down a dimly lighted hallway to their apartment. Outside of each room, people—usually women—were preparing their evening meal on coal burners. The air was dense with smoke and heavy with the smell of hot oil.

Their one large room contained a double bed and two small settees, which Frank had made. Their son slept on one of the settees. There were a couple of small tables, a wooden chair, and opposite was an entire wall unit, in sections, which Frank also had built. It included bookshelves, a desk, space for a radio and TV, and storage for their clothes and other items necessary for a family of three. That was it.

We ate across the hall in a borrowed room that belonged to a friend who was seldom there. They were lucky in that this room provided them a place for eating and study.

Once during a conversation with doctoral students, we were discussing people's feelings about age. I remarked that no one wants to get old.

Mrs. Zhang said, "Maybe in China they do because that way they can get a room." Note that she didn't say "apartment"; she said "room."

Emily's situation illustrates how long you have to wait for bigger and better housing. Emily, from the Waiban, is married to a teacher at the college and had a seventeen-year-old son and a twelve-year-old daughter. After twenty years of marriage, they still rated only two rooms, plus a kitchen. Housing conditions certainly must put a strain on family life.

If Westerners were jammed together in such close quarters and there were no privacy for work or study or separate activity, most would go berserk. I wondered whether there is a basic psychological need for space, or if we only think so because we are used to better conditions.

Some of my doctoral students said they take a nap in their offices or go back there in the evening and work till eleven o'clock or later. The reason: they have no room to work at home, especially if there is a young child.

Young people who are romantically involved find it difficult to find any privacy. Although young couples were fairly common on campus, their behavior was circumspect. Holding hands was about as much as you ever saw in the way of Western demonstrations of affection—in public, anyway. Judging from TV dramas, romantic scenes in China are much less torrid than on Western screens. Warm hugs—no mouth-to-mouth kissing—seemed to be the norm. It was interesting, though, that Don's students, average age about thirty, were very critical of the undergrad behavior they saw on campus. They thought students ought to be forbidden to fall in love! In fact, in 1991 kissing was banned on the campus of Beijing University and transgressors were fined.

Another difference in our cultures in that regard is the unself-conscious affection displayed between members of the same sex, perhaps brought on by the prohibitions against early dating and marriage. It was not uncommon to see both young women and young men walk down the street holding hands or with arms entwined. Even older women walked arm in arm.

When we had been on campus only a few weeks, we decided to check out the "Saturday night dancing party," as it was called, held in the students' dining hall. A live band performed on stage and the floor was crowded with couples—of young women, of young men, and some that were mixed. Although we immediately found stools on the edge of the dance floor and were content to be wallflowers, some of our students descended on us, beseeching us to dance. Both the young women and the young men asked each of us. We begged off, blaming our arthritic joints—not an empty excuse—but had we accepted, only we would have felt uncomfortable.

Just because we had learned to cope with many inconveniences I described earlier didn't mean we were resigned to them or accepted them uncomplainingly, at least not with each other. Especially Don.

Don, being the perfectionist and the practical person he is, has always had little patience with poor workmanship or ways of doing things he deems senseless. He found many instances in China that tested his patience. Sometimes things actually represented a safety hazard. In others it might just be inefficient or downright ugly. His not very explicit but colorful term for such examples is "dumb-ass."

I used to cringe at the crudeness of that expression, but I had become inured to it over the years, and after observing some things in China I decided that the term was probably apt in that case. Our apartment and the Guest House were full of examples.

Each of us had a desk, mine in the living room, Don's in the bedroom. Shortly after classes started, Don complained of back and shoulder aches for days after doing homework. Finally, he realized that the desk was the problem. The desks were both too high to work at comfortably while sitting on standard chairs. His solution? He got out his meager set of tools and started prying off the four-inch base at the bottom of the nice substantial-looking furniture. Once off, it was then a little too short. But with a little shimming, he built it up to a comfortable height. The backaches disappeared. I cringed when I saw the splintered discarded wood base and hoped we would be over the Pacific headed home before his handiwork was discovered. I declined his offer to "remodel" my desk.

The round folding table in the living room that we ate on was a similar example. It too was too high to sit at comfortably, which made me wonder if Chinese chair designers ever talk to desk and table designers. Now if this were only over-sized Westerners having to adapt to sensible native conditions, we would have had no grounds for complaint. After all, you can't travel halfway round the world and expect to find everything to suit your taste or done the way you do them at home. But given the size of the average Chinese, considerably smaller than us, none of this made sense.

The kitchen also had its problems. The stove, a two-burner gas model on a folding metal stand, stood about twenty-six inches from the floor, too short for this average-size American housewife. Setting it on top of the twenty-four-inch ceramic tile shelf made it too high—it was my turn to get backaches from stir-frying or lifting a heavy teakettle full of boiling water off the stove at that height.

The solution was to take the stove off the stand, place it on the tile shelf, and then build it up with bricks scrounged from a nearby construction site. We experimented until we got it just right, which meant Don made several surreptitious trips early mornings to get another couple of bricks.

All piping was on the surface of walls, and although most walls in China are brick or concrete and therefore concealing pipes does pose some problems, it is not impossible. That, of course, is purely aesthetic.

Another feature in our kitchen, however, we had a hard time figuring out. There was a three-inch drain pipe connected to the kitchen sink, which was set on a tile base and exposed in the front. The drain pipe stopped about three inches from the floor, and the contents flowed into the area where there was a floor drain. In other words, after being carried two feet in pipe, the water was then released to free fall into the drain below, but not without leaving a grimy mess. The reason for that kind of arrangement? Evidently it was to provide a drain for the washer hose, so that the water would be somewhat contained. But sanitary? Hygienic? I tried to avoid looking down into that recess beneath the sink. There was no way to clean it.

Another mystifying thing about our kitchen was a bolt lock on the inside of the door. I tried to think of any possible occasion when I might want to barricade myself inside that kitchen. There were times when I decided Don and I each needed a little space, but I would never have chosen to hole up in the kitchen, the most incommodious room in the apartment or anywhere else.

When we first came to China, we thought the water heater crude and Rube Goldberg-ish. But it was a good example of things that at first seemed dumb and hopelessly old-fashioned, even amateurish, but which we later realized were sensible adjustments, adaptations, or alternatives. We came to appreciate the water heater's efficiency. It produced almost instant hot water, eliminated the need for a tank, and was not using gas or electricity continuously to maintain a hot water supply. The amount of water available was limited only by the gas available. That water heater, like other things, made sense in light of China's economy and limited resources.

What was senseless, though, was the hookup itself. The water heater, about eleven by thirteen inches, hung on the wall in the entry way opposite the bathroom. Gas pipes feeding the apartment, as well as the gas meter, also decorated the walls of the entry hall. Now unless you are into galvanized pipe decor, this lacks a certain refinement, not to mention warmth.

Even putting aside the issue of aesthetics, the hookup still qualified for a dumb-ass award. In order to light the heater, you first had to turn on the water in the tub, then come out into the hall and turn the gas on and activate the igniter. When you finished showering, you reversed the procedure, coming out dripping wet into the hall and turning the gas off before turning off the water. Why couldn't they hang the water heater on the bathroom wall and save the dripping-water routine?

One of the nicest features of the apartment was its location on the bank of the canal. Both our living room and bedroom had window walls with French doors leading onto the balconies that overlooked the canal and the free market beyond. The French doors had steel screen doors inside, which given the proliferation of mosquitoes seemed like a very smart idea. However, they did not fit well and a mosquito and ten friends could easily flit through with no sweat. What made this feeble effort to screen insects even more ludicrous was that three windows on each side of the doors lacked screens.

To add to the incongruity, every other door in the apartment had ten good-sized louvres at the bottom, including the outside door, which could accommodate a whole tribe of mosquitoes if they chose to visit. In fact, the front door of the apartment opened into an inside hallway; but the opposite wall was completely glass, with many casement windows, most of which were always open and none of which were screened either. Neither were there any screens in the high small casement windows in the kitchen and bathroom. Therefore, installation of the two screen doors was pointless. Again I got the feeling that the apartments were built by many people, none of whom talked with each other about what they were doing.

As if that wasn't enough to encourage the insect population, there were three floor drains in the apartment, one in the bathroom, and two in the kitchen.

Few floors within the apartment were the same level; they varied from room to room. And another anomaly, to our eyes, were the nine- and ten-foot ceilings. What purpose does that serve, especially in a population of traditionally short people? Granted, that affords transoms, for ventilation, but we wondered if those were efficient or ever really used. Supposedly heat rises and high ceilings provide cooler rooms, but in Chengdu the problem was humidity more than heat.

Eight-foot ceilings have been standard for so long in the United States that higher ones seem strange. Since most buildings on campus are five stories tall, Don calculated that they could save the cost of one floor by reducing each floor by two feet. Construction money is scarce in China, and it seemed to us an unnecessary feature.

Since the college was built from the ground up, beginning in the mid-1950's, none of the buildings was more than thirty-five years old. But they looked much older. Chinese construction does not necessarily err in design as much as in execution. The buildings were basically sound but had been poorly maintained. It appeared that once up, the buildings were neglected. Yet four large new buildings had been built in the past five years.

The standard explanation was, "The government appropriates money for construction, but nothing for maintenance."

That is poor policy, but probably true.

Don, however, wasn't buying it. He saw a big maintenance staff and a large labor pool. With a little axle grease, some ingenuity, and determination, they could have fixed many things around campus at very little cost.

I dropped many a hint to anyone who would listen that Don had expertise along that line and ideas about how things could be improved, and if they were smart they would tap his brain. It was probably good no one ever took him up on it. Chinese-American relations, fragile at best, might not have withstood it.

30

Don and I are bird fanciers and feed many birds all year round at home. We get excited when an unusual one appears at our feeders. Birds in China, though, were something of a rarity. When I did hear them, they inevitably had a beautiful and, to our ear, unusual song.

Because birds were not common, their singing caught my attention immediately. But when it happened in class—the windows were always wide open—and I remarked about it, students were obviously unconscious of it until I mentioned it. They had little reaction. I didn't know whether they didn't like birds, found them uninteresting, or just insignificant. They always seemed a little surprised or nonplused at my interest.

Whether in class or at the apartment, I hurried to the window or out onto the balcony to try to get a glimpse of the music maker. The songs were thrilling. Even though we were on an upper floor, I seldom could see them—at best only a quick movement in the trees.

I wondered why there were so few birds. I know they are eaten, but were they also being deliberately killed? There was the infamous sparrow campaign in 1958, when the whole country turned out to kill sparrows and other birds because the birds were eating so much grain. It was part of a campaign to eliminate the four pests: flies, mosquitoes, mice and rats, and birds.

Killing the birds, however, turned out to be a bad move because the insect population increased, causing even greater problems. After they realized the short-sightedness of their policy, officials tried to retrain people. Considering the dearth of birds in Chengdu, at least, people must still be decimating the bird population.

Ironically, though, birds are about the only pets I saw in China. Parrots, parakeets, and a few other caged birds could be seen on balconies outside apartments. Sometimes the owners took them to a park or a teahouse. In a country that has limited housing and limited resources, there is simply not room for other pets. Whatever it costs to feed them, it would be a pittance compared to what Americans spend for dog or cat food. Chinese could live very well on what Americans spend on their pets.

Occasionally I saw someone with a dog and I knew one family that had a cat, but that was rare. You might see dogs running around, but they were usually skinny mongrels.

In the doctoral class I discussed a news feature I had heard on Voice of America about the controversy over using animals for research. The students had a hard time understanding the emotion behind this issue for many Americans. I also mentioned how important pets were for people, psychologically and socially, and how pets were used in therapy for the mentally ill, the elderly, and even the criminally insane.

This was probably even harder for the Chinese to grasp. Maybe because the Chinese are constantly surrounded by people and are therefore less likely to be isolated or lonely, they don't need, even if they could afford, pets.

One day in class, when we were discussing a lesson on food shopping in the United States, the text mentioned that ads for dog food meant food *for* dogs and not dogs *as* food. It also mentioned that Westerners not only had cats and dogs for pets, but regarded the eating of their "friends" as disgusting. I asked students if they were aware that Westerners felt that way. They were not, and I could tell they didn't quite understand what all the fuss was about.

I tried a different tack.

"What foods, animal or vegetable, would you not eat under any circumstances? What would you find unacceptable?"

They sat silently, thinking.

Finally, Miss Wang said, "I wouldn't eat cat."

When I asked why, she said, "Because they are so pitiful."

I think she meant "appealing." The other students still said nothing. Clearly they were not of the same mind.

I realized that in a poor country, where millions have died in famines, one couldn't be choosy. Judging by what I saw students eating, the Chinese diet seemed monotonous. While the choice of meats and vegetables might vary, rice was served in some form at almost every meal. When I commented on that, students said quite seriously, they thought they would die if they couldn't have rice every day. So monotony is in the palate of the beholder.

I was constantly trying to relieve the monotony in our own menus, which took some doing. Now that the weather was warmer, when time permitted, Don often took off downtown on Saturday morning, as he said, to "get away." He'd leave about ten, ride the buses, and be gone four to five hours. That gave both of us a little space, something there hadn't been much of in past months. I wrote in my journal, graded papers, or did a little cooking and enjoyed the luxury of a few hours of solitude.

The little expedition satisfied Don on two counts: he likes to shop and he likes to eat. (I liked the latter but not the former.) Therefore, he headed off with the backpack and lots of small bills for bus fare. Sometimes he would have to forage through a dozen stores to find the goods he was seeking. Now these were not quests for exotic or gourmet items, unless you think bread, saltine crackers, white vinegar, and raisins qualify. Actually, maybe in China they do.

I had always found Don's penchant for buying things in quantity maddening. When he did that in China, I found it doubly embarrassing, partly because it was spending money for things we might not use. One might conceivably go through two pot scrubbers in eleven months, but four? Once when Jilin was with us and Don bought a gross (slight exaggeration, perhaps) of pellets for the electric mosquito zapper, Jilin asked whimsically if he planned to take them back to America. His comment struck just the right note and even broke Don up, but it didn't stop his habit.

Nevertheless, in China I came to realize the necessity for buying something in quantity when you see it. The next time you went to buy that item, it might not be there, or the next, or the next. First I couldn't find oatmeal, then there was no tomato sauce for three months. Incidentally, when I next saw tomato sauce, I bought ten cans. Don couldn't believe it. In China, at least, I was converted.

One particular day in April was a shopping bonanza. Don got three items out of the four he sought, plus a supply of chocolate bars, which for him, in itself, considering his addiction to chocolate, constituted a successful venture. And he found a brand of saltine crackers we had not been able to locate since November.

That uncertain availability of products is seemingly a distribution problem in part. China has neither the communication nor transportation network to deliver goods on a regular basis. Given the planned nature of the economy, neither can it respond to demands of the marketplace quickly.

At any rate, that day Don was lucky. He bought eight pounds of crackers—sixteen eight-ounce packs. His backpack was already full by that time, so the store packaged them in two large, clear, plastic bags. Since the crackers were also wrapped in clear plastic, the contents of his package were obvious. He attracted lots of attention on the bus. Crackers are hardly a standard item in the Chinese diet, and the Chinese must have drawn some interesting inferences. For once I didn't criticize his buying in quantity. They were good crackers. I wish I had the franchise for North America.

31

Up to this time we went to church by car and made a day of it in town, but as spring came, we started going by bus. It took some doing, though, because we had to walk fifteen minutes to catch the bus, change buses, and then walk another fifteen minutes to the church.

Palm Sunday was a benchmark in that it was the first time in months I hadn't worn my long underwear to church and it was comfortable to sit once again. There were many people already seated in the courtyard when we got to the church and we squeezed into seats in the next to last row of the sanctuary, the first time we had sat in back. I'm sure if we had gone in a door closer to the front, well-meaning folks would have shooed some people out to make room for us, but I disliked that special treatment. I liked sitting in the back because we could watch everyone else and get a better view of the entire congregation. It was a good day for us—we knew two of the hymns: Holy, Holy, Holy, and Nearer My God to Thee.

There were many more young people than I realized when we first attended in the fall. It was amusing that day because many of the teenagers—young twenties, perhaps (I always underestimate Chinese young people's ages)—left shortly after the sermon started. People also got up frequently to go to the toilet and then came back. We knew that's where they went because the toilets were visible across the courtyard. Must be all that tea.

We were always greeted in English by someone before or after the service, and that day a young man who sat in front of us asked me to go ahead of him when we were going out and bade me to "Be careful." I had noticed over his shoulder that he had papers written in English and guessed he would probably speak to us. He had graduated from Sichuan University and was working in a factory.

On Easter Sunday we were glad we had asked for a car because it was cold and rainy, a disappointment after some warm sunshiny days the past two weeks. Even though we arrived at 9:20, forty minutes before the start of the service, we sat in the next-to-last row in some of the few remaining seats. Although some people sat outside during the service, there weren't as many as usual because of the rain. A big room across the courtyard where there was a speaker was also filled. There were probably about eight hundred people in attendance, many Westerners among them.

The Easter service was not quite as elaborate as at Christmas, but there were two numbers by the choir, and it was the first time since Christmas that there were flowers on the altar.

Stephen (Dr. Yang), our Quaker friend, had told us that baptisms were held on Easter, and so we were not surprised when we saw eight people lined up in front of the pulpit getting their picture taken right before the service began. The church confers baptism on about eighty persons a year, usually at Easter, Christmas, and sometimes in between. Members must come continuously for at least one or two years before joining.

In May we sat outside in the courtyard of the church for the first time, an entirely different experience. The sound of constant horn blowing in adjacent streets was distracting. Since it was a rare sunny day, it was pleasant, but there were other distractions closer at hand.

I felt like I was in the church nursery or "cry room," not just because there were many children, but because even though we could hear through the loudspeakers, people were talking quietly instead of listening to the scripture and the sermon, wandering around, getting up to go over to the toilets, and generally causing a lot of distraction. I wondered why a few even bothered to come.

However, there were some in the midst of all that who seemed completely engrossed. Some people wandered in late, stood around for a little while, and then left. One young man carried something wrapped in a newspaper. A Bible, perhaps? It probably isn't "cool," or maybe even politically smart, to be seen carrying a Bible out in the open. It reminded me of all the ads that promised that they would send you a copy of some titillating publication in a "plain brown wrapper."

A young girl, about thirteen perhaps, kept coming to an elderly man sitting in the row in front of us, getting something from his briefcase, and then going off again. After the sermon she brought him a cup of hot water. He greeted me in English after the service. He also talked with Stephen, who was sitting nearby, in friendly fashion. They seemed like contemporaries.

The sermon, according to Stephen, was about Adam, who had the freedom to enjoy everything in the Garden of Eden, but he and his wife ate the fruit that was not allowed. Although the scripture, prayers, and announcements were given by a young woman seminarian, the preacher was Pastor Fu, age eighty-one.

The sermons always covered very safe topics. How could it be otherwise? This was not the place for the preaching of the social gospel.

Most Chinese are not religious in any formal sense of the word. The *China Daily* reported that China had a religious population of about 100 million, decidedly a minority in a population of 1.2 billion.

The status of Christianity in China is hard to determine. According to Chinese Christian leaders' estimates, there are between three and four million Protestant Christians and about the same number of Catholics. A 1989 *Time* magazine report from Beijing estimated the number at more than ten million. The preponderance are in coastal areas, but the existence of three churches in Chengdu, two Protestant and one Catholic, is testimony that Christians can be found throughout China. The number has increased since 1949, and Chinese Christian officials claim that every thirty-six hours a new church opens somewhere in China.

Christianity has been in China for centuries, though it really only flourished during the nineteenth century. Protestantism was introduced at that time, along with Western colonial expansion. However, it was led, nourished, and financed then by foreign missionaries and denominations. The Chinese claim that missionaries worked "hand in glove with imperialist governments" probably cannot be denied in some cases.

Nevertheless, countless schools, colleges, hospitals were started all over China by those Christian missions representing several denominations, from several countries. Chengdu's Second Hospital, where Zhirong worked, was started by Canadian churches. West China Medical and Science University (Huaxie) is another church-founded institution. Most younger Chinese are probably not aware of the origins of these institutions because the government has taken pains to conceal them. The cornerstones have been removed from original buildings at Huaxie. For these reasons the Chinese in the past thought of Christianity as a "foreign" religion. Wanting to expel any continued or future bourgeois influence, the government forced all missionaries to leave after 1949. A friend, Helen Huntington Smith, who represented the Congregational Christian Church, was one of those.

The indigenous congregations that were left were in disarray. All denominations wanted to maintain their own traditions, but what happened in Chengdu was probably typical of what happened all over the country. On several occasions we talked with Stephen and Ruth, who were longtime members of the church. Stephen said that the church we attended in Chengdu had originally been Anglican. He called it Bishop Song's church. In the late 1940's Bishop Song and a few other Chinese Christians who were pro-Communist, realized the Communists were going to win. He proposed building up a new church in China. After 1949 he thought it would be a good idea to have all denominations merge.

The result of his efforts and those of other Christian leaders throughout China was the birth of the Three-Self Movement. Begun in the early 1950's, this movement takes its name from its nature: it made the churches in China self-governing, self-supporting, and self-propagating. The churches are entirely under Chinese leadership in personnel and in financial management. According to Bishop Ting, an Anglican who is president of the Chinese Christian Council, the Three-Self Movement is not nationalist or anti-foreign, but is merely the Chinese Christians' effort to achieve a Chinese identity for their churches.

During the Cultural Revolution, all the churches were shut down. After Deng Xiao Ping assumed office, new policies were enacted and religious freedom was restored. At the time of our stay, at least 1,600 Protestant churches had been reopened or built and the freedom of Chinese Catholics to practice the seven sacraments had been restored, at least officially.

The Chinese Constitution protects religious freedom and normal religious activity, but after a conference on religious affairs in Beijing in 1990, according to the *China Daily*, the director of China's Religious Affairs Bureau said that the government would step up efforts to regulate religious affairs.

All of that constitutional protection, therefore, is "in principle." Practice is something else. Woe to church officials who step across an acceptable line. Asia Watch, a United States–based human rights group, claims that China has since 1989 been engaging in its toughest crackdown on religion in decades. Both Catholics and Protestant leaders have been imprisoned. Their offense was to take part in meetings in house churches outside the religious bureaucracy. If believers worship outside officially approved places, they can face counter-revolution charges and ten years to life in prison.

The government fears that such meetings are open to "hostile infiltration" and "splittist activities." Beijing's rulers fear religion can harbor and breed dissent and are aware of the church's unifying role for Poles and other Eastern Europeans who toppled Communism.

Stephen told us that since he's a public and visible Christian, young people seek him out to ask questions. He tells them to read the Bible and, occasionally, he buys a Bible for a young person. He said younger people were more apt to ask questions. They want to know the difference between politics and religion. Older people in China have been oppressed and are afraid to do or say anything that might be considered wrong. When Don and I told Stephen that people we knew still seemed reluctant to go to church, he said that should not be the case; no one challenges belief. He reiterated that the Constitution now protects freedom of religion, and that a system of law has developed in recent years.

Neil, a British teacher at Huaxie, who participated in our conversation, said that, nevertheless, some of his students spoke about how going to church might be a little risky in terms of their future. Because of the degree of control over jobs and grades, going to church could be perceived as stepping out of line.

As I said earlier, it is difficult to judge the strength of Christian belief in China. Judging just from the activity at the church we attended, one might infer quite a lot. Because the congregation at the church we attended was overflowing, another church had been opened across town a year and a half before we arrived. But of the folks we were acquainted with, on campus, we knew of only one couple who professed interest in Christianity. A couple of our students expressed an interest in having a Bible and we obliged.

Although foreign evangelists are outlawed, some Western teachers use their contacts with students to spread their faith. A young teacher who spent two years in Nanchang held weekly Bible study regularly in her room, although surreptitiously. Dorothy, a teacher from Michigan, told us she was meeting with a few students who came to her apartment for Bible study. I said I understood that this was illegal, that no religious activities were to take place outside the church. We were having lunch in a hotel restaurant at the time. Her voice lowered and, conscious of the fact that there were people in the booth behind us, she said she knew it but would soon be going home, and she figured the government could do little but ask her to leave. Her defense also was that she had not initiated anything.

Another American mentioned that he had bought a Chinese-English Bible for one of the gatekeepers at his university at the gatekeeper's request. These were not isolated incidents.

In February 1994, China detained seven foreign Christians, three of them Americans. They were charged with violating a recent regulation that bans foreign missionary activity. In many ways, China has always engaged in an elaborate charade. China bars any foreign missionary activity, yet for years has welcomed teaching personnel from organizations that have a religious orientation, and even accepted missionaries themselves as teachers.

Jilin commented shortly after we arrived that there is a real crisis of belief in China today. Listening to and reading students' papers over the year convinced me that that was a perceptive observation. Although a few students said that Communism was their religion, students' disillusionment with corruption in the Party and with empty Marxist slogans has resulted in disappointment and disenchantment. It may be those same feelings which have driven many Chinese to Western religion.

32

Whenever we've traveled, whether at home or abroad, I've always liked to read the local newspapers. You can learn a lot about a community or a country by reading its newspapers. You can determine its problems, its politics, its concerns, its culture as mirrored in the local press. In my passion to learn as much as possible about China, I regretted that I wouldn't be able to read Chinese newspapers.

Nevertheless, the *China Daily*, the only English language newspaper, and the *Beijing Review*, a bimonthly magazine, both published all over the world, provided us with some information. *China Daily* celebrated its tenth anniversary while we were there. It had been launched after the open policy in the late 1970's made it important to share what was going on in China with the rest of the world.

The press in China is, of course, state controlled. There are about eight different daily newspapers. All are regulated by the government, as are radio and television. It goes without saying, then, that the information you receive is going to be limited and biased. Nicholas Kristoff of *The New York Times* described the situation accurately when he said, "The Communist Party treats all the nation's newspapers and TV broadcasts as advertising space to celebrate the glories of Communism."

One of the officially approved newspapers that seemed to be popular in China is the *Reference News*, which carried reprints of news items from newspapers around the world. Students were fascinated by it. Although it carried articles from newspapers in many places, usually when a student reported a news item from there it was from the US and something rather bizarre. That made me speculate that it must be China's version of the *Star* or the *National Enquirer*.

For instance, one item a student reported was a contest run by a local bar somewhere in the United States. Four women who were found not to be pregnant at the time entered a contest to see who could deliver a baby first. Only in America. That is not the kind of item that made me proud of my nationality. I responded with raised eyebrows, a shake of my head, and called on the next student. I suspected that items were chosen precisely because they showed a country in a poor light, but I was assured by English teachers that that was not necessarily the case. According to them, the newspaper usually did carry items of more substance and, surprisingly, it sometimes carried items about China not carried in Chinese newspapers.

Because we were in a provincial city, we did not get CNN, Western news magazines, or international editions of some of the newspapers available in cities in the east. We came to appreciate the Voice of America as well as other world radio services, and I sent letters off to our legislators to urge continued support. We saw and heard firsthand how necessary VOA is as a more objective source of news in other parts of the world, especially where the press is anything but free.

Many of our students listened to world radio services regularly. They may have been motivated by a desire to improve their English skills, but they were also getting information they would not otherwise know. We often heard news items about China on VOA or BBC World Service, which we saw no mention of on Chinese English TV or in *China Daily*. When we discussed news events and I mentioned a particular item about China, often students knew nothing about it.

For example, an editor of a Chinese newspaper was in Paris and called on his country to renounce socialism because it had shown itself incapable of meeting the country's economic needs. He was criticized at home for making such statements. His response was that he knew his comments would not be published or broadcast at home. None of my students had heard the item.

We also watched the TV English news broadcast each evening after the regular newscast, whenever we stayed up that late, that is. Most of the time it was on around 10:30, but it could be earlier or later, not unlike American TV in the early years. When it began depended on what had preceded it or how much news there was that day. The producers allowed as much time as necessary for what they considered news, which when you stop to think about it isn't a bad system. Unlike our way of doing things, they didn't have a set number of minutes to fill up or to squeeze the news into, apart from the commercials.

Of course what constitutes news has a different definition in that kind of society. In large part, the government only wants disseminated through both the media and the arts what will propagate the Party line and contribute to "developing socialism with Chinese characteristics." We heard that phrase over and over, in speech after speech.

Friends in the States occasionally enclosed political cartoons in their letters and I thought I would reciprocate. But the pickins' were pretty slim. There's the problem of language, first of all. The cartoons in the *China Daily* were bland and even when their topic was on the government, they were safe and self-serving. It was sort of an obvious "see how we can admit things aren't perfect here," but there wasn't the revealing incision of a Herblock or Mike Peters. It just illustrates once again that totalitarian governments don't have the capacity to laugh at themselves or tolerate anyone who does.

One cartoon that intrigued me depicted a black horse, with artist's brush and palette in hand, in front of a canvas on which the work in progress was a picture of a white horse. The caption read, "Some swear black is white." Hmmmm. That's what I thought the Chinese government specialized in. I remembered the story widely told about Deng Xiao Ping, who supposedly said, "White cat, black cat, what does it matter as long as it catches the mouse." Some officials in the government thought Deng's policies and reforms smacked too much of capitalism. I wondered if the cartoon's meaning was connected in any way to that.

People in the States have often complained about the predominance of bad news in the media. TV news has taken on many aspects of entertainment these days, and some years ago the idea of "happy talk" was introduced, particularly at the end of newscasts.

Well, the complainers ought to go to China. Although we could only guess the content of the story at the end of the Chinese news, we could tell that happy talk is also a practice in China. The last shots of the news readers always showed smiling faces.

And those complainers would love the *China Daily*. It *really* puts on a happy face. Here are some sample headlines: "Li: Leadership is Sound and Stable"; "Output Up in Rural Industry"; "China Sees Progress in Foreign Affairs"; Good Time Ahead for West China"; "Retail Sales Climb in the First Two Months"; "Energy Production on the Rise"; "Minorities Enjoy Better Housing." And those were chosen from just two issues.

One day in class I mentioned the chronic complaint of the American public that the newspapers were full of nothing but bad news. I read students the headlines from a recent issue of the *China Daily*. I said I wondered if they knew how lucky they were to live in a country where the news was always good. Although they remained silent, knowing smiles spread throughout the room.

Many of Don's students were not so reticent. If he cited the *China Daily* as his source for something, students scoffed and said, "Don't you know you can't believe anything you read in that? Just assume the opposite and you'll be closer to the truth."

The news wasn't always positive, though, and there were reports of official corruption, unemployment, hunger, and school dropouts. I assumed that information was probably reliable up to a point because while the government may not have admitted the full extent of a problem, officials were not likely to have exaggerated the facts they did divulge. Therefore, when the news media said government officials had been convicted of taking bribes, or accused of reporting inflated data, I figured they probably had the goods on them. I doubt if it could be in their interest to admit government officials were not the upright model citizens the socialist system was supposed to produce. Or that there was unemployment in a society dedicated to full employment.

We seldom watched daytime television, but we were surprised one afternoon in the spring to turn on TV and see a news conference taking place, with Premier Li Peng front and center. The Eighth National People's Congress had ended, and so the event was a report to the nation about that. Li and other officials were seated at a long table, Li's interpreter to his left. A large room was filled with reporters, some Westerners among them. We had not seen anything like this before, although I learned later that the first press conference was held about the time Chinese and American diplomatic relations were restored in 1979.

I mentioned to students the next day that we had watched it and asked if such press conferences were held often. They immediately said yes, they were held at the end of each National People's Conference—every five years. I remembered past complaints of American reporters and the public when American presidents have avoided press conferences for several months.

The questions from Chinese reporters were the kind American presidents would love to get—soft questions seeking information about policies. But those from Western reporters—among them *Le Monde, Die Welt, Christian Science Monitor*, VOA, and *The Washington Post*—were not so kind.

The *Christian Science Monitor* reporter (a Chinese-American) asked Li Peng why, when he had promised the student protesters in Beijing in May 1989 that they would not be punished, he had broken his word. He asked if clemency were not in order.

Li said the students had broken the law, and that besides, the judiciary was independent, and it had been their decision, not the government's.

The Washington Post reporter, also a Chinese-American, asked when the government was going to publish the number and names of students killed. Li replied that the government would be willing to do that but that the families of the students did not want their names to be made public.

The most abrasive question came from the VOA reporter who asked Li if he was proud that a Chinese film, *Ju Dou*, was nominated for an Academy Award and why that and other Chinese films were not shown within China. Was it because the government did not feel that Chinese are mature enough to decide for themselves whether a film was good or not? My journalist son John would probably consider that a good question, but I cringed a little. It seemed impolite, insulting of one's host. It's one thing to ask questions like that of one's own politicians. But, then, I'm not a journalist. Being too polite probably would yield pretty unproductive interviews. Li said he had not seen the film and the decision was made by the Ministry of Radio, Film, and Television.

I first heard about the film from the VOA. The first part of March, it was announced that *Ju Dou* had been nominated for an Academy Award for the best foreign film award. The film had already won an award at Cannes, but the Chinese government asked that it be withdrawn for consideration by the Academy.

The Gang of Four may be long gone, but this attempt says much about the state of the arts in China. Repression is not dead. Films are the most effective way to reach people, and Li Peng said in his response that the government wants more films that promote socialist values. We heard that refrain over and over in the year we were in China, and it is a stock answer that can be applied to every question. Ideology is the key to everything.

Ju Dou, set in the twenties, is a rather dark story that does not show China to good advantage. A Chinese writer who had seen the film was quoted in *The New York Times* as saying, "*Ju Dou* leaves one with a sense of tragedy, of sadness. The Government doesn't like unhappy films."

Ju Dou received Japanese financing, and at the time of the nomination, the China Film Bureau was considering stricter guidelines for films made with foreign cooperation. It will not tolerate extremely antitraditional films or ones that portray the backwardness of China to the rest of the world. The Film Bureau director emphasized that China's film coproduction should advocate patriotism and internationalism.

It just so happened that an assignment in the doctoral class that morning was to report a news item. I mentioned the controversy over *Ju Dou* as *my* news item for the day. The students seemed interested and between classes asked for more information. Those students in my classes interested in film found Chinese films boring. Not long after, my nephew sent an article about *Ju Dou* from *The New York Times*.

He also sent an article about a Taiwanese pop singer who is very popular in China, more even than at home. Her song, "Follow Your Feelings," was a big hit at the time of the Tiananmen Square democracy movement. The government shortly after that quietly banned it. The lyrics are hardly incendiary, but compared to such socially approved songs as "Follow the Communist Party" and "Socialism Is Good" and "Nightsoil Collectors Coming Down the Mountain," the idea of following your feelings is pretty subversive.

The New York Times article cited a Taiwanese film, *Mom, Love Me Again*, that bombed in Taiwan but was a spectacular success on the mainland. The author said that "some people in Taiwan sniff that this is because mainland Chinese are unsophisticated and are content with very simple and sentimental themes." That is probably very true. Several of our Chinese acquaintances spoke nostalgically about *The Sound of Music*, *Crocodile Dundee*, and even Shirley Temple films—no kidding.

The whole country was agog during the fall of 1990, when a program called "Expectations," the nation's first soap opera, hit the TV screens.

According to polls, ninety-five percent of Beijingers watched the show, and when it was shown in other parts of the country, it gained a large audience, also. I first learned about it from Mr. Jiang, a student from Beijing.

During Free Talk he mentioned a public opinion survey that had been taken in Beijing shortly before in which people were asked what three things they were most proud of in Beijing in 1990. He asked fellow students to guess the choices. Most everyone guessed the Asian Games for one, which had gone on for nineteen days in September and attracted worldwide attention. That was not even one of the three but what was, which surprised them even further, was the aforementioned soap opera, which was set in Beijing.

Since the program could then be seen in Chengdu, other students were enthusiastic about it as well. Mr. Jiang explained that he liked the program because it depicted a loving family and that society had become so materialistic he thought a program that portrayed those values was good for the country.

I was particularly interested then when *China Daily* a short time later carried an article titled, "Beijing Soap Opera Kicks Off Hot Debate." The program, described as a "tearjerker," was about "a kind-hearted worker, Liu, divorced by her self-centered husband with an intellectual background." The *People's Daily* praised the program, seeing it as "having a significant morally educative effect" and saying it amounted to an "ode to traditional virtue and as a kind of interpersonal relationship that should be advocated." In other words, women should watch Liu, and then go and do likewise.

Well, not everyone was buying it. Forums were held in several major cities in which critics, sociologists, and women's movement activists met and discussed what the drama reflected and some of its implications. The criticisms of all groups seemed to include the opinion that Liu was conceived by men with the intention of creating the image of an ideal wife. Many saw it as raising the conflict between traditional and contemporary ideas of women.

And, indeed, it was five men who had conceived the program. Their defense was that since it was the first soap opera, they felt it had to be a tearjerker and they wanted the female character to be a "symbol of China's traditional virtue and possess what most Chinese consider to be all the merits of a woman."

While the show obviously had its critics, it also struck a very responsive chord in the hearts of Chinese people. But the criticisms that were raised, even by men—that the tendency to expect a woman to be wholly virtuous and willing to sacrifice herself totally to her family was outdated—could have been voiced in dozens of other countries around the globe.

33

When we first came to China, I was surprised and impressed at how much housework the men did. Many male professors and married male students said that they did most of the cooking and marketing in their households. Since there are so many women in what have been non-traditional jobs in the West, it seemed there was real equality. Just the fact that there were many women engineers and geologists was striking. Most of the doctors and dentists in the hospitals we encountered were women. However, as had been the case in other Communist countries, those professions do not have the prestige that they have in the United States. Of course, when professions or occupations in the United States have become primarily populated by women, they decline in status and income also, so that should not be too surprising. Teachers and secretaries are prime examples.

Women on campus who were candid admitted that they are limited in the progress they can make. The "glass ceiling" also exists in China. One man said his wife received the highest score in the postgraduate entrance exam at another college but was passed over by three men. The college evidently did not want more women in geology, which is ironic since someone else assigned her to geology in the first place. Happily she had another chance.

A survey of women in Beijing and Guangzhou in 1990 by municipal women's federations found that respondents listed their two top problems as sex discrimination and having no say in their choice of job. A government report said that some units set much higher standards for women than men in recruiting new employees. Almost ninety-seven percent of women in Beijing and ninety-one percent in Guangzhou said it was hard for them to find jobs.

One male doctoral student, a young teacher, claimed that women teachers were lazy, partly because they were so tired from doing housework and taking care of the children—or in this case, child, since the population policy does not allow more than one child. The student saw no irony in his statement. He had stated previously in class that his wife was lazy and he evidently extended that judgment—assuming it was valid—to all women. (He, incidentally, was the laziest student in the doctoral class, in that his assignments were often late or not done at all and he was often tardy.) He always spoke about how busy he was. As a petroleum geologist, he could do research in his department for extra money. That department was the recipient of many contracts from oil fields and from the government and so those students had an opportunity to make extra money that some of the others didn't. (His classmates constantly made jibes about that, but if there was resentment in the others' teasing, I couldn't detect it.)

The underlying attitudes toward women are reflected too in parenting, when men said they prefer a boy. Many of our students, both male and female, wrote about their pride when they became parents of a son. I sometimes told them that attitude was related to agricultural societies, when people needed farm hands and in the West when men wanted sons to carry on the family name. But in China today, women also carry their father's surname, since they do not take their husband's surname at marriage. Also, these were educated men who said this, not farmers or peasants, which makes it even more ironic.

Although current marriage law in China says that a child may take the name of either parent, most take the name of the father. The custom of women keeping their names began with the Communists. I asked what name women went by before. To my surprise, women in the countryside, at least, had no surnames. They were simply the property of the men in their families and therefore not worthy of a name.

The *China Daily* carried an article that criticized the sexist nature of certain advertising and the way in which women in general are used to promote and sell products in China. One example given was the use of dancing girls to advertise heavy machinery. The writer said TV ads should "inform potential customers and urge them to buy," but they should not denigrate women in the process.

A group of teachers and students in Beijing wrote a follow-up letter to the editor announcing that they were attempting to look objectively at TV advertisements for evidence of sexism. They were going to pay particular attention to the images and stereotypes used, acknowledging that they would have an impact on the way viewers perceive the female role in modern society.

As I wrote in a previous chapter, there was a great controversy in China over a soap opera that began airing in the fall of 1990, the first of its kind in China. While older people and those less educated gave the program a high approval rating, others, particularly feminists, did not.

They argued that the heroine was an unselfish, submissive woman who though she copes with a series of hardships admirably, brings most of those hardships on herself. In the eyes of one critic, the heroine was simply a "weak-kneed, wimpish do-gooder." Another criticism was that most of the men in the show have the strong roles and all the other women—those who are "modern"—are portrayed as being arrogant and not very nice. Another reviewer accused the screenwriters of implying that unselfish and lenient women cannot achieve career fulfillment and that career-oriented women have to be disdainful and cold-hearted.

Nevertheless, the consensus seemed to be that the show sent a message to women that they should assume the nature of the traditional woman: devoted to her family to the exclusion of her own wishes and submissive to males.

One day in class I talked about attitudes toward women as representing a kind of cultural lag. The government had decreed after Liberation that women were to be equal. (Women had indeed fought alongside men to achieve Liberation, several of them, including the wives of Mao and Chou EnLai, on the Long March.) And women had moved into many of the professions. But that is not to say that public attitudes were changed.

Two students said that their wives had trouble getting jobs after graduation because the director of the units to which they had been assigned did not like to hire women. The government assigns women to their universities and dictates their majors, but the system breaks down when it is time for a job assignment. Unit heads refuse to take them or if they employ women, they give them a hard time, so that the women do everything they can to leave. Maybe that's the intention.

One of those same husbands who was due to become a father soon said he didn't care whether the baby was a girl or boy. But then, to me, smiling a little, he said that *in China* people preferred to have boys . . . and all but admitted that he too thought that would be nice. That was when I discussed and explained "cultural lag" and said that all the fathers of daughters ought to be concerned about this situation, too. Didn't they want their daughters to have an equal chance in life? How would they feel if their daughters had to take a back seat to a mediocre man?

One student said his wife was assigned to a unit downtown but that she wasn't wanted. Since she was a graduate of the College of Geology, she appealed to the college to take her back. It took the help of a half-dozen people at the college and about three months to make it happen. (If someone is unemployed, a student's alma mater is responsible for employing him or her.)

An auditor in the class, a library science major and graduate of another school in the spring of 1989, said that because of the student protest movement that spring no grads were assigned to government offices (libraries would be public). She was assigned to the Cultural Bureau in Chengdu, with the Sichuan Foreign Affairs Department. Her boss, however, did not want her, and did not like women, as workers anyway. She was miserable. Her parents helped her to get another job downtown where she worked four hours a day several days a week, but not as a librarian. A classic case of underemployment.

After I was in China for a while and observed Chinese students, it occurred to me one day that what Chinese women needed was an intensive course in assertiveness. Chinese young women fit the profile of a nonassertive person to a T. They are so nonassertive that I found it very unnatural to refer to them as "women." Most young Chinese men are hardly models of self-confidence and poise, either, but the young women are even less so.

That insight came to me when we were talking about the disinclination of employers to hire women in their geological units. I asked Miss Peng, the only other woman in the class that day what she thought of all that. She, with a coy sidelong glance at the men and a little toss of her head, said she thought she could get a job but probably not a very good job. She is attractive, dresses becomingly, and has a soft voice. I was constantly asking her to speak up.

Observing her behavior, I realized that all her nonverbal behavior discounted her words and that whatever professional competence she had would be undercut by her nonassertive manner. Although Chinese men also have some of these same characteristics, many Chinese women giggle, look down, seem to seek others' approval before speaking, and barely speak above a whisper. Some of it has to do with being unsure of their English skills, but not all. I wondered what they were like at fifteen if they were like this at twenty-two.

In the past fifteen years, I had conducted a number of workshops on assertiveness for women and included assertiveness training also as a regular part of the interpersonal communications course I taught. I had seen it help a lot of students of all ages, both men and women, to improve their self-concept, raise their self-esteem, and gain confidence.

I wondered what Chengdu's college deans would think if I started giving students assertiveness training. That probably would be labeled counterrevolutionary activity for sure.

Then again, I think about how disarming and spontaneous and guileless the Chinese are and I think it would be a shame to spoil that innocence. Assertiveness training would certainly affect their future relationships. As is, they're like delightful children. But, in the world of market economies and technological advance and fax machines, who's going to pay any attention to children?

It was never spelled out very clearly; but we thought Emily was in charge of the Foreign Affairs Office, which only shortly before we left had been raised to the status of a department. The staff included five men and one woman, besides her. Emily was a pretty assertive person, and seemingly dealt effectively with male peers. She appeared to relate well to the staff and was able to get things done. I was curious about how she managed and how she felt about such things.

When an opportunity arose, I asked, "I don't know for sure who is in charge of the Waiban. Is it you?"

She stalled and said, "We're all in charge. I'm really not the boss."

"But," I said, "someone finally has to make decisions and who does that?"

She finally admitted that she was in charge. What was particularly ironic is that although she didn't feel comfortable with or support the idea of strong women, she was anything but submissive by nature. She led by the force of her personality.

Newspaper reports shed light on the generally troubled and uncertain status of women in the country at large. Illiterate women number some 126 million, making up more than sixty percent of China's 180 million illiterate population. Women comprise thirty-seven percent of the total work force in China, and special commissions in major industries have been established to oversee protection of women in the workplace. A survey, however, showed that implementation of the regulations is lax. Providing for nursing periods for new mothers and the lack of such basics as toilets at rest places on bus routes for drivers are examples.

A much grimmer and growing problem is the kidnapping of women. Particularly alarming is news that networks of slave traders are terrorizing rural areas. In two provinces alone, in 1990, police rescued ten thousand women who had been sold into slavery. According to a

Chinese government report, gangs select their victims from among pretty shop girls, student dropouts, and rural women traveling alone. Farmers, for example, who live alone in isolated mountainous areas will pay a high price for a wife.

I saw television dramatizations on the subject attempting to make the public aware of the extent of the problem and acquainting unsuspecting young women with how they might be approached. Sometimes police have a hard time in rural areas getting the cooperation of unsympathetic neighbors in rescuing the woman because the neighbors feel a farmer has paid good money for his bride.

People we talked with, some sensitive students among them, were distressed about the growth of materialism and how even that was having an impact on women. The divorce rate is increasing rapidly in China, something that was relatively rare before the 1980's. This too is probably a consequence of the reforms begun in 1979. Although both sexes are rejecting their mates, more men than women initiate divorce in favor of someone with greater earning power or more status.

In China women are often referred to as "Half of the Sky," but in spite of the constitution which grants them equal status, one of my female students felt that women have to hold up more than their half. The Communist Party may have decreed that women are equal but old attitudes and traditions die hard.

34

When the weather warmed, we caught spring fever. If I wrote even one letter, I walked to the campus post office to mail it just for an excuse to be out. There was a deck at the other end of the hall on our floor that extended over the restaurant and conference rooms. The house staff hung the laundry there, but mostly it was a quiet little retreat in the open air. One afternoon when the sun shone, Don carried books and papers down there, took off his shirt, and did his school work in the fresh air among flapping sheets.

Sitting on the balcony outside our apartment, occasionally, was also appealing. Monique and Melinda, who lived downstairs, also made it a regular practice. Over the past few weeks, they had continued to make disparaging remarks about the Orange Dragon, and Don decided to avenge the little fellow.

One Saturday afternoon when M & M were perched on the banister one floor below us, Don tied a clothesline around the dog's neck and swung it in a high wide arc, so that it swooped down past them like an orange meteorite. Screams rent the sky, followed by laughter. This harassment was repeated a few days later, but this time the pooch came a little too close and Monique grabbed the small gold chain that adorned his neck.

Fifteen minutes later a loud knock sounded at the door. Outside was an empty beer bottle with a note attached from POOCH—Protection Organization Opposed to Canine Harassment. Not the most logical appeal, but we gave them credit for being quick on the uptake. The note demanded a ransom.

Two hours later another thunderous knock at the door. A small poster, lettered with magazine and newspaper letters, carried a menacing message:

> The target is fixed. Your dog is facing a bleak future. The mutt WILL be captured . . . plagued by injuries . . . receive violence . . . unless you meet our demands for the jewelry, we'll make a run for the canine. We know you do not have insurance for your loss. . . . Learn the way to play. No stoic resistance. No mediators. Don't call the police or the dog will be massacred. Cash deals only. How much money? Save a good supply of hard currency. Transfer all securities and $3 of personal savings into foreign banks.
> Warning: Do not try to contact POOCH for any information!

We hooted and howled. Then it was our turn.

I called up the Print Shop program on the computer and went to work. We proclaimed ourselves the Moral Minority: we would not yield to intimidation, fear, or bribery. Right and Virtue were on our side.

Adding a postscript, however, we offered to sell the pooch.

The next note, also taped to an empty beer bottle (there seemed to be no lack of beer bottles), was equally intransigent. They were out to get the mutt.

We knew they had recently announced their intention to sign on for another year at the college, so the Moral Minority countered: Who's going to protect your valuables next year?

Arm yourself with the Orange Dragon—an environmentally safe, efficient, and economical security system.

Next round: The next morning Don waited by our window that overlooks the drive the two passed on their way to class. He shoved the Orange Dragon through the open window (three flights up) and barked ferociously at the unsuspecting Canadians below. They exploded with laughter, then continued on their way, while numerous Chinese in the vicinity peered curiously at the upper windows.

We wondered what their image was of us and how this juvenile display squared with their perception of these supposedly advanced wai-guoren that their nation had resolved they should learn from.

The Chinese were getting spring fever, too, as the weather warmed. The men, students and professors alike, broke out in shorts, even wearing them to class, but the women, never. Women wore shorts only on the playing field. In fact, the women, students and staff members alike, turned out in dressy summery dresses. Long gone were the days of the plain blue Mao jackets.

I began to be more observant about other things. When we were first in China I marveled at all those black heads, particularly when I was in a crowd. There were occasional white heads, but there seemed to be few in between. Seemingly Chinese did not gray as early as Westerners. I thought perhaps it was a racial difference or attributable to diet. I commented admiringly about this longevity of black hair color to a Chinese friend.

She laughed merrily and said, "Just look around you sometime when you are caught in a rainstorm."

People were evidently do-it-yourself dyers and didn't necessarily use the most professional products. I had just assumed that since most women didn't use cosmetics, they wouldn't dream of using hair color. I became a little more observant. I was still not really aware of women coloring their hair, but I began detecting some not-so-subtle touch-ups among the men. Occasionally, some underwent an overnight transformation. Maybe they were just not as skillful as the women.

Perhaps incongruities are more apparent in another people's culture. In China a marked contradiction for me is the widely reputed importance of the family, so much a part of Chinese centuries-old tradition, and the reality of what contemporary life has done to the family. It was not at all unusual for families to have to live apart for many years and from the beginning of the marriage to have only a short time together each year. Because the needs of the country came first, individuals were assigned to work where the government thought they were most needed.

Before we went to China, I learned of a Chinese man, a teacher, who was visiting his wife at a Texas university where she was working as a visiting scholar for two years. After his visit there, he was going to go to Chicago to visit his daughter whose husband was in graduate school.

He was then going to visit another daughter who was in the United States as a student, before returning to China. I sympathized with the family's separation but learned that for them this was nothing new. The couple had never been able to live together in their entire married life. Obviously, those two daughters were conceived on holiday visits.

Our friends, the Hu's, had a similar story. When Jilin, a teacher, and Zhirong, a doctor, were married, they had to go separate ways. Jilin was teaching at the College of Geology and Zhirong had to go to the countryside. When their son was born, the boy lived with his maternal grandmother until he was seven. At that time, Jilin, who had been sharing a room with another teacher, was given a room of his own so that he could have his son with him.

A year later Zhirong was able to get an assignment at a local hospital and the college gave permission for her to live in Jilin's single room. It was the first time in the eleven years of their marriage that they lived together.

How do such situations arise? Since much of China is divided into work units and those units are in one sense little governments of their own, the employing unit controls not only everything pertaining to jobs but also to housing, medical treatment, ration cards, and a myriad other things. Therefore, it isn't only that one can not change a job without permission, but he can not get housing and many other things. Each factory, school, university, hospital, and business of any kind is a work unit with control over all those aspects of life.

Because both parents have to work to support the family and jobs may not have been near relatives, children were and are often reared by grandparents. Several of my students were reared by their grandparents and saw their parents only at Spring Festival.

One student, Mr. Liu, mentioned that he had never lived with his parents. In middle school, he began going to boarding school, and he was now in his fifth year of college. When he told about this, I could not hide my dismay. I asked him whether he felt closest to his parents or grandparents. He just smiled, a little embarrassed, and would not answer.

When we discussed the problem of family separation further, I said I thought it was very sad and it placed a great hardship on the marriage relationship, among other things. I asked students if they would be willing to have their parents raise their child. Mr. Liu shook his head no.

Chinese supposedly respect their elders and put great store by the family. Indeed students did talk and wrote frequently about their devotion to their parents and grandparents and I did not doubt their sincerity. What seemed to me contradictory or somehow inconsistent is that many husbands and wives did not seem to have a very close relationship. In response to a question about his wish for Christmas, Mr. Xi, one of my postgrads who was at the college without his family, spoke about how beautiful his three-year-old daughter was and how much he missed her. He said that he had never liked children until he became a father but now, for example, he noticed all the little children on campus. His wish to Santa Claus, in response to our little game, was that February were already here so he could see his little daughter sooner. When I teasingly asked if he also missed his wife, he quite matter-of-factly said he didn't miss her at all. Before he went home for that Spring Festival, he mentioned buying his daughter a couple of gifts. When I asked what he was taking his wife, he said, "Nothing."

One of Don's favorite students, respected by his classmates, wrote about his devotion to his eight-year-old daughter, and that his wife had said that if he had to choose between her or their daughter, he would probably choose his daughter. He didn't contradict her impression. When his wife came to the college as part of a business trip, we commented how nice that was, but he said he wanted her to hurry back home because their daughter was alone.

Although many couples seem devoted, perhaps part of the reason for the lack of warmth between some couples is that many have had little real choice over whom they married. One of the first pieces of legislation passed by the Communists, the Marriage Law, abolished concubinage, polygamy, and arranged marriages—all common by 1950. But traditions die hard. And even today, when young people, particularly in urban areas, demand the right to marry whom they please, their choices may be limited by circumstances. Because both custom and law have forced them to postpone consideration of marriage until their mid-twenties, speaking to someone they fancied may have been impossible. By the time they are in a position to speak, the person may already have been spoken for or be assigned to a work unit so far away that there is no way that they would ever be able to live together, at least for many years. The cost of transportation to see each other during their annual vacation would take all their savings and therefore they could never save enough money to get married or furnish a home. So, numerous practical considerations may actually have limited the field, and the final choice may have been a compromise or a resignation to fate. Some Chinese subscribe to the belief that love will grow and they hope for the best. Not exactly the stuff of which great romance is made, and yet Chinese legend and folklore is filled with stories of great romance. Several of Don's students wrote poignantly of not having been able to marry their true loves. Susan was typical when she said she was married to a good person and had a child, but she was still secretly in love with someone else.

Two of Don's students, Luke and Nina, a married couple, were in two different classes. Don did not even know they were married until we met them together at a party at a professor's home near the end of the first semester. They visited us the night before they left campus for Spring Festival, which they were going to spend with Luke's parents. Their six-year-old son was being raised by those grandparents, and they saw him only at these holiday times. After a few days they would visit Nina's parents and then Luke would go back to his unit to work and Nina would come back to the college to continue her English study. Even when Nina was not going to school, each worked for a different unit so that their little family was in three different locations.

Many student parents wrote about missing their families. Halfway through the spring semester, Nina mentioned that her mother-in-law had not written and so she had had no word of her son in all those weeks. Her roommate said that Nina often cried herself to sleep at night, lonesome for her son. Yet, to us she always seemed cheerful.

That afternoon after the morning barking incident, there was an ominous knock. Outside was another beer bottle with a note and a bouquet of pretty yellow flowers attached. The note read:

> Dear Ruth and Don,
> Thanks for dinner the other night. The quality of these flowers is no reflection of what we thought of the dinner. Yours until the food runs out, M & M.
> P.S. This has no bearing on the dog thing.

Although we met them at various times over the next few days, coming and going to class or at the Waiban getting the mail, we completely ignored "the dog thing." It was as if it had never happened.

The following Sunday, a group of American teachers we had met at church came out for a get-together, including hymn singing and Bible study. Monique and Melinda attended and left about the same time as everyone else, retreating to their apartment a floor below. As good hosts, Don and I went downstairs to the lobby to see the rest of our guests off and walked them part way to the bus stop.

When we got home, we found a note attached to the door. The

Orange Dragon had been kidnapped and the brownies left over from the afternoon refreshments were demanded as ransom. We were to leave them in an unmarked tin outside Room 207. Since the brownies were hard as rocks, a victim of my small Chinese oven, I didn't hesitate at the ransom. But I called up Print Shop for another message from the Moral Minority.

Since we had just spent the afternoon in Bible study, I decided to lay a guilt trip on them. The result was as follows, attached to a bottle of beer (and the brownies, of course): Matthew 5:44: Love your enemies. Do good to those who persecute you so you may become daughters of your father who is in heaven. Have one on us.

Pictures of doves bearing olive branches underscored the message.

I looked out the windows that lined our hall and saw M & M heading down the street. The coast was clear. I made the drop.

Half an hour later, there came a knock at the door. The Orange Dragon peeked its head around the door jamb, attached to an arm. Monique and Melinda followed, looking a little sheepish. We had obviously put the fear of the Lord into them, at least for the time being.

However, they still had the gold chain. We would have to even the score another day.

35

You can't be in China for long and not be aware of Chairman Mao. In fact, when we drove in from the airport that first night in Chengdu, we drove past a statue of Mao, which stands at the head of one of the city's main streets, Remnin Nan Lu, which means "The People's Street." He stands with arm outstretched in the pose known as "The Great Helmsman." Although many such statues were torn down after the Cultural Revolution, many still remain. We saw similar ones in several cities we visited. Mao may not be as prominent these days, but the statue still symbolizes the pervasive power and influence of the government over people's lives.

From what students said and wrote, I tried to piece together how they regarded Chairman Mao. One day the doctoral students had been assigned to tell about a person they admired. Although one student told about Victor Hugo, most spoke about Chinese patriots.

Mr. Lu spoke about Chairman Mao as a person he *used* to admire, with just that kind of emphasis. He said that when he was in elementary school, he was taught that Chairman Mao was the savior of the Chinese people, that all his speeches were "truth." As a school boy he must believe that. He told of a classmate who used words clipped from a newspaper to make a poster that said "Down With Chairman Mao." Even though the boy was ten years old, someone reported him to the police and he was arrested.

Mr. Lu admitted that if he had said then the things he was saying in class, he would have been arrested. He said that after 1978 people said that Mao had made mistakes, but he was a good leader. Lu challenged that claim. For one example, he pointed out that when Professor Ma, president of Beijing University, proposed a policy to limit the family to two children, he had been deposed by Mao, who thought the more people the better. That is partly the reason for the country's enormous population.

I asked students if they had ever heard of Thomas Malthus, the nineteenth-century British economist who said poverty and famine were unavoidable because population increased faster than the means of subsistence (geometrically instead of arithmetically). They said that they had and that Professor Ma was influenced by him. (In fact, that was probably his downfall. For Mao, Western ideas and people who espoused them were immediately suspect.)

Mr. Lu also said it was too bad that Mao did not die sooner or was not removed from power earlier. A few others agreed. Lu said he did not agree with those who thought Mao had been a good leader or good for the country. He said he preferred leaders who were concerned about civil rights like Martin Luther King and scientists like Einstein, and that he was glad when Mao died.

Since that happened only about halfway through the first semester, I didn't realize what a gutsy thing Mr. Lu had done in speaking up. No one else for the entire year was so candid in class in front of others and deliberately so. While some did agree with certain things Xiao Lu said, you could tell by their manner that this was not the usual class discussion. They laughed a little nervously and were obviously uncomfortable at times.

Mr. Jiang disagreed to an extent. He was still in the countryside when Mao died, since the Cultural Revolution was still going on, and he said he felt bad. He said he admired him as a poet and for his humanity. He does not admire the leaders now, believing they are too concerned with power.

Although we went on with other reports that day, an interesting addendum was made to that discussion a few days later. Mr. Xu, who had been absent when Mr. Lu spoke about Chairman Mao, also gave his talk on Mao. Although the students and I exchanged knowing looks when he announced his topic, we didn't tell him we had already had a report on Mao. He proceeded to give a brief biography of Mao's life. He told of his three wives and children and his poetry, in addition to his military and political record. He concluded that some people said he had made some mistakes and seemed to concede that, but he still thought he was a great man. A far different report than Mr. Lu's.

In the discussion that followed, I asked what were considered "mistakes." Mr. Xu said Mao's population policy was a mistake. He cited Professor Ma's warning and proposal concerning population growth and cited Malthus' theory. He explained Mao's position about the more children the better, and that that had now caught up with them. He also referred to the Cultural Revolution as a mistake. In his explanations he seemed to give these opinions as his own.

In an attempt to summarize what he had said, I asked if he thought Mao had been a good leader in the beginning but that later he had not. He said yes, that some people said it was too bad he wasn't replaced or that he didn't die sooner. I asked when he thought Mao had stopped being effective, and he placed it in the late 1950's.

Considering that Mao lived almost twenty years longer and is acknowledged to be responsible for the Cultural Revolution, his conclusions that he stated in the beginning—that Mao was a great man—seemed to be contradictory. But, I didn't challenge it. Most students agreed with his criticisms and offered others, but not all agreed with his conclusions. I don't know whether they didn't see any lack of logic, or whether they were still afraid to be too outspokenly critical.

Although students were more frank as the semester progressed and sometimes surprised me with their views, there was still a lot of vacillation. At times they would be spontaneous and forthright, voicing criticism. Later, even on the same or a similar topic, they wouldn't open their mouths. There have been so many different movements over the years, when openness has been followed by oppression, that they were still apprehensive about speaking up, particularly in front of others they didn't know well. Characteristically, when a student said something the least bit political, he or she would glance at others to gauge their reaction or laugh to soften a criticism.

There did seem to be consensus that current Chinese leaders were more concerned with maintaining their own power, although if they knew more about Mao's life, I wonder if that would hold up.

I thought of George Orwell's *Animal Farm*. Orwell, himself a British socialist, wrote about a revolution that starts out with the best of intentions, but which fails because the leaders succumb to the allure of power. The book, which Orwell called a fairy tale, is an entertaining and simple, but nevertheless brilliant, analysis of a revolution. What good discussions we could have had if only I could have used it in China.

The Party propaganda apparatus does obviously recognize the need to provide heroic figures to inspire the masses. Sometimes it works and sometimes it doesn't. Some of the ploys are an insult to people's intelligence.

One Sunday we had been downtown until late afternoon. After we returned home, we saw many people coming across the bridge, back toward the campus, carrying big loads of furniture on bicycle carts. The loads consisted of bookcases, desks, stools, and other items. Evidently there had been a great deal of activity in the market and housing area, and I was curious.

The next morning in class I described what I had seen. At first no one seemed to know what I was talking about. Then, little by little they told me it had been Lei Feng Day. Supposedly Lei Feng was a People's Liberation Army (PLA) soldier who had gone to extraordinary lengths in his service to the people. He was hailed for countless unselfish acts that came to light only after an unfortunate accident that killed him. Mao had heard about his exploits and held him up as an example for all. His diary was published, detailing his heroic deeds and his story spread far and wide.

That Sunday at the college had been devoted to people offering some service or performing some deed free of charge to the people as Lei Feng had done. People set up shop to tutor children, cut hair, sew on buttons, repair appliances and bicycles, and so forth, freely sharing their talents and abilities.

The students reported all of this with sincerity and seeming admiration. Later, when I gave an assignment for them to tell about someone they admired, a couple of students reported on Lei Feng and confessed that they tried to model their lives after his.

All of that sounds quite impressive, and I was impressed. What I later learned, however, is that the Lei Feng story is an invention of the propaganda agency. Many Chinese know this and are openly scornful, but I don't know whether my students knew it. If they did, they evidently thought it safer to go along with the ruse. Whether or not such a person ever existed, there are too many inconsistencies and incongruities for the story as circulated to the masses to be true. The story has even been updated to make him more relevant to young people in the 1990's.

One night the doctoral students had to cut short our conversation session at the apartment. They left after less than an hour because they were going to the theater to see a film for which everyone at the college had been given a ticket. There were continuous showings of the film, which was about Zhoau Ya Lin, who had been general secretary of a county in Henan province. The province was extremely poor; the river flooded frequently, the water was salty, the soil very poor, and the people had little to eat. Zhoau took great pity on the people, went out into the province to see their problems, and did what he could to help. He worked long hours and died at the age of forty-three after only eighteen months in office. He won the respect of the people.

A few people grumbled about the command performance aspects of the showing of the film, another political propaganda piece. But the next morning in class when I asked for a summary, everyone spoke in admiring terms of the man and one student said he shed many tears while watching it. Mr. Liu said that he was a leader people could respect but, in effect, that leaders at the present were not so selfless. I told them that was a cry that many people in the world could make about their leaders today; that leaders were more interested in getting reelected and staying in power than doing the kinds of things that would be best for people or their country in the long run.

Everyone in the room seemed to acknowledge the importance of selfless leaders and to express regret that there were so few. Once again, however, I wondered whether they really admired Zhoau Ya Lin, or if they were saying only what was expected in front of their peers.

From written assignments to class discussions to Free Talk sessions, I encouraged students to tell me about their country. This served a number of purposes. They could talk best and easiest about things they knew, and I was genuinely interested in learning about China.

I had done some homework before we left the States, but there was much to learn. The students genuinely appreciated what I did know about their country, and at times I knew more than I let on, but I wanted to get their views of events. I have studied much more since coming home. What amazes me, looking back, is how much they did know about what went on at various times, in spite of government attempts to withhold information.

For example, Mao lost confidence in and distrusted his handpicked successor, Lin Biao. When Lin realized his predicament, he supposedly tried to assassinate Mao. Failing in his attempt, he stole a plane and tried to escape to Moscow. The plane crashed, killing everyone aboard. Although it has never been acknowledged by the government, when students told me about this, they were frank in saying the plane was sabotaged. Some claimed that Lin Biao was even dead before the plane took off.

Zhao Ziyang was General Secretary of the Party, the highest office, until the events in Tiananmen Square. He was removed from his post, having invoked Deng's wrath, and made the scapegoat for those events. He angered Deng because he told Soviet Premier Mikhail Gorbachev, who was visiting, that Deng had a veto on everything (which students were aware of, also). Even though it was true, he was banished because he told a "family secret." When I asked in class if Zhao Ziyang were in prison, one student said he was living quietly in his house and playing golf. When I expressed surprise, the student said Zhao probably would be brought back into the government again in the future.

The other students did not disagree.

The government may control the press but it is unable to squelch all information.

36

"Tomorrow your assignment is to explain to me how your government works. I listen to the China television's English news program regularly and I've read *China Daily* for the last eight months, but I still don't understand the structure of your government. When we're finished, I want to be able to draw an organizational chart, in the same way I drew one for you when I explained the American form of government."

That was my charge to the doctoral students one morning. Students sensed my genuine interest in their country and I often only half-facetiously told my classes that when we went home we would be expected to be China experts and that they were responsible for my Chinese education.

The next day I opened the topic and stood expectantly at the blackboard. We got off to a slow start. When someone began, mentioning the Central Government, the National People's Congress (NPC), the State Council, the Central Military Commission, and their relationship, others immediately challenged his statements.

When I attempted to make an organizational chart, asking who was answerable to whom, the discussion dissolved into a half dozen separate intense conversations at high volume. The students could not agree on the relationship or the power structure of various arms of government such as the various ministries.

After some minutes they agreed that the NPC was the legislative body and that the Central Government was the administrative arm of the NPC. They agreed also that the ministries were the agencies which carried out the policies decided by the NPC.

"But where does the State Council fit in here? And who sits on it? And how about the military? And the judicial system, the Supreme Court, which you say is independent? How did Li Peng and Jiang Zemin and others get their positions? What determines how long they keep them?"

Again, they argued among themselves. There was no consensus. And they hadn't answered the biggest question of all. "Where does the Communist Party fit into all this?"

Mr. Wei said, "They're equal to the NPC."

Mr. Tang, who had disagreed from the beginning but had remained still during all the others' discussion, broke his silence. With some finality he said, "There are three separate systems: the Party, the NPC, and the government, but the Party dominates everything."

No one challenged his conclusion. When I said, as the class drew to a close, that I still wasn't sure I understood, that I was still confused, they said they didn't understand, either. They promised to continue the discussion that night during our conversation session.

That night, Chang Shugun announced he had talked with some people in the college political office—that was the first I knew there was one—and had brought a reference book.

He attempted to explain the relationship of many of the pertinent bodies. I followed as best I could. I wished I could take notes or that I had a tape recorder, but it wasn't appropriate.

What I learned from those sessions was how complex the government of the People's Republic is and that even with all their political studies, the students still have difficulty grasping it. But while I still didn't understand the workings of the government, I *was* beginning to grasp the extent to which the Party indeed controlled everything in the country. The General Secretary, Jiang Zemin, was indeed top dog. Jiang has recently assumed the presidency as well, an office that has been largely ceremonial.

The students mentioned later that evening that Deng Xiao Ping had studied and done a lot of writing about the American form of government (as well as others) and that he didn't want the same kind of government because he didn't want capitalism. I pointed out that I didn't think that was relevant since the form of government was a political system and capitalism and socialism were economic systems. After all, many European nations had a high degree of socialism but still had democratic political systems. The students seemed a little surprised to hear that. Few systems were pure forms of anything, and certainly not China's, though I did not say the latter.

Even before we went to China, Chinese people we met in the United States talked about the "political studies," which everyone had to attend at his or her place of work. There is renewed emphasis on this since Tiananmen Square. The government's conclusion was that indoctrination of the youth had not been effective enough and "politics" as a bona fide course had to be strengthened. (Of course, the history of China since 1949 has been one kind of campaign after another at various intervals so this isn't really all that new).

At present, at regular intervals, employees in China have to engage in political studies. At the college employees of every stripe, be they professors or clerks, meet in their departments several Saturdays a month. When discussing tentative plans for the weekend, staff members at the college mentioned that they would have to attend political studies on Saturday afternoon. The meetings consisted of individual reading time or separate little conversation groups going on while someone read aloud to them from an official publication. If no one "official" was present or in charge, there was never even any pretense of carrying out what was expected. Staff members felt comfortable discussing personal matters or even criticizing the Party.

One particular Saturday, people were given the option of going to their department office or staying at home to view a film on socialism versus capitalism. Whether the faithful actually did watch the political film or switched channels was probably never known, but the film reportedly stated that thirty million people in the United States lived below the government's poverty line, thus proving the failure of capitalism. Never mind that the *China Daily* had run numerous articles citing the number of Chinese farmers and others whose incomes were below the Chinese poverty line.

One day one of the doctoral students in the fall semester class came early to afternoon conversation. He said he wanted to explain that from the time students took the entrance examination for college at the end of high school, they were faced with political questions. Regardless of the score on the entrance exam, it was important to answer those political questions to the satisfaction of the examiners if they were to be allowed the opportunity to study further. The same was true of succeeding levels of study.

When I asked about the doctoral exam, he said it was also true of that. He knew of a student who had passed the exam, hoping to begin study with the spring semester class. But because of things the person was known to have said, he had not been accepted in the program. It seemed important to my student that I know this.

One Saturday afternoon I ran into a young man from the Waiban. I asked if he were headed home. He said no, that he had something to do in the office. I asked if they were having political studies. He hesitated, perhaps surprised that I knew about the studies, but then said yes quite decidedly. He said they had to read a report, written by a high official in the Communist Party. He said rather heatedly that he didn't like it because Saturday and Sunday ought to be his, but that he and his colleagues always had to do some reading, or other things. I was surprised at his candor and said quite matter-of-factly that I knew that many others on the staff complained about the same thing. I merely indicated I was aware and was sympathetic. I think if I had initiated criticism, it would have backfired or people would have clammed up out of fear, conditioned over a lifetime.

Rich, the young man who had preceded us at the college and taught some of the same classes, mentioned that he had been censured for political comments he had made in class. We felt relatively free of monitoring. We hadn't had any undue sense of being watched or scrutinized, although several unannounced visits to my classes were a little disconcerting. Whenever my department head at home had observed my classes, I was usually told about it in advance.

Soon after classes started in the fall, Mr. He, from Foreign Affairs, had unexpectedly visited my class one morning. He evidently pronounced me acceptable. Young Mr. Li, who worked in the postgraduate department, was the doctoral class monitor and had sat in on my class the first few weeks. It was not until later that I realized his purpose and that he was not even a doctoral student. I thought he, like others, was merely auditing the class and wanted to improve his English. I only realized later that all the postgraduate classes included their own monitors who were, I'm sure, reporting on what was going on in class. And when I say reporting, I mean to the political office, read *Party*, not the Foreign Language Department.

I had one situation, however, that made me very uncomfortable at the time. I had auditors in all my classes, but more in the doctoral classes. In fact, there were as many auditors in the second semester doctoral class as there were students, partly because some of the first semester students continued to come. I had to give permission for the auditors to attend the class, and I found it hard to say no to students who so desperately wanted to learn. That is an experience few teachers have had or can resist. Supposedly it was up to the teacher. The class was still only about twelve in number, and I thought the students could all learn from each other. The first semester class had not seemed to mind. However, in the second semester, Mr. Kong, our Foreign Language Department liaison, mentioned that one of the students had contacted him about the large number of auditors, which gave me a clue that all were not happy.

Then one morning I walked in a little later than usual and found that Mr. Li, the postgraduate monitor, was back, sitting among the auditors. I sensed by the rather strained, half-embarrassed smiles that this was an "official" visit. I sensed also it might be better if I did not include the auditors in the discussion that day.

Mr. Li left during the break without a word to me. I asked the auditors to stay afterward and tell me what was happening. They said they would have to get permission from Mr. Liu, the head of the postgraduate department, to continue.

The frustrating thing was that no one had ever spelled out to me clearly whether I was to allow auditors in, and if so, how I was to treat them. I, as the teacher, had been ignored and kept in the dark. The auditors were a little embarrassed by the proceedings and for me as well. They didn't know whether they would be back or not. I vowed to talk with Mr. Kong and try to find out what was going on.

This seemed to go along with a recent discussion in class about Japanese and Chinese culture—that the Eastern way is indirect, which is very frustrating to Westerners. It seems not only secretive, but downright sneaky. I wondered if I dared go so far as to say that and give what happened in class that day as an example of cultural differences. Why couldn't someone have contacted me directly about this? I decided to wait to see what developed.

As it happened, only a few auditors received permission to stay. None of last term's doctoral students even applied, and on hindsight I realized that it had been a mistake to allow them to stay because they were perceived as a threat to the new doctoral students. But again, that would have been better decided by the department ahead of time.

A week later, after the five-minute break, we had just resumed class when the door opened and in came a middle-aged man I hadn't seen before. He nodded to a couple of the students but ignored me and headed for a back seat. I looked questioningly at a student in front of me and he whispered that the man was—he searched for a word—a monitor from the postgraduate department. Since the man had not acknowledged my presence, I took my cue from him and ignored him as well. I proceeded to lead a discussion about an article on robots. The class sprang into action, and a very lively discussion followed. I thought at first he was probably there to monitor me, especially after the auditor issue had surfaced. When even Mr. He, who usually spoke only when spoken to, also jumped in, volunteering several comments, I began to suspect the nature of the visit. I had voiced some reservations to Mr. Kong about whether Mr. He, who was repeating the class, and not participating very much, would be able to pass even after a second semester. Whether the purpose of the visit was to observe Mr. He at close range or not, he too must have suspected it was.

When class was over, everyone including the visitor filed out, the visitor still not so much as nodding in my direction. When I asked a student exactly who he was and mentioned that he hadn't spoken to me, the student said he didn't speak any English. Here I had been inwardly gloating about how good the students were making me look with their animated discussion. What a letdown.

Nevertheless, I resented his not even looking my way, not to mention giving me a nod or a smile. Even if he didn't speak English, a smile carries a universal message.

Imagine our surprise when after being on campus for about nine months we learned that we were supposed to have all videos shown to students approved first by the Political Office on campus. For several weeks we had been getting videos down at the American consulate. The monitoring was evidently standard procedure, but no one had ever told us. I found out about it in a rather casual way, as often seemed to be the case. Xiao Lin, from the Waiban, and I were shopping in the market.

Emily and the others in Foreign Affairs had known about our getting the videos from the consulate library as soon as we got them. We asked their help in making the viewing arrangements with the A-V Department in Building 3. Emily offered the Foreign Affairs Office VCR to us to preview the videos and asked if the English speakers in their office could see some of them at the same time. We had a triple-feature matinee the very next day in our apartment, replete with popcorn and Pepsi.

Two of the videos, a Blue Angels promo and an Alistair Cooke one titled *Gone West: the Settlement of the American West*, we showed in Building 3, in the Audio-Visual Department. Mr. Kong made the arrangements. At our request, however, they showed the second one at night because many of the students were not able to come during the day. I decided that the videos had limited usefulness. Most were beyond the students' language capabilities and I ended up showing carefully selected things only to doctoral students.

If the videos were documentary in nature, the subject was either too unfamiliar or the sound may not have been clear enough for students to understand. They had an easier time with fictional works.

One movie I really misjudged. I showed the movie *The Gods Must Be Crazy* to some of my doctoral students in the apartment at night and since they enjoyed it immensely, I decided to show it to the postgrads in a classroom. Since there is a very articulate narrator for some parts of the film, and there are many uproariously funny visual scenes, I thought they could handle it.

I thought I prepared the postgrads for *The Gods* by giving them the setting ahead of time and then stopping the film at least three times to check on their understanding. The film is set in South Africa and Botswana, and the actors speak in obviously British accents. The students laughed uproariously at the obviously physical things, but a couple of days later in class some of their questions revealed some gross misconceptions. They thought that the movie depicted the United States, that the bushmen were Indian Americans, and that the coup d'etat took place in the jungles of the United States. I stuck to slides with the postgrads from then on and supplied my own narration.

Despite their less than complete understanding, the doctoral students persisted in their request to see more videos. They thought it tested and challenged their listening comprehension in a way that was useful. One auditor in the class said she had a tape of *Mussolini*, a six-hour American TV special shown several years ago. Since it had been taped in Hong Kong, it had Chinese subtitles and therefore was particularly useful. Even those whose English listening comprehension was poor could follow the story. The students were eager to see it.

So began Monday Night at the Movies. The first Monday daytime class after we had finished the Mussolini tapes, students asked if we were going to continue the video showing that night and were disappointed when I said I was cooking a birthday dinner for Monique that evening. I promised them I would see what I could come up with for next week.

It was on a day when Xiao Lin went with me to the market that I learned that videos shown to students had to be screened and approved ahead of time. He first asked if it was difficult to get videos from the consulate. I jokingly said no, the hardest part was getting to the consulate. He had trouble with the idiom. When he finally understood, he said that a department on campus wanted to know what I was using and that it was supposed to see them first. (I assumed it was the Political Department. Maybe I had alarmed them with my questioning the students about the government.) I said no one had told me that, and that Emily knew what I was using because the people in the Waiban had already seen some of the videos. Anyway, he insisted that I talk with Emily when we went back.

She was half apologetic but said I should bring the videos over. I took them, informing her I would like to have one of them back by Monday morning to use for class, assuming they passed muster. Actually I warned them about the one I was planning to use. It was on immigration, one of the Alistair Cooke American History series. In it an immigration officer asks a Hungarian doctor who is applying for citizenship if he is or ever had been a member of the Communist Party? I thought that might ruffle somebody's feathers.

Later, when I went over on another matter, various staff members were listening to the tapes in another office. I got the videos back on time and we all were happy—I, because I didn't have to come up with something else for Monday's class, and they, probably because they could get the Political Department off their back. The Party motto evidently is you can't be too careful, or else, intimidate just enough to always keep people on guard.

Although no one had objected to the film, one student wanted to know why the question about communism was asked.

I said, "Isn't it true that communism was dedicated to world revolution?"

His only response was a small smile. I said our government thought it legitimate for any nation to ask that question of someone who was seeking to become a citizen.

One thing we had observed was that even when people we knew well said something critical about the system, no matter where they were, their voices automatically lowered. We noted it time and again, even in our apartment. One evening, we were taken to a provincial fashion show. It was the finale to a week-long exhibition by the provincial clothing industries, quite a big deal. We were perched in bleacher seats high up in a big exhibition hall and watched a bevy of models from various cities parade their fashion entries. The models, both men and women, minced down the runway, wearing what to my matronly midwestern eyes looked like very avant garde styles. I hadn't seen anything like it on any Chinese street or even on television.

I leaned over to Mr. He and said, "I wonder what Chairman Mao would think of all this."

He said quickly, rather flippantly, "But Chairman Mao isn't here any more." I noticed that as he spoke, however, he shot quick glances behind us to see if anyone else had heard.

It's hard to overcome the conditioning of a lifetime.

I did cook that birthday dinner for Monique. And after she and Melinda and Jean Sesiano left that evening, we discovered the Orange Dragon was missing again. The kidnappers had been aided and abetted by Jean. This had become an international incident of growing proportions. Since we were certain the Dragon hadn't left by the front door, he could only have catapulted over the balcony.

We were offended, not to mention embarrassed, that security had been breached right under our noses, but decided this called for a change in strategy. We would await the right opportunity.

37

Beginning in the early spring, the Foreign Language Department sponsored a Tuesday evening lecture series in English, in which any of the visiting professors or foreign experts could make presentations. They had asked if I would organize it, and I did, enlisting other presenters. It was a way for the students to test their English comprehension and to learn more about another subject or culture. The lectures were held in a large lecture hall and were amazingly well attended. There wasn't a lot of social life to interfere, although there were some night classes.

One night our lecture was preempted by the Communist Party,

although I didn't realize it at first. On Monday, when I reminded Post-grad Class 1 of the lecture that week by the Canadians, someone said they could not come because there was a Party competition. I asked how many would be affected and they said every postgrad at the college. I was astounded.

I asked who had scheduled the competition for Tuesday. Someone mentioned Miss Shi (the young student who said initially that they couldn't come) and Mr. Lou, from Class 3, the student who had told me the previous semester that he was an officer in the Young Communist organization. (Miss Shi looked a little embarrassed.) I said I considered it thoughtless to schedule something in competition with the lecture series when supposedly the purpose was to give the students a chance to improve their listening comprehension and to learn a little about Western culture. Those of us who were doing the lectures were going to considerable trouble to prepare, and it was unfair to the speakers.

That afternoon I wrote a note to Mr. Kong telling him about the conflict and asked if he could do anything about it. He did, rescheduling the lecture for Thursday night, which meant *my* postgrad classes still missed it because they had an English review class for the national English test they would take in June. My doctoral class would also miss out on our Thursday night conversation session. If the students were unhappy about it, they could complain to the Party.

At our Wednesday evening Free Talk session with the postgrads that week, I learned what the competition was about. The information came in a roundabout way. Sometimes I learned something indirectly about Chinese society by the questions my students asked about the United States.

The first question came from Mr. Jia. "Do American students organize sports events at colleges and universities?

I said, "There are college teams for most sports but other than that, students exercise or play games on their own.

"Even when there are intramural sports," I added, "students usually sign up on a volunteer basis."

"But," he asked, "how do universities in the United States organize students?"

I didn't know what he meant and said so.

"Who are the class monitor, secretary, and so on?"

I said, "There isn't such a thing."

Pursuing that still further, Miss Wang asked, "How do universities control students?"

I said, "They don't. College students are adults and expected to take care of themselves and do what they are supposed to on their own. If not, they don't have any business there. There are academic requirements, of course, and there are academic advisers at most schools. And teachers spell out the rules for their individual classes."

Mr. Jia, having a hard time believing me, persisted, "Maybe universities elsewhere organize students."

I told him I had attended one college, two universities, and taught for almost twenty years at another, and what he referred to just did not exist. I said American students would not put up with being told what to do and where to go. For example, American students would probably climb up and tear down those loudspeakers on campus that are always blaring music or announcements at all hours of the day, I said.

That prompted me to ask, "By the way, what was that competition about that was held last night? The one that displaced the lecture?"

I had a hard time getting them to talk about it or to give straight answers. It was like they were a little embarrassed about it. Mr. Deng, who I knew was a Party member, was particularly reluctant.

Little by little, by asking very specific questions I learned that it was a kind of "political bowl," in celebration of the 70th anniversary of the founding of the Communist Party, which was coming up soon. There were eight teams: two from each of the three 1990 postgrad classes, a doctoral class team, and a young teachers' team. The questions tested the students' knowledge of Party history.

Of those who showed up for Free Talk that night, I learned that four were Party members. A fifth laughed and said "maybe." I presume that meant he had applied.

They asked me about political parties in the United States. I briefly explained the differences between the two major parties, commenting that a big complaint was that the two parties were not different enough to give people a real choice. They were absolutely delighted or astounded, I'm not sure which, when they learned Don and I have different party allegiances.

When they asked how I had joined and how much it cost, I realized there was still a lot of explaining to do. Being a Republican or Democrat in the United States is a lot different than being a "member" of the Communist Party. Although you can join the Communist Party at eighteen, you have to be sponsored and then approved by an appropriate body. Your credentials have to be above reproach or you have to have connections. And, there are dues.

I explained that one didn't join a party in the United States in the same way that they do in China and that one didn't *have* to pay or even donate. Party contributions are voluntary. The "party faithful" get a certain amount of pressure to contribute to the party or to various candidates, but contributions are still voluntary, and certainly support of a political party is voluntary.

When I told them I was a Democrat, they assumed that I was a party member and I had to constantly correct their assumption. I told them I was not really active politically, that I had merely helped in a few local campaigns, and that I frequently wrote letters to legislators.

When I said I had contributed money to political campaigns from time to time, they were shocked. One student asked why the candidates needed money.

"They ought to give money to the people," he said. (That comment in itself was revealing.)

I explained that it took a great deal of money to get elected and what the money was spent for. I alluded to the problems created by the high cost of elections and that many people sought to reform the system.

Turning attention to their system, I said, "Do you vote?"

They said they had voted.

I asked, "Where?"

They voted in class.

"Do you ever meet the candidates? Are you told what the vote tally was afterward?"

The answer was no to both questions. They said sometimes there was information on the bulletin boards about the candidates.

I still wasn't sure what kind of party membership they were talking about. Were they members of the Young Communist League or the Communist Party itself. My curiosity was peaked and I vowed to use the first opportunity to find out more.

A few days later, Lin Xiao Guo, a doctoral student, came for conversation. Since he hadn't attended class that day, he didn't realize the session had been canceled. I invited him to stay and talk. It proved enlightening.

As a young teacher, one of his duties was to supervise the postgrads. I learned who some of the student officers were and was surprised at some. The class Party secretaries are the conduit from the Communist Party to the students. When I asked how many of the students were members of the Young Communist League, he said he thought all of them were. I got the feeling from him and others that it was expected.

He himself was a Party member and paid fifty fen (ten cents) a month to the Party. It was deducted from his pay. The postgraduate students had told me earlier they pay thirty fen.

Xiao Lin reitereated what the students had said at an earlier time—that it's hard to understand how the system works and that most people don't know.

Don's students, being older and having job experience, were a little more realistic and objective about conditions in the country, even those who were Party members. They were unquestionably patriotic, and a few still cheered the socialist system, but most were more observant and more questioning.

Although reform had been in progress for ten years, they had a few reservations about how effective or deep the reforms were. One remarked on the inequalities that had sprung up, such as the creation of the special economic zones where regulations were waived, which allowed some people to get very rich.

"This makes the common people very angry in such a socialist country," he said.

He also disliked what he called the "heavy moral lock." He meant by that the tight constraints imposed by the government, what Americans would call the absence of the freedoms guaranteed by the Bill of Rights.

"It is like an invisible net, spreading to every corner of our life," he explained. "We are all bound tightly by it. Before doing a thing or saying a word, we need to think it over and over, or maybe we'll be trapped in the net. This can even destroy our whole life."

He went on to make a concession, though.

"On the other hand," he said, "perhaps it is the moral net that helped the government to rule us and make our society stable and peaceful. I appreciate this kind of social environment."

Another student regretted the way in which people treat those who succeed. They don't admit or accept others' success, but "will also try to bring you down," he said.

A characteristic of Mao's Revolution from the beginning was the distrust of knowledge and education, and those who possess it. Another student mourned the continuation of such attitudes.

He said, "There are some very ironic sayings in China: a person who uses a chopper earns more than a person who uses the operating knife. A person who uses a steelyard earns more than the person who uses the pen. In Shenzen, one of the special economic zones, people say that you are poor like a professor and a fool like a doctor. So that is one of the reasons young intellectuals hope to go abroad."

One student said he is careful to keep secret his desire to go abroad. He said his boss and colleagues regard people who go abroad as if they were abandoning a poor mother for a rich one, and if his desire were known he would have little chance of being trained or promoted.

He added, "If your boss or others criticize you and tell the authorities something bad about you, you may never have a chance to go abroad." And so he keeps his secret.

When I wanted to expand my knowledge about a particular topic, student writing assignments and class discussions were valuable sources. They not only provided information but unique personal experiences. Before going to China I had thought there was universal health care. I soon realized that was not true, but I was interested in finding out what health care was available.

I said to my postgrads, "Your writing assignment for next week, which we'll discuss in class, is this: tell me what you know about health care in China and what your experience with it has been."

The students at the college have medical care, as do those of Don's students who are employed, all for a tiny sum. Most took pride in that they would be taken care of if they were sick, but others recognized that though that is true for them, it is not true for most Chinese. Mainly only those in the cities are covered adequately, but many of the students' families live in the countryside, where medical facilities, personnel, and medicines are woefully inadequate.

In another assignment we asked students to discuss the best features of their social system. Many of them cited the full employment policy, but many also saw that it could foster inequities. They complained about corrupt officials and bosses who stifled growth. They chafed under the ceiling on their income, no matter what they did, as the following writer indicates.

"The good point in our country is that almost all graduates can make money with ease. The bad point in our country is that almost all graduates can not make any *more* money."

He went on to say that in the beginning he worked very hard at his job, but it made no difference.

"Some colleagues do nothing, but they get more wages than I. People with senior professional titles and high salaries have less professional knowledge and capability than those of junior status and low salaries. So I become lazy day by day. In our country, someone who has not entered college can make far more money than the graduates. For example, salesmen often receive far more money than a professor. People who sell books often receive far more money than people who write books. *The more you read books, the less money you make.* So more and more graduates give up books to become businessmen."

One could say, so what? China isn't the only place where those things happen. In other places, though, ambitious, enterprising persons have options not available to the Chinese. They could seek a job where their skills and abilities would be appreciated and suitably rewarded.

The students all acknowledge that though the government has tried to change these situations, it has had little effect.

Another thoughtful young man confessed to deep misgivings about the system; but as he had watched the loss of discipline that occurred with greater freedom in recent years, he began to suspect that freedom destroys the inner disciplines that make freedom possible. But that was before events in Tiananmen Square.

He wrote: "I had about decided that maybe the government knew best after all until the Chinese Government took violent measures to put down the pro-democracy protests in June, 1989. I have completely lost faith since then."

38

Our most memorable travel experience—not necessarily the most pleasant—was our last in China. The first week in June, the Waiban took Monique, Melinda, Don, and me to Jiuzhaigou, north of Chengdu. Our travel book said it was a nature reserve in a remote area of Sichuan, that it has beautiful lakes and forests, but it was "isolated and difficult to reach."

They weren't kidding. Until we went, we had no conception of how difficult or remote. When Emily said the road was rough, I assumed it would be like the road to Emei Mountain.

Actually we had no desire to go to Jiuzhaigou, as scenic as it was reputed to be. But Emily kept pushing until we felt obligated and ungrateful. (Although these tours were ostensibly for us, they amounted to a "perk" for the Waiban staff as well.)

Eight of us, four waiguoren and four Chinese, and our luggage were crammed into a four-wheel drive Nissan van. I sat between Don and

Mr. He in the middle seat, three rode in front, and Melinda and Monique sat in the back.

It took two days to get there and two to get back, about fourteen hours of driving all told, covering a distance of less than three hundred miles. As you might gather, the road was next to impassable in many places. I felt like I was riding a bucking bronco most of the time, taking a proficiency exam for the Cheyenne rodeo. Don said he knew what it must have been like to go west in a covered wagon. Those wagons may not have had pneumatic tires or shock absorbers, but the description couldn't have been far off. We hit bottom several times.

The roads were narrow and mostly dirt. We often had to wait for other vehicles to be pulled out of mudholes before we could proceed. As we neared our destination, we met huge lumber trucks. The drivers, including ours, seemed to be trying to qualify for the Indianapolis 500.

There were many rock slides where we had to wait for the workmen to clear the road or because they were blasting to repair and improve the road. In many places the mudholes were so big that if we had not had four-wheel drive, we wouldn't have made it across. We got out several times and walked ahead while the driver drove the car through.

It was cold in the mountains, and it even snowed half an inch one night. We had no water most of the two days we were in the hotel inside the reserve at Juizhaigou and, of course, never any heat. We noticed that the chipped brown painted floor was dirty, and that one of the single beds was two inches lower at the head than at the foot. We discovered later that the floorboard at that spot was broken, and so the headboard was anchored in place in the hole. We dismissed that lightheartedly, thinking one of us could just reverse ends, but that was before we realized how cold it was and that we would have to move our beds so we could sleep together for warmth. When we moved the other bed away from the wall, we discovered dirt that must have been there since last year. When we surveyed the bathroom, I was sure of it.

When it got dark and we turned on the lights, we found the voltage was low and we had only very dim light. We played euchre with M & M by candlelight. Although it was early, there was no hope of reading—we could barely find our way around—and since it was cold there was nothing to do but go to bed at nine.

We were supposed to have water from nine to ten, but it didn't come on till 9:30, for half an hour, and even then it was cold. The stool hopper didn't fill so we couldn't flush the toilet, and the bathroom odor, bad when we arrived, only got worse.

The next morning we poured several pans of cold water in the hopper so we could flush it. There was a ring that was cross-threaded on the pipe that led from the tank to the toilet bowl and when the toilet flushed, the water ran across the floor to the drain near the door so that the floor was perennially wet.

Melinda and Monique were next door and our bathrooms joined, also—literally. The partition did not reach to the ceiling, and we soon discovered we could hear each other's conversations. I warned them before anything too personal could be divulged.

I was ready to break out of there at the break of dawn but Emily had already paid for two nights, and in China I guess one doesn't complain or ask for a refund.

Before we left that hotel, I developed chills and nausea, one of the few times I had that problem. This was not the high point of our China travels.

There were some compensations. The mountains and lakes and waterfalls were beautiful. But the most interesting feature was the minority groups who live in the area, chiefly the Tibetans. Driving along where they lived or strolling through their villages, I felt like I was in the middle of a *National Geographic* special. Observing them at work in their colorful garb, I realized their clothes were not just costumes donned for tourists.

Their many layers of clothes were made of wool. Men and women alike wore long wraparound coats, and the women wore a colorful wide band around the middle. Even though the outer garb was dark, a colorful band usually trimmed the sleeves and the neck and the hem. The women wore a kind of hood or sometimes a colorful scarf over their heads. The men and boys either wore a conventional green army cap or a traditional wide-brimmed hat.

We saw men and women alike astride horses, small rangy animals, at various points along the way. June 1 is Children's Day in China, a holiday, and some of the groups of riders along the way appeared to be out on a lark. They waved to us in friendly fashion as we drove by. The fields were full of sheep and yak, leading me to think of the area as China's wild west, range country. The horses were no doubt used to herd the animals, as well as for general transportation.

Although the clothes appeared cumbersome, the Tibetans wore them while performing their regular chores. When we walked through a tiny settlement down the road from our hotel, we watched two old women, with marvelously wrinkled brown faces, industriously sifting wheat through a large sieve. They were winnowing the grain, allowing the chaff to blow away in the brisk wind. Their heavy clothes were dark and none too clean, but around their waists were heavy silver belts, made of large round medallions. They appeared to be wearing their accumulated wealth.

They smiled at us at first, but chatted away and seemingly paid us no attention. The minute we aimed our cameras, however, they frowned and immediately put up their hands to block the picture. We retreated.

Another group of women gathered near a mountain stream were busily screening gravel in order to add to a growing mound of sand. They were similarly garbed. Although they were some distance away, they saw cameras and hid behind a tree or a building to avoid having their picture taken.

We moved to a relatively new hotel right outside the reserve the last day before we started home. I stayed in bed all day under three comforters and that night finally stopped shivering. The room decor was attractive, the water was both hot and abundant, the double beds were comfortable. The bathroom? The toilet seat was loose. Oh well.

I realized something even more clearly about myself during that trip. I remembered why we never take package tours, even when we go abroad. I do not like to be in situations where I have no control. For six days, all our actions were proscribed by someone else and eight people were together—very much together—every hour of the waking day. There were no options, few choices. I felt angry and frustrated for having gotten into such a situation. And then, later, it occurred to me that that is the situation that most Chinese are in every day of their lives. After six days I could go home, but even in China I had more privacy and comfort than did most Chinese. I wouldn't make a very good Chinese.

Those hotel experiences, accumulated over months in China, prompted my writing a letter to the editor of the *China Daily* shortly after that trip. I had read numerous newspaper articles throughout the year about efforts to improve tourism and I couldn't resist. I had noticed similar letters from Westerners in the past, written in a spirit of helpfulness, and hoped they would see fit to print it. The letter follows:

> Foreign Affairs Department
> Chengdu College of Geology
> Chengdu, Sichuan 610059

Dear Editor:

My husband and I have been teaching in China for the past year. We have enjoyed our experience very much and have been interested in learning as much as we can about this country. We have a keener appreciation of and are sympathetic to its many problems.

I have read many reports of China's efforts to increase tourism. Given China's beautiful scenery and unique heritage, this would indeed be a revenue source with great potential. I applaud the efforts made in this direction. While many more hotels and restaurants are undoubtedly needed, there is another aspect that needs attention if China is to truly attract many Western tourists.

We have traveled in many scenic areas in the past year and have stayed in hotels of all classes. While the sights are spectacular, the accommodations were sometimes appalling. I am referring not to how modern they are, but to simple cleanliness. Carpet and floors and bathroom walls were sometimes filthy. Even in nicer hotels, we have yet to find a hotel room where all the plumbing worked satisfactorily.

Many improvements cannot be made because of a lack of money, but one thing China does have is a surplus of labor and I'm not aware of a lack of soap and water. There seems little excuse for such conditions. We have traveled widely in Western Europe and even where accommodations were simple, even primitive, they were spotless.

Although individual Chinese are unfailingly friendly and courteous, service personnel, whether flight attendants or shop clerks, are often surly and even discourteous. Western employees are trained to offer prompt, cheerful service.

Until there is an improvement in such basic hygiene in the country, and service personnel are more accommodating, China's tourist industry will not attract large numbers of Westerners and become the bonanza it could be. The need for advanced technology is widely recognized but perhaps there are other simpler lessons which China can learn from the West.

Sincerely yours,

The letter was printed, with considerable editing, in November 1990, four months after we returned home.

39

As we suspected, the Orange Dragon was on display in a prominent place in Apartment #207. When we called on M & M, we studiously ignored the brazen affront and awaited an opportunity to retaliate. It came, as we knew it would.

Monday evening I peeked over our balcony railing and noticed their big enamel cups sitting on their balcony railing below. An idea blossomed. I had seen them ride away earlier on their bikes and I goaded Don into taking one of the hooks from the kitchen, attaching it to a length of clothesline, and fishing for their cups. Don plied his skill and in no time had both cups in hand. Now we would have some bargaining chips with which to negotiate the return of the Dragon.

We heard them come home, but all was quiet for the rest of the evening. Perhaps they hadn't discovered their loss. The next morning, we thought surely they would discover it at coffee time. No response. The same at noon when they came home for lunch. Don couldn't stand it. That evening, when he assured himself they were out, he returned one cup. The next day, the cup had been taken inside. Surely this would tip them off. We still had one cup: one cup for one dog.

Still no response. This was no fun. Didn't they know where their cups had gone or did they know but just didn't want to give us the satisfaction?

He returned the other cup. Nothing. Either they underestimated Don and didn't suspect us or else they were deliberately frustrating us. Whichever it was, it was working. Anyway, we still didn't have the dog back and we had given up any leverage we had. We knew the CIA would never recruit us for intelligence work.

To this day, M & M don't know why or where their cups disappeared for two days in June 1990. Or do they?

There was no more vital topic in our classroom discussions, just as between our two governments, than the subject of human rights. It was a paramount issue as it bore on the Most Favored Nation trading status that China sought to have renewed. Students were listening to the Voice of America and were aware of the debate going on in Washington between President Bush and Congress. Some members of Congress had also been in China complaining about China's human rights record.

The same issue had been discussed the previous summer before we went to China. There were persuasive arguments on both sides and I leaned toward withholding Most Favored Nation status. After I was in China a while and read the government's official line in the *China Daily*, which presented happenings and events mostly in a positive light, I thought that even more strongly. The government interprets willingness to trade as unconcern about, if not approval of, their domestic policies. Most nations that fell away after Tiananmen Square had renewed ties with Beijing, and it was business as usual. Would withholding trade really make any difference, however?

One morning in the doctoral class when we were discussing news items, a student mentioned that he had news about Fang Li Zhi, heard on Australian radio. Li is the Chinese physicist who was a leader of the student movement that resulted in the protest movement that led to the demonstrations in June 1989. He was the one who, with his wife, holed up in the American consulate for about a year, before they somehow got out of the country. The students said it probably was a result of a deal between the Chinese and American governments. The news item was that Fang had given an address at an American university recently in which he had said that China could not progress economically until she made some political reforms.

I used that report to set the stage for our conversation that evening. I asked the students to be prepared to discuss what reforms they would like to see and what they would prefer the United States to do concerning the Most Favored Nation status. They were already aware that some Chinese people in the United States who were upset about human rights wanted the United States to discontinue the trading status.

Although I had been opposed to continuing the status before we came, I had recently written a letter to my representative saying I thought we ought to renew but keep the heat on human rights in other ways. Removing it would hurt the Chinese economy, which was none too good, and might only make the government more repressive.

We had done a lecture on American history and government the previous week. I don't know how much the audience had understood, but my thought was that if they heard some explanation of our Constitution and the provisions in the Bill of Rights, plus how our government functions, they might be more apt to question their own. We would have been in trouble if we had made comparisons or were openly critical, but there were various ways to make a point.

Later that evening in our conversation session, I asked if they were satisfied with the status of human rights and the degree of democracy in the country. They said they really didn't know.

I reminded them that they had said that the mayor of Shanghai had handled the student protesters in Shanghai much better than was done in Beijing. They halfway agreed but said Beijing was different than Shanghai. And they again said they didn't know enough about what happened in Beijing to judge.

I told them that TV cameras and reporters from the United States as well as other nations were there and that Americans were revolted by what they saw. One student said he was told that reporters filmed the same scenes over and over, making it appear worse than it was. I said the West's information came from many different quarters, much of it from Chinese observers. And it was that information that Americans responded to.

Students immediately got into the human rights issue and talked about the impossibility of democracy in China because of the large numbers of rural people who have little education. People in the countryside are so poor, and even when the children want to go to school the parents may not be able to send them. Schooling in China is not free; tuition for elementary school is only twelve to sixteen dollars per year, but considering that annual income may be anywhere from forty to one hundred and fifty dollars, the cost can be prohibitive. Even though the government has mandated nine years of education for every child, that goal is far from being realized.

Li Yong told about staying with a family in the mountains in Shaanxi province, in central China, when he was doing fieldwork. There were nine children in the family. Only two children went to school. One, a nine-year-old boy, walked two hours down the mountain to school, spent four hours in school, and spent two hours walking home. He said that all the family had to eat was potatoes and corn, only one common dish for everyone. The children were always tired because of poor nutrition. After two days he moved to another place that was less convenient and cost him more travel time each day, but which offered him better living conditions.

In other words, what they seemed to be saying was, "We can't afford democracy or concern for your human rights now."

Only Yin Guodong, who was silent at the beginning of the evening, finally said he thought they needed more democracy.

The next week, though, that same student, Mr. Yin, asked why Americans were so concerned about human rights in China. I plunged in, describing our heritage grounded in Western-oriented civilization and all that that meant: the odyssey beginning with (for want of a better starting point) King John and the Magna Carta to our Bill of Rights, that there were states that were only willing to ratify the Constitution on the condition a Bill of Rights would be added later. I also discussed how people's religious beliefs influenced their thinking.

I was a little bothered by the whole conversation since it rehashed things I thought we had discussed before. But after some reflection and remembering who had asked human rights questions, I thought perhaps it was deliberate in that he wanted to hear more discussion of the issue and perhaps wanted others to hear, as well.

Once when we discussed the idea of a generation gap, in response to my question about whether they and their parents disagreed on anything, Yi Chao said that his parents had had some bad experiences during various political movements. Because of that, they advised him to concentrate on his education and stay clear of any political expression. He disagreed but said nothing so as not to offend or worry them. He admitted that he had taken part in the protest movement in Chengdu in June 1989. I don't know to what extent it took courage for him to confess that in front of others.

I still felt my explanations of why Americans were so concerned about this issue were probably inadequate and unconvincing to the students. The Chinese government adamantly claims that how it treats its citizens is an internal matter and some of those students seemed to buy it.

Still I decided to try a different tack. The next morning in class I described the events that led up to the demonstrations at Kent State and the horrified reaction to the killings there in an attempt to show that Americans were not just picking on China. I followed up with this analogy: if someone moved in next door to you and wanted to be a friendly neighbor, you would welcome them and try to make them feel at home. But if those people abused and beat their children, you might not like them very much or want to associate with them.

I don't know whether my analogy meant anything to them (I didn't dwell on it), but it seemed appropriate to me. I tried once again to help them understand that though people in the United States differed on the issue of Most Favored Nation status, everyone was motivated by what they thought would help Chinese people the most.

On a Voice of America broadcast about that time, I heard an interview with a member of an American relief agency who had worked in Africa for several years. He discussed the plight of people in Ethiopia and how many had to choose among their children as to who to feed and who to leave behind when they had to move on. At times old people gave their rations to children at the cost of their own lives. He pointed out that other people in the world were more concerned with the survival of the group whereas Americans are much more individualistic.

He said, "What we consider rights, much of the rest of the world considers privileges."

That is, to a great extent, true with respect to China. Given their bouts with hunger, disease, deprivation, and oppression in the not too distant past, the Chinese feel they have made tremendous strides. They still have not solved all those problems, however, and to allow the kind of freedoms we Westerners demand would result in extreme instability in China. The chaos that developed in the former Soviet Union is a lesson China is heeding well.

Neither Don nor I had ever asked our students point blank if they had participated in the June 4 demonstrations. The event in Tiananmen Square was a topic that never came up directly. However, when the end of the year came and both they and we were ready to go home, the inhibitions seemed to loosen.

When one of Don's students came to the apartment to say good-bye, he told Don out of the blue that he had participated and had been arrested and had had to write many papers to show that he had corrected his thinking. Several others had the same experience—endless discussions followed by written statements—so that was evidently common procedure.

Some students, who at the time of the demonstrations had been at different colleges and universities, described similar activities at their schools. In April and May of 1989 they had talked for days in their classrooms about what was happening in Beijing and the issues under protest. Then classes were dismissed for a while. In some cases students demonstrated in their own town centers, and in others they boarded the trains for Beijing. As in the Cultural Revolution, they could ride the trains free. One young woman, a student at Zheizhang University in Hangzhou, wanted to go to Beijing, but when she called home her parents forbade her to go, fearing for her safety. One student from Xian said that he went with friends to Beijing for two weeks, but they ran out of money and had to go home on June 2, just two days before the crackdown.

Those who participated in Chengdu told similar stories. About two hundred young teachers from the college participated in the demonstrations in downtown Chengdu. When I told one student participant that the *Chicago Tribune* reported eight people had been killed, he verified the story: two students and six townspeople. He said that a thousand people had been injured, several from the college. The police had been called out to block off the streets so that people could not get to the center of town. The townspeople tried to reason with them and told them what had happened in Beijing. Some of the police were sympathetic, but they had their orders. They clubbed the students, but did not shoot.

From our conversations with students we gleaned that people at the college were generally sympathetic to the protest. But as at all other colleges, the students who participated were ordered by teachers, probably at the behest of officials, to write about their intentions and what they had actually done in the demonstrations. Those who were Party members had to reapply to the Party for membership. They may or may not have been accepted.

Students told us also that government controls were tightened after the crackdown on June 4. It became harder to get passports of all kinds, and political education was stepped up. Government officials concluded that they had not done a good enough job of indoctrinating the youth; otherwise they would not be questioning the system. To show how little things change, after the disintegration of the Soviet Union in August 1991, political studies for undergraduates on campus were increased by one hundred hours. The government seemed to be running scared.

When another of Don's students from Beijing came by to say goodbye, I asked if he had been in Beijing in June 1989 at the time of the demonstrations. He said yes and that he had seen many people shot, probably several thousand altogether. He said that was why the people hated the leaders and why the young people were so discouraged and wanted to go abroad to study. He was hopeful that with more business involvement with other nations, conditions would eventually improve.

More than once students asked us what had happened in Tiananmen Square. Most knew only what was reported in the Chinese media: that only three hundred people were killed. We found that no one really believed that, however.

Thinking about my students' seeming lack of concern for human rights, it occurred to me that China's defense of her beliefs about human rights might be related to Maslow's hierarchy of need fulfillment.

Psychologist Abraham Maslow held that human needs generally recognized as universal could be arranged in hierarchical form. That is, one cannot or will not be concerned with satisfying some needs until the others, the lower or more fundamental ones, are met.

Li Peng and company keep saying that in China the fundamental human rights are the people's right to live. They see the primary task of the Chinese government as solving the food, clothing, and housing problems for a population of 1.2 billion. This is what the government perceives as the basic human rights of the Chinese people.

Solving those problems is indeed a monumental task. To open up or change the system quickly is to invite chaos and instability, and that would upset a balance which is tenuous at best. In other words, the Chinese government's position is not wholly indefensible.

40

July 1, 1991, was a big day in China—the seventieth anniversary of the founding of the Chinese Communist Party. Two nights before, in the college theater, the college held a choral competition between departments. Since it was hot by that time, several groups had rehearsed outside under the trees, giving us a preview of the competition. I told Emily that we wanted to go, and indeed the whole contingent of foreigners attended. How often do you have a ringside seat at such an event?

Twenty groups, all attractively costumed, performed. It was a long evening, especially since the majority of the groups sang one of the same songs: "No New China Without the Communist Party." They had to choose among four songs for one of their selections, and there were even some duplications in their second number. All the songs in some way commemorated either the revolution or Mao or some famous event in Chinese history. For example, there were songs that were popular during the "anti-Japanese war."

The theater was filled most of the time, and the performance of the audience was consistent with what we had observed everywhere. In spite of our second row seats, we still could not hear well because of the buzz of conversation, particularly from several noisy children behind us. (Since we were in the college theater, I wondered if audiences are quiet during a film. I asked a student about this later and he said yes. Maybe that shows more discrimination than I'd given the Chinese credit for.)

It was ludicrous to bill this event as a competition. Obviously, the judges, who were seated in the row ahead of us, could not hear the singers, either. Nor did they seem to care. They made no notes during performances. Another feature which made the competition aspect phony was that the groupings were so contrived. The fellows in the Foreign Affairs Department, for example, sang with two groups because they needed male voices. The judges, who were Party officials at the college, also could hardly be considered impartial. The Party had entered its own singing group which, upon taking the stage, was joined by most of the judges. I wondered if any of the other contestants considered filing a complaint about a conflict of interest.

It struck me during the event that, similar to the Speech Contest, Chinese authorities only introduce competition when it is meaningless or trivial. The event was not about singing. It was about political indoctrination, part of the ongoing process of instilling Communist philosophy. I thought this was a big deal because it was the seventieth anniversary, but I learned later that such a competition is held every year. Although winners were announced the next week and there were monetary awards for the winning departments, hardly anyone I talked with knew who had won. They obviously did not take the competitive aspect seriously.

And I question whether any of those judges in the front row really listened or if there was a musical ear in the whole bunch.

One evening, in the next week, Xiao Peng, Xiao Wang, and Ge Jiangping dropped by unexpectedly. These were all students from the fall semester class with whom I had remained close. Xiao Peng was a pretty young woman, a little shy until you got to know her. She had a way of tossing her head and looking sideways at others for affirmation as she spoke, smiling all the while.

Xiao Wang was a tall, thin young man who had a flair for things modern. He wore his few clothes with style, turning up a collar or cuffs, affecting a different look. His moods were mercurial. He could look very somber and a moment later break out in quick laughter at something going on around him.

Ge Jiangping, also tall, had rather prominent cheekbones, and I imagined Mongol horsemen in his ancestry. He looked at you with an appraising and intelligent eye. He listened carefully, and when something struck his fancy, his eyes would dance merrily. He too could joke and make fun, but there was a quiet steadiness about him that invoked others' respect.

He had been in the field for several weeks and I was really glad to see all of them. The timing was good since Don had gone to bed early and I was doing some mending and listening to music.

I had seen Xiao Peng and Xiao Wang in the postgrad chorus the previous week at the seventieth anniversary celebration, and I commended them on how good they sounded and how nice they looked. They didn't think they sounded good at all and said the songs were awful, but I reassured them it was all relative since I had heard all the groups and they hadn't.

I had been surprised to see Xiao Wang with the choral group. I asked if he had volunteered to sing. He said a little indignantly that he was asked, that he wouldn't have done it otherwise. When I asked if they had a choice, they chorused a resounding "No."

I asked about the Young Communist League. Young people can join at age fourteen and most do because they want to conform. Not belonging makes you suspect or shuts you out of certain things. In China you had always better be on the right side of an issue or activity. Nonetheless, you have to be recommended for Party membership.

Xiao Wang said that he would probably join the Party in the future. He speculated that I was probably surprised to hear that. I answered no, but asked why he wanted to join. Xiao Peng, who is a Party member, half teasingly told him he wasn't joining for the right reason. They admitted that joining the Party is the only way to get ahead.

I told Xiao Wang I wasn't surprised at his wanting to join and that I thought he could probably convince others because I remembered his participating in the speech contest in which he had gotten first prize. I'd also heard that he had taken part in the doctoral team in the Party Information Bowl that had been held in May. When I asked if he had volunteered for that he said, again rather indignantly, that he had been asked.

The three kept repeating that I probably couldn't understand things in China. I did say that Americans—and most Westerners—would simply not put up with such control over their lives.

I asked Xiao Peng why she was a member of the Party. She said she was asked as an undergraduate. She was a good student (and Xiao Wang added that she was a beautiful girl, intimating they wanted pretty young girls in the Party) and she was recommended by her professor. She was flattered and wanted to conform, but admitted she had not really understood very much about the Party at that time.

Ge Jiangping had been quiet during most of this conversation. When I asked him what he thought about it, he said he had no interest in such things, that they could only talk about such things among themselves. He is a little older and had gotten in on the tail end of the Cultural Revolution. He is also a teacher and family man, and I suspected that his experience and maturity had taught him it was better not to be vocal.

I mentioned the importance of being "on the inside" if you want to change something. As China continues its open policy there are bound to be changes. Yet, none of them felt there was any hope of change—at least for them—and said they get very discouraged. I expressed amazement because they seemed happy.

Their low pay demoralizes them, for one thing. Grad students got about 70 yuan ($14) per month and doctoral students got about 100 yuan ($20). Xiao Wang said he was embarrassed to tell me how much he made, it was so little.

Although I had had intimations of their views before this, this still was the most candid conversation we had ever had. Maybe it was because there was no one else around and they trusted each other and me. When we had talked about how the Party officials didn't really seem to take their duties seriously at the singing competition, one suggested that even the officials didn't really think it was important. It was just something which had to be done all over the country. They said perhaps no one really believes communism was the best system but that they couldn't do anything about it.

Chinese have to consider the implications of everything they say from childhood on. One young woman whose mother was a junior middle school teacher told about an incident she remembered from her childhood. One of her mother's students came to their home and confessed that he had been asked to spy on her mother. He was not to tell his parents or anyone, and he was distressed by the assignment. Her mother had reassured the young boy, trying to relieve his anxiety.

Knowing that in the past children had been asked to monitor their parents' behavior, and that children innocently repeat parents' remarks or behavior, I asked Chinese parents we met in the United States and in China if that had been a problem. All said that they had been lucky in that regard. Their relationship with their children had been such that the children sensed what needed to be kept confidential.

Only within families and with close friends can people be candid even today. To others they must dissemble or even lie. If you get into the habit of lying, how do you know when anyone is telling the truth? It's difficult in China to separate pretense from reality.

Some individuals seemingly get tired of pretending and just drop out. In July, two nights before we were to leave for home, one of my postgrads came by quite late, the first he had ever come to our apartment. At the beginning of the year he and his buddies had been eager to begin Free Talk sessions and had been regular and enthusiastic participants. Along the way, however, they had stopped attending. I was disappointed but didn't ask why. I was sorry I hadn't. That evening, he told me they had stopped coming because of the monitors and the "stooges" in the class who kept them from speaking freely. He wanted me to know.

Another of my students in China has since come to the United States to study. She then told me of her activities in May and June of 1989 and of other incidents. I had had no hint of this in the year I knew her in China. She had seemed apolitical.

Amazed, I said, "You never said anything about those things before."

She said, "Ah, but I'm free now."

One morning in Class 3 students worked in pairs to explain the meaning of proverbs. Miss Luo illustrated "Haste makes waste" by saying that in 1958 China had had the Great Leap Forward, but that things were done too quickly and not done well. Not only had the country failed to make progress, it had made mistakes and had fallen behind. I thought it a marvelous example and wanted to yell "Bravo," but I dared not. I simply praised it as a good example and called on the next student.

While the students were conferring, Mr. Tuo had come up to my desk to see if his particular example was a pertinent illustration of his assigned proverb: "Actions speak louder than words." The example concerned his mother's impatience with his repeated empty promises to study harder. I assured him it was pertinent. When he spoke in class, however, he gave an example provided by his partner, Mr. Lou, to wit: In 1989 Western powers had criticized China for opening to the outside world and tried to get China to change from socialism to capitalism. But China had shown in the past year that great progress has been made, thus "actions speak louder than words." In other words, China had shown *them*.

Well! I hadn't been listening that carefully in the beginning because Mr. Tuo's pronunciation was hard for me to understand and besides I thought I already knew what he was going to say. But when I heard "Western powers" I began to pay attention and then thought I had better ask him to repeat the example. Everyone was watching me closely. How would I comment?

Although delivered by Mr. Tuo, I considered this a challenge from Mr. Lou, officer in the campus Young Communist League. He had mentioned this in a personal interview that was part of the final exam the previous semester. Although he had never been unfriendly to me, neither was he as warm or spontaneous as the other students.

I said, first of all, I thought the premise was wrong. I knew of no

Western nation that did not want China to open to the outside world, that I thought all nations thought it was a good idea. From the standpoint of their own economies, they welcomed it, and wondered why China had waited so long. I also said I knew of no country that had tried to get China to switch from socialism to capitalism, even though many probably hoped it would happen. It was China, I said, that had decided to open the door ten years ago and to invite other countries to help it develop its economy. It was the businesses in those countries from which China hoped to learn new technology, businesses that are decidedly capitalistic.

I went on to say that the criticism that Westerners made in 1989 was over the issue of human rights. Other nations had been horrified at the way students were treated in Tiananmen Square.

As I talked, the students sat quietly, with little change of expression. Perhaps because the comment caught me by surprise, it irritated me more than I wanted them to know. Still, I thought I had better leave my response at that. Some battles are better left to be fought another day. I called on the next student.

Something rather subtle occurred over the course of the year with some students. Perhaps I imagined it but I don't think so. There were several students who were very open, warm, and spontaneous in the first semester, but who, by the second term, had cooled considerably. They held me at arm's length. I don't think it was any coincidence that by spring they had definitely identified themselves with the Party. One young woman, who had not even had enough money to go home during Spring Festival, suddenly in the spring had a bicycle. Her director had had some part in getting it for her. She also seemed to have more and nicer clothes. A young man wrote in the second term that he probably was going to become a teacher at the college. He was much more reserved in his attitude toward me in the second semester.

Perhaps it was my imagination, but I felt as if someone had said to those students, in effect, "Don't get too involved with any waiguoren."

41

The semester was almost over, and while I was eager to go home, there was still much I wanted to learn about China. My students were my teachers.

From the very beginning, I had started the doctoral class off each morning with an "opening question," announced the day before. One day a week it was on a news item they had read or heard. Occasionally I asked about a childhood experience or their field of study. Some days they had to have a question for a classmate. As the semester progressed and the students became more fluent, the questions became a little more involved.

One of my last "opening questions" was a political one, if they chose to take it that way: What would you ask Premier Li Peng if you had an opportunity?

Only six students were present, but their questions were interesting and varied, although not unexpected. Three had to do with the state of education, particularly higher education, and what Li Peng would do to improve it. When I pointed out there had been improvement in terms of the rate of illiteracy and number of students enrolled in schools and colleges, they replied that it still wasn't enough. They, of course, complained that workers made more money than intellectuals. (Chinese define "intellectual" as anyone who has higher education.) And they complained that the drivers at the college were able to make more money than they did as teachers.

One student's questions were wholly personal in nature: he wanted to know about Li's family, where he lived, what his salary was, and where his children lived and worked.

I had commented once that we Americans probably hear more about our politicians and their families and activities than is either healthy or relevant, but it was the other extreme in China. Although you do see officials' wives in the pictures when they go abroad or entertain state visitors, there is no information on the personal lives of public officials. Chinese public officials lead very private lives.

One student wanted to ask Li about his claims that the country was becoming more democratic and about his emphasis on stability. She didn't think you could have real stability or security when people were not allowed to speak out.

I followed up with a *China Daily* article on a Kettering Foundation report about Americans' disenchantment with politics and their cynicism about political leaders. Whereas only 36.4 percent voted in our last midterm elections in 1992, eighty-nine percent of the people in most European countries vote. I was quick to let them see that our system has many flaws, that there are troubles aplenty in paradise, and that we are not hesitant about pointing them out.

One of the more significant responses I got came early in the semester, when I assigned this opening question: "Tell me some perceptions you have of the United States."

Some of the answers were predictable: wealthy, technologically advanced, militarily strong.

Deng Ron Gui, though, said, "America is a country in which law is very important. That is definitely not the case in China."

That is something most Americans might not think to mention if asked to describe their own country because we know how we fudge on speed laws and how some public figures flout the law and get away with it. Nevertheless, compared to people in many other nations, Americans do usually pay their taxes and protest when laws are flagrantly violated.

We who grow up in Western culture take the rule of law so much for granted that we have a hard time comprehending a society where there are few codified laws. China had never had a clear system of law until the latter part of this century. Chinese people could never be sure what was legal and what wasn't. Western businesses learned that to their sorrow when they first went to do business with China. Binding contracts were not in the Chinese experience. Even now when China has a constitution and laws, those laws and even constitutions are only as good as the people who enforce them.

Copyright and patent laws, too, have been slow in coming. When I first went to the college library, the journals and other publications in the reading room seemed to be wearing uniforms. All the periodicals had plain covers. China passed a copyright law which was to go into effect in June 1991, but until that time, it freely pirated publications of all kinds. I made some assignments in *Reader's Digest*. Every page of the library's issues was the product of a copy machine. Foreign computer software manufacturers, also, were unhappy with China's theft of their materials.

I was startled one day while browsing in a very modest little shop to find a Liz Claiborne label on some skirts. The price was a mere $8. Wholly apart from the price, I don't think the Liz Claiborne people would have been happy to see their label on the quality of merchandise that was offered.

It was not only foreigners who were cheated out of recognition and rightful compensation. Chinese authors and composers were victims of piracy, too.

Another occasional class opening was a question exchange: I had a question for each of them and they each had one for me. One questioner was clearly puzzled over the controversy that surrounds abortion in the United States. Considering their burgeoning population and crowded conditions and the fact that China has only seven percent arable land, the students and people, generally, view abortion as a necessity. Zhirong, a gynecologist, estimated that there were approximately one thousand abortions a week in Chengdu hospitals. While contraceptives are free, often dispensed at the workplace, according to news reports supply cannot keep up with demand. Central planning isn't without its failures in that regard either, it seems. I explained that most opposition from Americans is motivated by religious convictions, a distinction that Chinese find difficult to relate to.

Another question took me by surprise: Tell us about your beliefs.

Well, that isn't something I had pat answers for, particularly in two minutes or less at 8:30 in the morning. I first asked what kind of beliefs he was talking about: political, family, religious? I wanted to clarify what he had in mind so I didn't get accused of trying to corrupt them in any way. His answer was equivalent to "all of the above."

I don't think I made it in under two minutes, but one I did include was that while I could offer no scientific proof, I believed in God.

As I said, the question surprised me. I would have been timid about asking their beliefs, even if I had thought of it, but once the question was raised I decided to turn the tables. I made it their next writing assignment.

One student affirmed his belief in the Communist Party. The student who had initiated the question was quick to say that he did not believe in God; he believed in science and knowledge. He seemed to equate the two and felt that through knowledge we could solve the world's problems.

I commented on his paper that knowledge brings no guarantee that it will be used to solve problems or even be used for good. We already have a great deal of knowledge that would solve many of the world's pressing problems, but the motivation and the will are lacking.

Teachers always have the last word.

Although they were all patriotic young people, in previous discussions the students conceded that Chairman Mao had used poor judgment in many of his policies. There were things in the country they were dissatisfied with, so I thought it might be interesting to see what they thought might have been done differently. The very last writing assignment I made was this: If you could turn the clock back to 1949, what would you have China do differently?

Two students surprised me by their responses. One, in that he would not change a thing. Since that student had expressed less than complete confidence in the government, and expressed frustration with certain policies, I didn't know whether he had thought my question was limited only to 1949, or whether he was playing it safe to the very last.

The second surprised me not only in the content of his assertions but in their boldness. This student was a milquetoast character, speaking only when spoken to in class, and expressing only the safest views. First, he would have had China stay out of wars. For instance, he regretted not only the money but the half million lives lost in the "War to Resist US Aggression and Aid Korea." He had been a soldier in the People's Liberation Army. That information was startling and enlightening on three counts. I had no idea how many Chinese were killed in the conflict. Nor did I previously know their name for what we Americans call the Korean War. One man's war is another man's aggression. But in addition, I was startled by the firmness of his conviction. He stopped just short of calling the participation stupid. About that same time, he spoke, in Free Talk, about his brother who was a county official, who somehow was able to afford a twenty-room house. When I asked how he could do that, he just laughed evasively. But it gave context to an additional complaint in his paper that intellectuals received neither equal political treatment nor equal pay.

Others repeated familiar refrains: the sorry results of past reform movements, population policy, a wish for more openness, getting rid of the "iron rice bowl," developing the market economy further, more support for education, and allowance for private ownership. Perhaps more significant than their beliefs that China should have done things a lot differently after 1949 was their willingness to say so.

While I sympathized with those students, they had never experienced anything but Communist rule. I had even more compassion for those of their fathers' and grandfathers' generation who had been buffeted by the winds of many political changes.

One man, in a lengthy chance encounter we had at an airport, gave us some insight into his experience. Almost of retirement age, he said that while the world was changing, referring to events in Eastern Europe and elsewhere, he felt like his surroundings were "as if frozen" and would remain so "until the world's last day."

He was a college student in the 1950's and studied Russian. At that time, they were to "learn from the Soviet Union," because the Soviet Union was considered as the only example in revolution and construction.

In the 1960's, things Russian were out. The Party fought against Soviet Revisionism, believing that China was carrying out the true socialism and communism. Then, after the Cultural Revolution, in the 1980's, the wide gap between the People's Republic of China and the Soviet Union narrowed. They were drawing closer again, based on their common socialism and some common language. But by the 1990's Eastern Europe had rejected communism and tremendous change was rocking the Soviet Union.

He ended this recital, punctuated frequently by rueful laughter, saying, "I am confused now. I have seen devout Communist leaders pledge they will work and fight all their lives for communism, but they use the system to benefit themselves, and order people about. We have no rights. I have stopped believing in their doctrine and suspect their sincerity."

Having observed how reticent Chinese people were to say something negative about the government, and to waiguoren at that, it seemed to indicate how demoralized he was to have risked opening up to us in this way. It could only be that he knew he would never see us again and that he needed to let someone know.

I thought of him again when only a few weeks after we arrived home the Soviet Union was dissolved. Still more change to add to his confusion. From the very beginning, students had been eager to learn about the United States, but they had many interesting misconceptions. For example, one asked if it were true that all young people moved away from home at eighteen and got their own apartments. Another asked if it were true that when the young people went home to visit, they were required to pay for their food.

The one that left me speechless, though, was something one of my doctoral students mentioned one night at our apartment. He asked if it were true that when the first American walked on the moon in 1969, he had an argument with NASA officials. When he said, "one small step for man, one giant step for mankind," there was a blackout for four minutes afterward. The astronaut was ordered to claim the moon for the US and he refused. As a result, the other astronaut was named "director." After they landed back on earth, the first astronaut disappeared for a couple of weeks. Supposedly he was being punished for his refusal. The story was so ludicrous I sat there with my mouth open.

Finally I said, "In the first place, what would anyone *do* with the moon? And if such a thing were true, the press would have picked it up and made a big deal of it. There's nothing reporters like better than that kind of story. And it would not have been surprising for Neil Armstrong to have dropped from view just for a little R & R, especially since he is such a private person.

Don was in the next room, and I called him in for support. It turned out that he also had heard the story from his students. He pointed out that the Antarctic and other places were shared by many countries.

I don't know whether we convinced the students or not, but I was so intrigued by the story that after we returned home, I called the NASA library in Washington to ask about it.

After the woman at NASA finished laughing, she said there was a UN treaty signed in 1967, two years *before* the Apollo landing, saying that moon exploration and benefits thereof would be shared; no country could claim exclusive rights. That treaty was signed by many countries, including the United States *and* China.

There is even a postscript to the story. I had asked a young Chinese man in Chicago about the story. He was a doctoral student and had been in the United States for about six years. He said that he had never heard such a story, so it couldn't have been a government claim.

However, a week or so after I asked him about it, he read that same story in the February 1990 issue of a Chinese digest. The article had first appeared in a Chinese magazine called *Contemporary Youth*.

The title of the article was, "The Secret of the US Moon Landing." The two men who were supposedly on the moon in July 1969 were "Mr. Wilson" and "Mr. Harridan." (Neil Armstrong and Buzz Aldrin will be surprised to learn that.)

The dates of publication surprised me. I had assumed the story was circulated sometime in the 1970's before we had any relations with the Chinese. It amazed me that the Chinese would still be circulating that kind of propaganda in the 1990's.

42

I dislike saying good-bye under any circumstances and I was dreading good-byes in China even more. They could be protracted, to say the least.

Numerous visitors to the college had come and gone and their leave-taking had created quite a stir, particularly when they were old friends of the college. Several parties and banquets were held, often involving the same people each time. Then as many of those same people as the van would hold also went along to the airport to see the person off. We would have sneaked out of town if possible. We instructed Emily that we wanted to leave with as little fanfare as possible. That is, if we were ever able to leave.

A year before we had sweated the arrival of our formal invitation to teach from the Ministry of Geology and Mineral Resources in Beijing, which oversees the college. We could not get our visas from the Chinese consulate until then. Now, a year later, we worried over getting tickets on China Air. As the college instructed the year before, we had bought only one-way tickets. The college was to provide our transportation home after a year of satisfactory service. So now it was up to the Waiban to book our flight.

Early in June we decided on a date in late July for our departure. Usually someone from the Waiban would go to Beijing by train (a two-and-a-half-day trip) and stand in line for two or three days to buy airline tickets. The staff member would have to take the travelers' passports along in order to get the tickets. (We never got over our anxiety in letting go of our passports for even a few days.)

In this case the Waiban contacted the Ministry in Beijing, which somehow was going to be able to get our tickets without our passports. The head of the Ministry's Education Department had a nephew who worked at the airline and supposedly he would get them for us. No problem! That was using *guanxi*, in the best Chinese tradition.

That sounded fine to us and we waited to hear. Days went by and June was running out. The Waiban staff could not schedule our flight from Chengdu to Beijing until they knew exactly when we were leaving the country. Since China Air flew only to San Francisco or New York, we opted to fly to New York in order to be nearer Dayton, Ohio, our final stop where son Doug would pick us up.

June turned into July and there were still no tickets. We began to think it would be easier to scale the Great Wall than to arrange transportation. But Beijing had promised the Waiban that things would be taken care of. Not to worry. No problem.

Enviously we watched the Canadians go home July 1. In the meantime we had a party for Don's classes, which finished earlier than mine. Then the students came by in two's and three's the day or night before their trains were to leave with yet more tearful good-byes.

John Smith and four friends dropped in before he left for home. John Smith from Tibet, that is. He wanted to show his regard for Don, his teacher, and he presented each of us a *hada*, a filmy silk stole. He had had his wife send them from Tibet. The gift of a *hada* is a special Tibetan tribute. In a simple little ceremony he placed it around our shoulders and shook hands while his friends took pictures. We were touched by his gesture.

While we appreciated and enjoyed getting to know our students and reading about their experiences, we were troubled by some of their stories and concerns. We still think about Ben, a quiet, sensitive young man.

Like many students in our classes, Ben lived for the first twenty years in the countryside. He described it as a life of "hardship, poverty, and closed surroundings." By qualifying for a university education and a subsequent career in geology, he has been able to leave that kind of life behind him.

In a paper he wrote that he now has a "light decent job, a beautiful wife whose parents are rich by Chinese standards, and her parents' help allowed us to become a modern new family." He said he thinks he should be happy. But he confessed he is deeply troubled by his social status. He has left the hard life behind him but his parents haven't.

He wrote: "Quite often, after a happy time, I lie in bed, staring at the ceiling and think of my old father, my brothers and sisters. I know they must still be working hard, and they will never have such a wonderful time as I. I should help them but I am only a common person without any power. I am not able to change their life. The only thing I can do is to help them with some money, but as time goes on, this must displease my wife. All these troubles give me sleepless nights."

He felt he was leading a double life. His family regarded him as very lucky and very happy. His wife "knows only a good life and love." He wondered if anyone could understand his feeling, if it was peculiar to traditional Oriental culture. What did we as Westerners think about it?

He began and ended his paper with the same line: "I need help from a good psychologist."

We were moved by this writing and relieved when Hy Zipkin, an old friend of the college paid a lengthy visit about that time. Hy is a retired school psychologist and seemed an answer to the young man's plea. Hy agreed to counsel him, and Don conveyed the message.

Although Don made several attempts to arrange a meeting, Ben always had a conflict and he and Hy never did get together. Even though his pain was real, he evidently could not overcome the inhibitions of a lifetime.

Still no airline tickets. Don bugged the staff and they promised to call Beijing. For two days, however, all the lines to Beijing were tied up.

In the meantime the weather was the same: hot and humid every day. The temperature hovered around ninety degrees and we were running the fans almost around the clock. In the winter the kitchen was downright cozy; cooking and washing-up had certain advantages.

But definitely not in June and July. KP duty in steamy Chengdu gave new meaning to the famous line, "if you can't stand the heat, stay out of the kitchen."

That new air-conditioned Guest House that was to have been completed before we came was pretty well finished by spring, and new furniture had been bought and delivered. Occupants still could not move in, however, because the building had no gas. The powers that be had never approved the allotment of gas for the building.

Arrangements and provisions for utilities are usually made before construction ever starts, at least that's standard procedure in the United States. But there was no piping in the wall for the gas. When we left, workmen were beginning to drill holes in the walls so that pipes could be installed.

It seemed incredible: drills, hammers, and chisels were making holes in a new building when it *could* all have been done beforehand. For those who don't mind decorating against a backdrop of galvanized pipe, I guess it wouldn't matter.

Don was making daily trips to the Waiban office to see if there was any progress on getting tickets. No word. Mr. He probably felt he was under siege. He had no leverage over the Ministry, of course. In fact, he was beholden to the staff there for getting the tickets, and they just kept saying, not to worry, they would take care of it.

Yet here was Don, bugging him every day, reminding him we needed to know so we could order our other tickets in the United States. Don told him repeatedly that last year when we got ready to buy our tickets I had merely picked up the kitchen phone and ordered them. Three days later they were in our mailbox. Mr. He kept reminding Don that he was in China now.

And then, finally, we got the word. We were to leave Beijing on July 24. Now we could buy our other tickets. In China it is not safe to schedule a flight on the same day as a connecting flight for fear the first flight will be canceled. If you miss the connecting flight, who knows when you can get another ticket. Therefore, Emily booked our flight out of Chengdu on July 22. She would accompany us to Beijing and make sure we got on the plane two days later.

Our early morning flight required that we leave the College at 6:00 A.M. My students who had not yet gone home themselves came around the night before to say good-bye. Some vowed to see us off, but, sensing my horror at the idea, their good sense prevailed and they slept in. At six, Mr. Chen arrived in the blue Toyota van. The Hu's and

Professor Zhang arrived, too, and helped us load the van and accompanied us to the airport. We appreciated their help with our considerable luggage. We were taking home more than we brought.

There was, however, one item we were leaving behind. We decided we didn't have room for the Orange Dragon. So he was placed in a nice box and left in #207 to await Monique's return in September.

The last we heard, he is alive and well.

It was still dark as we drove off, and when we got to the front gate of the campus, Mr. Chen had to wake up the gatekeeper to let us out.

43

Once again, we were high above the Pacific, almost a year later, heading east this time. Once again, I had a book to read. This time it was Michener's *Texas*. I'd deliberately held off finishing it so I'd have something to read on this long flight. We'd eaten, Don was napping, and I settled down to read. But I could not put China behind me yet.

For one thing, since we were flying China Air, we were surrounded by Chinese. There were only seven waiguoren on the flight. The young Chinese man in the window seat beside me was on his way to Columbus to begin study for a master's degree in computer design at Ohio State University. He had just received his bachelor's degree from Qinhua University in Beijing.

I expressed surprise at his being able to go abroad immediately after graduation. After Tiananmen Square, the government had decreed that graduates must work for five years before going overseas for graduate study. He admitted that relatives in Canada and other places had made it possible. They had paid the government $10,000. In effect they reimbursed the government for his education, a common procedure and justified considering China's limited education funds. He confessed, though, that he felt guilty about the unfairness of the policy, which allowed some to go but not others.

Then the on-board movies started, distracting me still further. One was Chinese, one Russian. The films had English subtitles, an advantage we had not had in China. You didn't have to be a film connoisseur to recognize what the film buffs among my Chinese students claimed: that Chinese films are terrible and the Russian ones not much better. The plots were simplistic and transparent and the acting, amateurish and predictable.

On a trip to the restroom, I struck up a conversation with two other waiguoren, a couple from Michigan about our own age. He was a retired businessman, she a retired teacher. They too had been teaching English in a teacher's college in Beijing. They were going home for a year and then perhaps would go back again, to a different location.

Back in my seat, my mind wandered. Would we go back again?

That was a question I knew we would be asked once we got home and another question would be, Was it worth it?

I decided the answer on both counts was definitely yes. But, I also recognized that this kind of experience is not for everyone.

We had numerous expressions early on from people at the college saying they hoped we would stay another year—some formal ones from official sources, and other informal but touching ones from students. They may all have had a selfish motive. Administrators like to solve their staffing problems the easiest way possible and if they already have people who are reasonably satisfactory, the easiest thing is to retain them. Students want the best possible chance to continue to improve their English and with someone they have gotten used to. But we also thought most were sincere.

When college officials accepted that we were going home in July, they asked if we had any friends or colleagues who would be willing to come to China to replace us. In other words, "Are there any more at home like you?"

Teaching there was particularly satisfying to me, but not all would find it so or be willing to put in the necessary time or endure a less than comfortable life-style. How many people would be willing to withstand the constant cold for four months (without central heating), the constant heat for four (without air conditioning), do without seeing a movie or concert for a year, or the convenience of a car, telephone, or TV—not to mention things like convenience food, video players, and microwave ovens? Many of these, after all, are things most people in China have little experience with and get along well without.

I copped out and said that people probably would be willing to come for less time but not a whole year and that unless people are retired, they could not leave their jobs or financial obligations for that long.

People who do that kind of thing fall into two age categories: those who are just starting out in life and have little vested interest at home in terms of jobs or property; or those at the other end of life, who have retired from careers, have an income, and can make the necessary practical arrangements to leave home for an extended period.

And there were times when we became weary of China. However, whenever life became a little too heavy, usually something unexpected popped up to give us a little boost. One day in late spring, when Don was feeling depressed and eager to go home, he went to class and as an opening, did a sentence completion: "At this moment I feel . . . ."

Two students said ". . . sad because in two months you will be leaving."

Two students who had to leave the class early wrote him warm notes full of regret. One, who went home to Beijing because his father-in-law had died and his mother-in-law could not live alone, found when he got home that things were much better. He was on a train, heading back to Chengdu, within a couple of days. Being in Don's class was a big drawing card. He even brought us a little gift.

In fact, I was wholly surprised that Don had been as successful as he was in "this teaching game," as he put it. As I wrote earlier, when we first planned the China adventure, he was just going along for the ride. But he was a hit with his students. They genuinely liked, admired, and appreciated him. They thought of him as that kind old man. (Remember, the Chinese respect their elders.) He was corny and full of baloney and told the same jokes over and over. For example, when he gave his students a quiz and they groaned and complained about how hard it was, he told them it was mere child's play. For about the fiftieth time, that is.

He told them where all he had been and what he had done, embellishing considerably, of course. They hung on his every word and if they suspected he was full of blarney, they didn't let on. When I occasionally heard him make a grammatical error, I cringed. Yet, along with helping his students improve their English, he fed them a lot of motivational lines, pepped them up, and made them feel a little more confident about the future.

Whenever they asked his advice about something they wanted or hoped to do, he always responded, "Why not?" The students latched onto it as a kind of mantra or rallying cry. He reminded them that they were intelligent and that they should think for themselves (not necessarily the safest advice in a totalitarian society).

They were always hoping for "good lucky." He made them memorize a saying: "Luck is what happens when preparation meets opportunity."

He also made them laugh and feel good for a little while. I dubbed him the Harold Hill of the Chengdu College of Geology.

Teaching as a career is still not anything he regrets missing. I think, however, that he has a new respect for the teaching profession, which

I suspect he, along with the rest of the world, always secretly thought was a pretty cushy job.

For me, teaching had been a continuing delight. Students wanted to learn what I had to teach and expressed their appreciation of our coming to China in little ways. If the blackboard wasn't clean when I walked in a classroom in the morning, scarcely before I could lift an eraser a student would bound forward, take the eraser from my hand, and finish the job.

When winter came on, like everyone else I brought a tea jar to class. During the five-minute break between periods, someone would take my jar to the service room found on every floor for a refill of hot water.

Seldom did students leave the classroom without a comment, a good-bye, or at least a smile. If I had many things to carry back to the apartment, a couple of volunteers sprang forward as bearers.

We knew that we were appreciated, but we got a very nice surprise at the college farewell banquet. We were each given an Outstanding Teacher Award and a small bonus which the college had never before given to foreign teachers. I had twenty years' teaching experience and had never received such an award. Don taught one year and walked away with an award and some prize money besides.

Maybe it was growing up in a simpler time, but I had not felt terribly deprived of all those modern conveniences I referred to earlier and that many of my fellow Americans find indispensable. As much as anything, I was looking forward to getting home to my hairdresser, settling myself into the chair every Thursday, and letting her work her will with me.

When we went, I had resolved that if we could just stay well, keep cool when it was hot, warm when it was cold, and keep my hair colored, we'd have it made. We didn't have much control over the first three, but we had actually done pretty well on all counts. Don was not thrilled when I first apprised him of the fact that he was going to have to learn a new skill when we went to China. And when he first started his career as hair color technician, I was anxious about the results, fearful that I would appear in class the next day with hair three shades darker than before..But I came home with hair reasonably the same color as when I went, thanks to Don's capable assistance. He could have added yet another item to his vita. I suggested that he set up a shop in our garage and solicit a little trade in the neighborhood. He was unenthusiastic.

We knew too that people at home would probably question how we could possibly have spent a year in China, speaking only a few words of Chinese. We had blithely reassured friends before we left and indeed had experienced few difficulties even when we ventured out on our own. But Don wasn't sure he would tell anyone about one incident.

A few weeks after we had come to China, we were visiting on the campus of Huaxie, West China Medical and Science University, at the invitation of some American. When we had first arrived at a building in which there was a special exhibit, we had all signed in and had our pictures taken with some of the Chinese.

Because a car and driver from the college were to pick us up at a prearranged time, we were forced to cut short our tour of the exhibit and say good-bye to our friends so that we would not miss our ride. When we passed the table at the entrance, the same folks called us over, gave us some gift products, and wanted to take our pictures again. Not being able to explain to the Chinese our reason for being in a hurry, it was easier to comply, since the picture-taking would not take long.

Not only did they take one, but two sets of pictures, each time asking us to hold up a product and giving the thumbs up sign. These people had seemed acceptable to our friends earlier, and since they were very friendly, we did our best to be accommodating and enthusiastic. The pictures done, they got our names and promised to send us pictures. We thanked them for the free gifts and hurried to meet our car.

We forgot the encounter until weeks later when we received prints of the pictures in the mail, along with a pamphlet in English describing the products that were being exported to the United States and other Western countries. The pamphlet claimed that the Chinese product had already found favor with Americans. (Oh? Anyone we know?) In the pictures they had taken of us, in which Don was seen giving an enthusiastic thumb's up, it appeared that we were giving an unqualified endorsement of the product.

The next time Jilin dropped in we showed him the free samples and the pamphlet. It seemed Don had been enthusiastically endorsing a feminine hygiene product.

Other more serious questions some of us waiguoren had discussed among ourselves were what is going to happen in China? Is there likely to be any loosening of control, greater democracy in the foreseeable future? And if there is to be change, how is it most likely to come about? I suspected others would ask those questions, too, when we got home. Mao said in the 1950's, "The Soviet Union's today is China's tomorrow." In the light of what has happened in the Soviet Union, China's present leaders are probably taking Mao's words as a warning.

Professor Zhang often said, "The Chinese people are too tolerant." While that is true, if they weren't, they would go crazy. But it amounts to a kind of Catch-22. If they are too tolerant, they'll never change the system.

We had no sense of any kind of underground, of course, and our students, while dissatisfied, didn't seem ready to rock the boat. There's too much to lose. But there are undoubtedly things going on in China. Students who have escaped seem to indicate as much. One little incident we do know about gives a hint of surreptitious activities.

In May we had a letter from Brett, our ten-year-old granddaughter in Florida. It was a thank-you letter for a birthday gift, but enclosed in the envelope was a full page of Chinese writing. She had made no mention of the enclosure, and we were puzzled about what it was and where she had gotten such an item.

Curious about the content, I asked a young man to translate it for me. It was from a group of soldiers within a particular military district in China and was a criticism of the Communist Party and its use of the Army as its political tool instead of fulfilling Mao's promise that the Army would serve all the people. It referred to the events of spring 1989, when soldiers fired on students, as an example of that.

My translator was curious about where the paper had come from and said it must have been typed by computer in the United States. He seemed certain it had not been faxed from China because the fax is being monitored and it would have been illegal to send such a thing. He was a little alarmed that I had it in my possession and said it was not the kind of thing which one should show around. It appeared to be a big mystery. A letter by return mail from John informed us that the enclosure did not originate in Tampa. He was as puzzled and intrigued as we.

My translator had asked if he could keep the paper, saying he didn't think it wise for us to have it. Consensus seems to be that the letter was opened in, perhaps, Hong Kong and the enclosure inserted. We had not noticed that the letter had been opened.

It was all rather disconcerting. China scholars and almost everyone we knew in China conclude that the Chinese Revolution was inevitable. The more I learn of China's history, the more I see that. I also have more appreciation of the concept of "New China." While there is much of their past that is glorious, the century before their Revolution was one of intimidation and subjection and oppression by outsiders— and done to them right on their own soil. It is no wonder they sought to regain their dignity and that they feel great pride in what they have attained.

It is unfortunate that since the Revolution they have at times done stupid and counter-productive things, which have impeded their progress and made them the laughing stock of other nations, but there are explanations even for that. And what they have accomplished in the past forty-five years is remarkable. The Yangs, among those we've talked to who knew China before, not to mention writers like Han Suyin, speak about the tremendous improvement in health, sanitation, and food production. The Chinese have done it primarily by themselves, with little or no help from outside. Even the Russians who initially helped them turned on them.

In the summer of 1991 before we came home, several provinces in eastern China experienced terrible floods. One student said, considering the floods and earlier typhoons, that this was a very bad year for China. For the first time ever, China would be asking for help from World Relief agencies. Always before, despite devastating earthquakes and other natural disasters, the government had stubbornly refused to seek help. They prided themselves on their "pride."

In 1979, for example, the earthquake in Tangshan completely destroyed the city and resulted in 250,000 deaths. I told my students that sometimes such actions, like refusing to ask for help, resulted in "cutting off your nose to spite your face," that such an attitude hurt Chinese people even more.

What I didn't say was that some of the past "natural" disasters were exacerbated by stupid policies that produced famine and flooding and that the Chinese government would not have been willing to admit that or submit to the criticisms of world opinion that receiving aid would have precipitated. For instance, thirty million people died of starvation in the late 1950's during the Great Leap Forward. Peasants were too busy making steel in backyard furnaces to harvest crops. Nevertheless, the record shows the ability to survive terrible ordeals and the resilient nature of the Chinese people.

It was disheartening, though, to hear people tell about their optimism in the beginning of the Revolution, how hopeful they were, and then to realize how disillusioned they had become. Even those who did not favor the Communists recognized that Chiang Kai Shek was so bad they needed someone to lead the way. They were willing to go wherever they were sent, to work, to study, because they were rebuilding the country. They realized they needed to stop being so dependent on foreign imports and manufacture things themselves.

Today's leaders constantly speak about developing socialism with "Chinese characteristics," and I see the sense of that, even while I hope they have gotten past the automatic rejection and suspicion of everything Western. We both have had knee-jerk responses—we to anything smacking of Communism, and they to anything connected with the West. Given their experience, one can understand why they were so xenophobic, but they now suffer if they "throw the baby out with the bath." (I wish I'd thought to use that idiom in class!)

I read Robert Fulghum's book, *It Was on Fire When I Lay Down on It*, when I was in China, and one of the little essays in it struck a responsive chord.

It is about a citizen of Crete named Papaderos, who founded an institute which provides a conference setting that is dedicated to human understanding and peace. It is near a site in Crete where there were fierce battles between Nazi paratroopers and local Cretans. The institute is the result of a dream that if Germans and Cretans could find it possible to forgive each other for the horrors inflicted on one another, it could be an example for others.

Fulghum attended the institute and at the close of the two-week seminar Papaderos asked if there were any questions.

Fulghum asked him the meaning of life. Papaderos, sensing it was a serious question, responded by taking from his billfold a very small round mirror the size of a quarter. During the war, as a small boy in his remote village he had found broken pieces of a mirror from a German motorcycle that had been wrecked in that place.

He said, "I tried to find all the pieces and put them together but it was impossible, so I kept only the largest piece. This one. And by scratching it on a stone I made it round. I began to play with it as a toy and became fascinated by the fact that I could reflect light into dark places where the sun would never shine—in deep holes and crevices and dark closets. It became a game for me to get light into the most inaccessible places I could find.

"I kept the little mirror, and as I went about my growing up, I would take it out in idle moments and continue the challenge of the little game. As I became a man, I grew to understand that this was not just a child's game but a metaphor for what I might do with my life. I came to understand that I am not the light or the source of light. But light—truth, understanding, knowledge—is there, and it will only shine in the dark places if I reflect it.

"I am a fragment of a mirror whose whole design and shape I do not know. Nevertheless, with what I have I can reflect light into dark places of this world—into the black places in the hearts of men—and change some things in some people. Perhaps others may see and do likewise. This is what I am about. This is the meaning of my life."

I found that a very meaningful story and hope it isn't too presumptuous to think that we did a little reflecting of our own in Chengdu. However, in our case it definitely was a two-way mirror. We got as much as we gave.

At any rate, our year in China was a record year in many ways: for Don, the most pounds gained, lost, and regained; for me, the shortest and straightest my hair has been in fifty years when I used to go to the barber shop instead of the "beauty" shop; the most time we have ever spent together in our married life—and in a three-room apartment, at that; the longest period that we've not driven a car since we each got our licenses at fourteen; the most days we've gone without a bath; the most consecutive days we've worn the same clothes; the first time I've ever included on my syllabus, "Spitting in the classroom will not be tolerated"; the longest time in my life I'd gone without *ice cream*; the greatest number of hours I've gone without going to the bathroom.

No matter how frustrating and unsavory China is in many ways, her saving grace is the natural sweetness and unself-consciousness of her people. They made it all worthwhile.

This book was set by Skid Type of Savannah, Georgia, in Adobe Systems' version of the Bembo typeface, which had its origins in a type cut for Aldus Manutius by Francesco Griffo. It was used by Aldus in 1495 to print *De Ætna* by Pietro Bembo, and was revived and then recut in 1929 under the supervision of Stanley Morison for the Monotype Corporation. The Chinese calligraphy is by Professor Shiao-Ping Wang Chu, also of Savannah.